W9-BWB-633

DATE DUE

JAN 14 1981
APR 6 1981
APR 20 1983
APR 18 1983
APR 18 1983
MAR 28 1984
MAR 16 1984 B R
MAR 19 1984
MAR 23 1988
AUG -5 1991
AUG 16 1991
DEC -7 1995
MAR 25 1996
APR 26 2000

DEMCO 38-297

The Cognitive–Developmental Basis of Human Learning

STUDIES IN HYPOTHESIS TESTING

DEVELOPMENTAL PSYCHOLOGY SERIES

SERIES EDITOR

Harry Beilin

Developmental Psychology Program
City University of New York Graduate School
New York, New York

LYNN S. LIBEN. *Deaf Children: Developmental Perspectives*

JONAS LANGER. *The Origins of Logic: Six to Twelve Months*

GILBERTE PIÉRAUT-LE BONNIEC. *The Development of Modal Reasoning: Genesis of Necessity and Possibility Notions*

TIFFANY MARTINI FIELD, SUSAN GOLDBERG, DANIEL STERN, and ANITA MILLER SOSTEK. (Editors). *High-Risk Infants and Children: Adult and Peer Interactions*

BARRY GHOLSON. *The Cognitive-Developmental Basis of Human Learning: Studies in Hypothesis Testing*

In Preparation

ROBERT L. SELMAN. *The Growth of Interpersonal Understanding: Developmental and Clinical Analyses*

The Cognitive–Developmental Basis of Human Learning

STUDIES IN HYPOTHESIS TESTING

Barry Gholson
Department of Psychology
Memphis State University
Memphis, Tennessee

RECEIVED
JUN 10 1980
MANKATO STATE UNIVERSITY
MEMORIAL LIBRARY
MANKATO, MINN

1980
ACADEMIC PRESS
A Subsidiary of Harcourt Brace Jovanovich, Publishers
New York London Toronto Sydney San Francisco

COPYRIGHT © 1980, BY ACADEMIC PRESS, INC.
ALL RIGHTS RESERVED.
NO PART OF THIS PUBLICATION MAY BE REPRODUCED OR TRANSMITTED IN ANY FORM OR BY ANY MEANS, ELECTRONIC OR MECHANICAL, INCLUDING PHOTOCOPY, RECORDING, OR ANY INFORMATION STORAGE AND RETRIEVAL SYSTEM, WITHOUT PERMISSION IN WRITING FROM THE PUBLISHER.

ACADEMIC PRESS, INC.
111 Fifth Avenue, New York, New York 10003

United Kingdom Edition published by
ACADEMIC PRESS, INC. (LONDON) LTD.
24/28 Oval Road, London NW1 7DX

Library of Congress Cataloging in Publication Data

Gholson, Barry.
The cognitive–developmental basis of human learning.

(Developmental psychology series)
Bibliography: p.
Includes index.
1. Learning, Psychology of. 2. Cognition in children. 3. Human information processing in children. I. Title. II. Series. [DNLM: 1. Cognition--In infancy and childhood. 2. Learning--In infancy and childhood. 3. Models, Psychological. 4. Information theory. 5. Child development. WS105.5.C7 G427c]
BF318.G46 155.4'13 80–307
ISBN 0–12–282350–8

BF
318
.G46

PRINTED IN THE UNITED STATES OF AMERICA

80 81 82 83 9 8 7 6 5 4 3 2 1

Contents

443977

Foreword

During a research career of two decades, I employed a single post-doctoral fellow. To my very good fortune, that young man was Barry Gholson. He was then a brand new developmental psychologist from Iowa, steeped in the conditioning tradition. He arrived in the late 1960s to learn the new cognitive theories of discrimination learning and concept learning. These views held that people (adults) were active processors of information in learning tasks, that they tested hypotheses in order to locate a solution. Barry's mission was to apply the new theories to children: To study how the dynamics of hypothesis testing emerged and became more sophisticated as the children grew. He brought to the task not only intelligence and a flair for technical analysis but also energy and zest. Barry was indefatigable. The first signs of his almost inevitable success appeared in what is now a well-known series of experiments describing strategies of hypothesis testing at different ages. (For the reader who is not familiar with them, they are nicely reviewed in this book.)

Barry became a young master of this new intellectual tradition, but did not regard his knowledge as complete. He was now in New York City, holding his first academic position. There he studied and worked with the foremost Piagetian in the area, Harry Beilin. Barry was soon accomplished in two cognitive characterizations of children's problem solving: the American tradition, focusing upon instrumental-learning tasks, which described the information-processing and hypothesis-testing characteristics of children; and the Piagetian tradition, with an informal interview method centering on classification and conservation tasks, which emphasized the changing logical capabilities as children matured. Barry took up one of the most important challenges in the developmental analysis of cognition: The need to interrelate these two traditions.

This book is a product of that undertaking. As the reader will learn, the insights of Piagetian theory help to organize a vast amount of findings about the hypothesis-testing process. Here Barry displays many of his experiments, performed since he left my laboratory, in the framework of this theoretical synthesis. Although the new theoretical statement is not complete, this book demonstrates that an important step has been taken, that important goals lie ahead. Along the way are to be found many fascinating facts. The spectacle is lovely to behold.

Marvin Levine
State University of New York at Stony Brook

Preface

Since the early 1970s Piaget's structural theory and information-processing theory have dominated mainstream developmental learning. Each approach presently claims many adherents, and each theoretical view has certain advantages relative to the other. Information-processing models are clear on the relationship between executive functions and performance, but because they provide no structural or operative basis for the executive functions, they are not developmental in scope. Neo-Piagetian models are clear on the structural basis of operations and, therefore, they provide an account of development; but they are vague on the relationship among structures, operations, and performance.

This volume presents a developmental model of learning and performance that involves a synthesis of the two; that is, Piaget's structural theory and information-processing theory. The model derives executive functions from structures and specifies the relationship between executive functions and performance. Thus it is a developmental theory and is, at the same time, precise enough to be easily tested.

The text is divided into three sections. The first contains four chapters. Of these, the first two chapters present a brief overview of the historical events that shaped the Zeitgeist in the United States in about 1970, when cognitive theory entered the mainstream of developmental learning. The model itself is presented in Chapter 3. Assumptions of the model and its implications are explored in the context of an extensive review of the relevant research in Chapter 4.

The second section is divided into three research chapters. Each chapter contains experiments that were designed to examine previously untested implications of the model. The last section of the book summarizes the results of experiments presented in the research chapters and presents a refined statement of the model based on those findings.

A major concern of mine since graduate school has been the problem faced by educators and education theorists in designing curricula that complement and build upon the cognitive capabilities of the developing child. Thus, although this book was written with the advanced undergraduate in mind, it is primarily aimed at an audience of graduate students and professionals in child development and education. Although the book is a monograph, not a guide to either child development or education, the work was conducted with an eye on the classroom and what has become known as "instructional psychology."

Acknowledgments

The factors that lead an individual into a particular field and line of research are diverse and multiply determined. However, I would like to single out a few individuals who encouraged my interests and made this book possible. First, I owe a special debt of gratitude to my teachers, most especially Ken Hoving, Ray Hohle, Marvin Levine, and Harry Beilin. The first two men introduced me to the science of psychology. The second two introduced me to the scientific questions addressed in this book and inspired me to search for answers. Second, a number of my students and colleagues contributed to the research that is reported. Their individual contributions are acknowledged in the authorships of individual experiments presented in the research chapters. I am also indebted to Bob Cohen, Frank Leeming, Stu Offenbach, and Ted Rosenthal for their helpful comments on various chapters.

We are also sincerely indebted to the many children who played our "games," and the many public and private school personnel who cooperated so closely with us in the research reported herein. We are in debt to Joyce B. Weddington and O. Z. Stephens of the Memphis City Schools Division of Research and Planning and the following city school principals: James Adkins, Newberry Elementary School; Gerald Beibers, Winchester Elementary School; Ronnie Bynum, Westwood Elementary School; Lee Hopkins, Fox Meadows Elementary School; C. C. Jones, Lakeview Elementary School; Don Jones, Ridgeway Elementary School; and Faye Lane, Richland Elementary School. Jim Paavola, Mary Berk, Martha Taube, and James Olds of the Memphis City Schools also worked with us on more than one occasion. Grady G. Woody and Bertanrene Young of the Memphis State University Campus School have been involved in many of our projects, as have Robert D. Lynn of The Hutchison School and Jack Stanford of Presbyterian Day School. Finally, we thank Minor Perkins, Henrietta Stainbrook, Margaret Wilson, Ruth White, Glynis George, and Mona Kernan of the Educare Child Care Centers for their cooperation. The Memphis State University Computer Center provided facilities for data analysis. Lawrence Erlbaum Associates and Academic Press permitted us to reproduce figures and tables. Specific authors whose work is reproduced are acknowledged at appropriate places in the text.

I
THE THEORY BASE

1
Introduction

Historically, in this country at least, most researchers and theorists concerned with children's learning have conceptualized the acquisition process within the framework of conditioning theory, following the traditions of Guthrie (1935), Hull (1943), Skinner (1938), and Watson (1914). This theory accounts for learning in various concept-identification, discrimination-learning, and problem-solving tasks in terms of the conditioning and extinction of specific stimulus–response associations. The varying strengths of individual associative bonds determine which overt response occurs. Recently, however, a competing view called "hypothesis-testing theory," or simply "hypothesis theory," has received increasing attention. Most broadly stated, this theory posits that the child has a repertoire of hypotheses (or rules) that are tested in an attempt to attain the solution to a task. The child's overt response is determined by the hypothesis being tested. The hypotheses are tried and rejected until one is located that consistently results in correct response.

This latter conception presently enjoys growing acceptance, but a few years ago hypothesis theory could claim few adherents among active researchers concerned with children's learning. A decade ago, for example, influential theorists routinely offered accounts, albeit sometimes critical, of children's learning couched in the framework of association theory (see Estes, 1970; Gagné, 1970; T. S. Kendler & H. H. Kendler, 1970; Reese & Lipsitt, 1970; Spiker, 1970; Stevenson, 1970; White, 1970). The mainstream of developmental learning, then, has only recently felt the impact of hypothesis theory.

While the theory elaborated in this monograph is concerned only with developmental issues, modern versions of hypothesis theory derive largely from research conducted with college students during the 1960s (e.g., Bower & Trabasso, 1963, 1964; Erickson, 1968; Estes, 1960; Levine, 1963, 1966, 1969; Restle, 1962, 1965; Trabasso & Bower, 1968). Consequently, some of that work and the resulting theoretical formulation will be described in Chapter 2. It should be explicitly stated, however, that while it was always on the periphery during the heyday of associationism, hypothesis theory actually had its beginnings a half century ago. Thus in order to put events that took place during the 1960s in perspective, a few developments that preceded modern statements of the theory will be highlighted (for a more thorough historical treatment see Levine, 1975, pp. 1–141).

Historical Antecedents

The movement may be said to have begun in 1929 with some musings by Lashley in his book, *Brain Mechanisms and Behavior*. In pondering the behavior of his rats during the acquisition of a brightness discrimination, Lashley offered two casual observations. First, he said that "attempted solutions" such as position preference, position alternation, or reactions to other cues irrelevant to solution frequently preceded acquisition of the "correct association." Second, he added that so long as the animal exhibited these attempted solutions, training had *no effect* on the final acquisition of the correct association. Although Lashley had little more to say on the issue, Krechevsky, a graduate student working with Tolman (Tolman, 1932, 1948), was much influenced by his (Lashley's) observations. There followed a series of research reports in which Krechevsky investigated systematic reponse patterns exhibited by rats prior to solution in various discrimination tasks (Krechevsky, 1932a, b, 1933a, b, 1937). He labeled these reponse patterns "hypotheses" and discussed them in a cognitive language.

K. W. Spence, and others representing the associationistic view, were quick to respond to Krechevsky's challenge. In a series of very influential papers, Spence (1936, 1937, 1940) argued, convincingly, that any response patterns observed prior to solution were an uninteresting by-product of the organism's earlier conditioning history. Because reinforcement and extinction processes were presumed to account for *all* responses that occurred, systematic response patterns themselves were of little intrinsic interest. In the ensuing dialogue, to which many on both sides contributed, the emphasis shifted, therefore, to Lashley's second claim—that training produces no effect on final acquisition so long as presolution response patterns persist. Consequently, the continuity–noncontinuity controversy was born, and the analysis of response patterns—Lashley's and Krechevsky's original concern—for the moment at least, died.

By the mid 1940s the aforementioned controversy was temporarily resolved in favor of association theory. Although an occasional experiment was reported (e.g., Bruner, Goodnow, & Austin, 1956; Postman & Bruner, 1948, 1952), the influence of Hull and Spence was at its zenith, and hypothesis theory was effectively eclipsed for the ensuing decade and a half. There were, however, other events taking place that foreshadowed the rebirth of the theory during the 1960s. One of these involved Harlow's (1949) demonstration of learning set in monkeys.

Error Factors

Harlow presented each monkey with a lengthy series of short (six-trial) problems that all involved a common type of solution. A pair of stimulus objects was presented on each trial, with the left–right position of the correct object varied randomly. A learning set was said to be acquired when the solution to each new problem was immediate; that is, when the monkey needed feedback from only the first-trial response to obtain solution. This research provided measures of learning efficiency within each individual problem, and measures of the cumulative improvement in performance across a series of problems.

While some viewed the demonstration of learning set primarily in terms of its challenge to association theory (cf. Reese, 1964; Restle, 1958), Harlow was more intrigued by systematic response sequences he observed in his monkeys prior to the achievement of learning set. He observed, as had Lashley, that interfering response tendencies, which he called "error factors," served to mask the learning process. Thus Harlow concluded that it was important to identify the various error factors and to chart their course during the acquisition process. He chose the individual problem as the unit for analysis.

Initially, Harlow (1950) identified four error factors:

1. *stimulus preference*, a repetitive choice of the incorrect stimulus object, or avoidance of the correct object;
2. *position habit*, persistent response to either the left or right position, regardless of the position of the correct object;
3. *response shift*, a shift to the incorrect stimulus object following a series of correct responses;
4. *differential cue*, an error on the trial following a change in the position of the correct object.

Each of these error factors occurred in some of his monkeys, and it appeared that different error factors dominated the monkey's behavior at different phases of the acquisition process.

In the next few years Harlow, his students, and other primate researchers performed error-factor analyses upon data derived from various kinds of learning-set problems. As a consequence, the number of published accounts increased very rapidly, as did the list of error factors. By the mid 1950s the domain had become somewhat cluttered; each article seemed to specify a different set of error factors and the factors that were identified never seemed to be related to each other.

The next episode in this scenario involved the work of Marvin Levine, a graduate student working with Harlow in the late 1950s. Levine (1959) systematized error-factor analysis. He defined error factors in a way that permitted a standard mode of measurement, and provided a quantitative theory from which the measurement was derived. To accomplish these ends, Levine introduced a number of changes relative to what previous researchers had done. He maintained the "problem" as the natural unit for identifying particular response patterns, but he limited the number of trials submitted to analysis, first to three trials per problem (1959), then to two trials (1963). He enlarged the class of response patterns to be considered, and redefined the means by which each was identified. This involved reference (*a*) to the outcome of the Trial 1 response, either "win" or "lose"; (*b*) to the dimension responded to on Trials 1 and 2, either object or position cues; and (*c*) to whether the Trial 1 and 2 responses were to the same cue, "stay," or to the other cue, "shift," on the given dimension. This redefinition led to an eightfold classification of the kind illustrated in Table 1.1. In Levine's system, for example, Harlow's "stimulus preference" error factor became "win–stay, lose–stay" with respect to a particular stimulus object. Unlike previous analyses, Levine's enlarged system also included a response pattern that reflected acquisition of the learning set, "win–stay, lose–shift" with respect to the stimulus object. Correct responding, then, was treated simply as another response pattern. The label "error factor" was no longer appropriate for the class of all response patterns, and Levine (1959) substituted Krechevsky's term, "hypothesis."

Mathematical Learning Theory

During the decade of the 1950s another movement, at first at odds with hypothesis theory, but important to its rebirth in the 1960s, was taking place within the mainstream of conditioning theory. Contributors

TABLE 1.1
Levine's Eightfold Classification of Response Patterns [a]

1. Win–stay, lose–stay position	5. Win–stay, lose–shift position
2. Win–shift, lose–shift position	6. Win–shift, lose–stay position
3. Win–stay, lose–stay object	7. Win–stay, lose–shift object (problem solution)
4. Win–shift, lose–shift object	8. Win–shift, lose–stay object
	9. Random responding

[a] The ninth category was included for response patterns uncorrelated with stimulus changes.

to this movement (e.g., Bush & Mosteller, 1955; Estes & Burke, 1953; Restle, 1955), which is commonly known as statistical—or mathematical—learning theory (Estes, 1959), presented highly polished theories that made precise quantitative predictions. They elaborated a version of associationism called "stimulus-sampling theory," which was based upon Guthrie's contiguity theory (1935, 1942). This theory proposed that various stimuli, or cues in the environment, were sampled at the moment of response, and when the response was executed the sampled cues gained their full associative strength on the occasion of this one pairing.

To illustrate the general approach, consider a two-choice task in which the subject must learn to push a button located to the left side following the flash of a red signal and to push a button located to the right following a green signal. The stimulus cues included all the discriminable features of the environment: details of the walls and floor, features of the apparatus, kinesthetic cues, etc. When the red signal occured, then, the universe of cues consisted of all the aforementioned features plus the elements corresponding to redness. To the green signal the universe was similar, differing only in the cues corresponding to green. Thus the two universes had many elements in common. Each environmental cue was assumed to be conditioned, in an all-or-none way, to one response or the other before learning began. For convenience, it was assumed that half the cues were conditioned to the left-button response and half to the right-button response at the outset.

At the start of each trial the subject took a random sample of the cues available in the environment. Two features of the sample were important. First, the sample determined the response: the probability of the left-button response, for example, was equal to the proportion of cues in the sample that were conditioned to that response. Also, all the conditioning produced by the reinforcement applied only to the cues sampled on that trial. On the next trial the sample was returned to the universe and a new random sample was taken, etc. The notion was, then, that all the cues that corresponded to the red signal would eventually become conditioned to the left-button response. Similarly, all the cues that corresponded to green would eventually be conditioned to the right-button response. Thus the probabilities of correct responses would increase incrementally over trials.

Quantitative predictions derived from this simple but elegant formulation were applied successfully to numerous tasks and subject populations, ranging from simple conditioning in rats to complex concept identification in college students. Consecutive statements of the theory broadened its scope, and solved the problems of earlier versions, it seemed, almost before they were even identified as problems (cf. Bourne & Restle, 1959; Restle, 1955). Since the formulation was mathematically cast, rigorous, and clear in its implications, it set a demanding standard for competing theories.

At about the same time, however, Rock (1957) published a challenge to the very foundation of conditioning theory: the assumption that learning is incremental. He compared two groups of college students in a paired-associate task. One group of students went through a standard list of eight paired associates on successive study and test trials until the correct response was given to each stimulus item. The other group began with the same list, but each time an incorrect response was given that particular item was removed from the list and replaced with a new pair. The latter group, then, had to learn a few new items on successive presentations of the list. If each pair was learned by a gradual, or incremental, associative process, then the group that received the same list of paired associates throughout should learn faster than the group for whom pairs were substituted following errors. Rock, however, found no differences between his groups. Thus he argued that prior to the acquisition of a given stimulus–response pair, the strength of the associative bond was zero. It followed that learning was an all-or-none process.

If learning was not an incremental process, then conditioning theory, no matter how elegantly formulated, was suspect. Thus the finding was critically examined by many active researchers, and although this brief sketch greatly oversimplifies the ensuing history (cf. Battig, 1962; Bower, 1960, 1975; Brackett & Battig, 1963; Clark, Lansford, & Dallenbach, 1960; Postman, 1962; J.P. Williams, 1961), the next events of importance to the rebirth of hypothesis theory were produced by conditioning theorists. Estes, for example, a leading figure in the mathematical learning movement, was one scientist who took the issue seriously. Rock's results, along with some of his own findings, led Estes to conclude that learning was indeed an all-or-none process, at least in some tasks. In 1960 he announced this view, provided supporting data, and, at least tentatively, rejected an incremental view.

The next episode of importance to hypothesis theory may be considered a restatement of stimulus-sampling theory. According to this latter view, conditioned cues that are sampled from the environment determine the subject's response. Thus it seems, in retrospect, almost a natural transition to place the response-determining cues in some repertoire inside the subject to be selected and tested until one is located that always results in correct response. This theoretical advance was presented by Restle, another leading mathematical learning theorist, in 1962. Restle (1962, p. 342) remarked that his model was similar in intent to Krechevsky's, and because the label "conditioned cues" was no longer appropriate for the class of all response determinants, Restle substituted Krechevsky's term "hypothesis."[1]

Therefore, spokesmen for two different lines of research and theory—Levine for error factors and Restle for mathematical learning—had in rapid succession converged upon a theoretical statement in which "hypothesis" was the central construct. Most would probably agree that these events and the ones that engendered them were impelling forces in the rebirth of hypothesis theory in the 1960s. There was, however, one subsidiary movement that should be mentioned in this context, not because it contributed to this rebirth but because it has, so to speak, provided sustenance during the theory's adolescence.

Hypothesis Testing

Beginning in the 1940s, Bruner was one isolated spokesman for hypothesis theory (e.g., Bruner & Goodman, 1947; Bruner & Postman, 1947, 1948). In the early years his important contribution was in the area of perception, where he argued that the way a person achieved a stable perception was by testing hypotheses until one was located that was consistent with all the perceptual input (see Allport, 1955, pp. 304–463). In 1956, however, Bruner and his colleagues (Bruner *et al.*, 1956) presented a monograph concerned with concept learning in the college student. A variety of procedures were used, but a summary description will illustrate the general approach. They presented stimulus materials that could be easily analyzed into dimensions and values. The subject was explicitly informed about the makeup of the stimuli and the required kinds of solutions were illustrated. Following the presentation of each stimulus card the subject's task was to write down a "best guess" (hypothesis) about the solution to the problem. The set of hypotheses that was to be considered was restricted by a list of symbols that was provided: each symbol represented a specific value on a given dimension.

Bruner *et al.* took the hypotheses presented by their subjects as the units of analysis. Individual hypotheses were, however, of no intrinsic

1. Actually, at the time Restle (1962) referred to the response determinants as "strategies," but later (Restle, 1965) adopted the more conventional term, "hypothesis."

interest. Instead, they analyzed sequences of hypotheses as a means of inferring their subjects' "strategies of decision making [p. 54]." The individual's *strategy* was inferred from the sequence of hypotheses generated during the problem. Bruner *et al*. described two basic approaches that their subjects used (or attempted): *focusing*, which involved the simultaneous evaluation of all possible hypotheses; and *scanning*, which consisted of testing one hypothesis at a time. The new procedures permitted the identification of specific strategies used by different individuals. In addition, the procedure provided a rich analysis of the influence of various task demands upon the problem-solving process.

The immediate impact of the work upon mainstream learning theorists was, it is fair to say, minor. Bourne and Restle (1959), for example, reported research in which they used concept-learning tasks that were essentially identical to those used by Bruner *et al*., but provided an associationistic account and concerned themselves only with choice responses. In the ensuing decade, however, as cognitive approaches became more influential, the impact of the work was widely felt (cf. Hilgard & Bower, 1966; Levine, 1966, 1969). More recently the general approach has been very influential among researchers concerned with various developmental issues: memory (A. L. Brown, 1975, 1978), attention (Wright & Vlietstra, 1975), problem solving (Gholson, Levine, & Phillips, 1972).

2

Hypothesis Theory: Developments during the 1960s and Preliminary Applications to Children's Learning

All of these are the sorts of results that Krechevsky was claiming to find for his rats learning their mazes back in 1932. One may take issue with the restrictive arrangements of Levine's experiments or note some opposing data from lower animals regarding the "continuity" position. But it is undeniable that the "hypothesis-testing" approach propounded by Krechevsky and Tolman has very strong experimental support and theoretical devotees on the current scene. The theory is still very much on the books [Hilgard & Bower, 1975, pp. 142–143].

During the 1960s, hypothesis theory flourished. After its abrupt reemergence in the early part of the decade, events moved so quickly that by 1969 it was characterized, fairly, as "the leading theory of discrimination learning by the adult human [Levine, 1969, p. 101]." Many scientists, of course, subscribed to the theory and contributed to its development during the intervening years, and general summaries are readily available (A. S. Brown, 1974; Hilgard & Bower, 1975; Kintsch, 1977; Levine, 1975). The version of the theory adopted by developmentalists in the early 1970s, however, derives mainly from the work of Bower, Levine, Restle, and Trabasso. Thus their work will be emphasized in the brief historical sketch drawn in this chapter.

Hypothesis Theory

Bruner *et al.* (1956) offered a wealth of descriptive material in their book, but they presented no real theory of concept learning. The subjects selected hypotheses that were consistent with stimulus input: Some used a strategy that tested one at a time, others tried to test all hypotheses simultaneously. Often, however, no particular strategy could be detected in the subjects' protocols. In addition, different subjects, and the same subject at different times, used different strategies. The strategies that were observed, then, did not explain much; instead, it was the strategies themselves that needed to be explained. Clearly, a more precise statement was needed as bedrock for further theory construction.

Restle

Restle's (1962) model, although restricted in scope and somewhat oversimplified, provided a solid foundation for subsequent developments. Restle proposed that a problem gives rise to a set of hypotheses, and that the subject samples from among this set in an attempt to achieve solution. He subdivided the set of hypotheses into three subsets: *correct*, those which always lead to correct responses; *wrong*, those which always lead to incorrect responses; *irrelevant*, hypotheses that lead to correct and incorrect responses with equal frequency. The subject's task, then, was to somehow obtain a sample that contained at least one correct hypothesis, but none from either the wrong or irrelevant subsets. Restle's goal was to provide a precise theoretical account of how this was accomplished. For illustrative purposes the model is described in terms of a two-choice concept-learning task.

The model he proposed had three forms. The first form was based upon the assumption that the subject samples and tests only one hypothesis at a time. If the response dictated by the hypothesis is correct, the hypothesis is retained and it dictates the next response, etc. If the response is incorrect, however, the subject returns the hypothesis to the original set and randomly resamples before the next response is made. This last assumption implies that the subject may resample a hypothesis that was just rejected. In fact, if the total set consists of n hypotheses, then the one that was just rejected will be resampled with the probability $1/n$. Because this implies the subject has no memory about the hypothesis that was just rejected, it became known as the *zero-memory* assumption. The subject continues to sample and test hypotheses until one from the correct subset is located and, of course, the problem is solved. Because the correct hypothesis may be located only when the subject resamples, the model also implies that opportunities for learning occur only on error trials.

At first glance the second form of the model looks radically different from the first. In this version Restle assumed that at the outset of the problem the subject samples all the hypotheses from the entire set. The process of obtaining solution, then, would involve narrowing the set until all hypotheses contained in the wrong and irrelevant subsets were eliminated; that is, until the sample being tested held only hypotheses from the correct subset. Restle specified how the narrowing-down process was accomplished. On the first trial of the problem the subject considers the entire set of hypotheses. All hypotheses in the correct subset and some in the irrelevant subset will, of course, lead to a correct response on that trial. Those in the wrong subset and the remainder in the irrelevant subset will lead to an error. The subject decides which response to make, then eliminates all hypotheses from the test set that would have led to the other response *before* the first-trial response is actually performed.

If the first response is correct, the hypotheses that dictated the response are retained. The subject examines these, decides which response to make, eliminates those hypotheses that would have led to the other response, etc. In this way the subject may eventually eliminate all hypotheses from the wrong and irrelevant subsets and, of course, solve the problem. If, however, the subject makes an error on this or any subsequent trial, the process begins all over. Following any error the subject resamples the entire set; all hypotheses contained in the three subsets are resampled and the process starts again. Thus, this model, like the first version, implies zero memory, and that opportunities for learning occur only on error trials when the subject resamples.

For completeness, Restle provided a third form of the model that was a variant of the first two. The subject was assumed to take a random sample of hypotheses at the outset of the problem, and following any subsequent error. The size of the sample could range from 1 to n hypotheses, and could vary for a given subject from one sample to the next. The dynamics of the acquisition process were the same as those in the second form of the model; or the first form in cases in which the subject sampled only one hypothesis.

Restle (1962) then proved that all three forms of the model lead to the same theorems; that is, they make identical predictions about sequences of correct and incorrect responses during learning. For this reason, and because of its simplicity, the first form of the model received the most attention during the next few years. The equivalence of the three models is qualified, however, by two considerations. First, it is due to two of Restle's assumptions: Sampling is random, and sampling is with replacement. If these assumptions proved incorrect, and were modified, the models would not lead to equivalent quantitative predictions. Second, the three models make identical predictions only about sequences of correct and incorrect responses. If they were applied to different experimental questions—for example, attempts to identify specific cues that are used in obtaining a concept—then the three forms would make different predictions.

In any case, Restle applied a quantitative version of his theory to maze learning in rats, position and object learning in monkeys, and paired-associate learning in college students. Precise quantitative predictions derived from the theory were extremely accurate in all cases. Despite the relative simplicity of the model, and the counterintuitive zero-memory assumption, the theory predicted sequences of correct and incorrect responses among college students, as well as rats and monkeys.

Bower and Trabasso

Bower and Trabasso (1963, 1964; Trabasso, 1963; Trabasso & Bower, 1966, 1968) began testing and refining the assumptions and implications of Restle's model immediately following its publication. They applied the simplest form of the model, which assumes the subject tests one hypothesis at a time, to the behavior of college students in two-choice multidimensional concept-identification problems. Their first experiments were concerned with the probabilities of correct and incorrect responses prior to solution, with solution defined in terms of a lengthy criterion run of consecutive correct responses. According to Restle's model, when a correct hypothesis is finally sampled, the subject responds correctly on that trial, maintains the hypothesis, and responds correctly on the next trial, etc., producing the criterion run that defines solution. Thus the subject never makes another error once a correct hypothesis is sampled. Conversely, any observed error implies that prior to that trial the subject had sampled only incorrect hypotheses; that is, hypotheses drawn from the wrong and irrelevant subsets. The pivotal error, then, is the last error the subject makes before solution. Before the trial of last error (TLE), the subject has sampled only incorrect hypotheses. Following the TLE the subject must hold the correct hypothesis, because incorrect hypotheses lead to correct responses only by chance. Thus, in a two-choice task, the probability of a correct response on each trial prior to the TLE is .50.[1] Bower and Trabasso aligned their data around the TLE by combining all their subjects' protocols and obtaining the proportions of correct responses one trial before TLE, two trials before TLE, etc. Restle's model, of course, predicts that the resulting *backward learning curve* should be flat, or stationary, fluctuating around .50. This result, illustrated in Figure 2.1, is exactly what Bower and Trabasso (1964; Trabasso, 1963) obtained. The finding has since been replicated many times (Erickson, Zajkowski, & Ehmann, 1966; Holstein & Premack, 1965; Levine, Miller, & Steinmeyer, 1967; Wickens & Millward, 1971).

Bower and Trabasso (1964; Trabasso & Bower, 1964a, b, 1966) then tested other implications of Restle's one-hypothesis model and, in

1. The probability should be constant, but its exact value depends upon some subsidiary assumptions (see Levine, 1975).

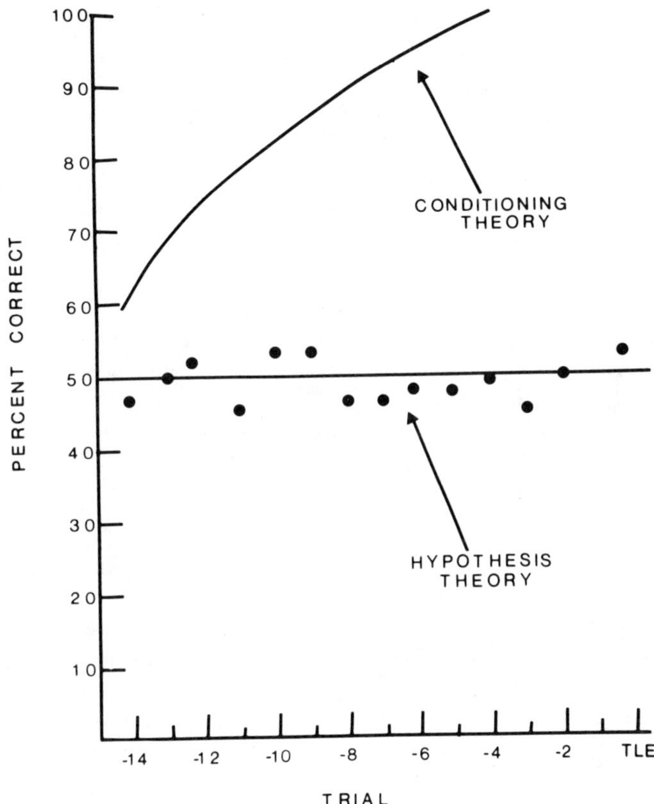

Figure 2.1. The points show the percentage of correct responses on each trial before the last error (TLE). The curves are theoretical (after Levine, 1975).

general, demonstrated its robustness. They showed, for example, that stimulus–response pairings could be changed on error trials without impairing learning; that the theory predicted observed error distributions almost exactly; and that the stationarity assumption held in a variety of tasks. This work culminated, however, in a monograph (Trabasso & Bower, 1968) in which they demonstrated important weaknesses in the one-hypothesis model and presented a refined, alternative theory.

The refined theory had several features in common with Restle's (1962) model: mathematical precision, stationarity before TLE, opportunities for learning only on error trials. The processes involved in hypothesis sampling, however, were modified in important ways. Hypothesis sampling was not strictly random, nor was it with replacement. In addition, rather than simply assuming that the subject held one hypothesis, or more than one, the theory provided a mechanism for estimating the average number of hypotheses that was sampled.

During a concept-learning task the subject was said to operate alternately in two modes: the search mode and the test mode. The subject is in the search mode for a brief time following errors and, while in this mode, makes decisions about which dimensions to sample. The subject could, for example, sample the size, color, and shape dimensions after some error. The next step would be to determine which values on these dimensions, or hypotheses, were included in the designated stimulus array. The stimulus complex designated as correct on that trial might, for example, contain a large, red, square, two borders, a single dot, and a striped background. The subject would then determine that "large," "red," and "square" were viable hypotheses, given the dimensions that were sampled. This assumption, that subjects sample only among those hypotheses that are included in the correct stimulus array following errors is called a "local-consistency" sampling rule (Gregg & Simon, 1967). Trabasso and Bower (1968, p. 53) refer to the resulting set of hypotheses as the *focus sample*.

Once the focus sample is selected the subject switches into the test mode for the next trial. While in this mode the subject is testing the correctness of the hypotheses in the current focus sample. When a response is correct, or receives positive feedback, the subject retains the hypotheses in the sample that dictated the response and those that would have led to the other response are immediately discarded. In this way the focus sample may be narrowed down until it contains only correct hypotheses. If, however, the subject makes an error on this or any subsequent trial, the focus sample is given up and the search mode is reactivated. New dimensions are selected, hypotheses to be included in the new focus sample are designated, and the testing operation begins again.

Restle's assumption of replacement sampling, then, was definitely abandoned. In fact, the description of the search mode offered by Trabasso and Bower implies that the subject has perfect memory for the immediately preceding events. Because the subject selects hypotheses according to a local-consistency rule, not only are those hypotheses in the sample that led to the error eliminated from consideration, but so are any other hypotheses that would have dictated the response on that trial. In addition, Trabasso and Bower abandoned the assumption that the sampling process is completely random. Instead, they argued that some dimensions, those that are more salient or noticeable to the subject, are more likely to be sampled. In order to represent saliency in their theory they assigned weighting coefficients to the dimensions that were used. The greater the relative weight of a particular dimension, the greater the probability that it is sampled following any given error. Thus Restle's zero-memory assumption was renounced; but the theory proposed by Trabasso and Bower is, in an important sense, also a no-memory model. This is because once the subject makes a response, any hypotheses in the focus sample that would have led to the other response are eliminated. If the response is in error, the subject cannot recover those just-eliminated hypotheses, but must re-enter the search mode, select dimensions, assign hypotheses, and begin the narrowing-down process again.

Trabasso and Bower (1968) applied a mathematical model based upon their assumptions to the behavior of college students in various redundant relevant-cue problems. In these problems two redundant cues are used to specify the solution. The stimulus complex designated correct on each trial might be, for example, both red and square, with the composition of the stimulus complex otherwise varying randomly from trial to trial. Thus the subject could attain solution by narrowing the focus sample until it contained the hypothesis red, or square, or both red and square. Single-cue transfer tasks are then used to determine exactly which hypotheses remained in the focus sample when solution was attained. Quantitative predictions derived from the model accurately predicted various facets of the subjects' performance during learning. Trabasso and Bower estimated that their subjects sampled, on average, two or three dimensions each time they entered the search mode. The narrowing-down process of the test mode was such, though, that in most instances the subject's focus sample included only one hypothesis at the time solution was achieved.

Dozens of additional scientists, of course, contributed to developments in mathematical learning theory during the 1960s. Wide acceptance of hypothesis theory by this group is illustrated by a few examples of the issues, and researchers who addressed them: effects of positive and negative feedback upon hypotheses (e.g., Dodd & Bourne, 1969; Erickson, 1968; Erickson & Zajkowski, 1967; Suppes & Schlag-Rey, 1965); effects of errors on hypotheses (e.g., Cotton, 1972; Dodd & Bourne, 1969; Schwartz, 1966); strengths of hypotheses (Coltheart, 1971; Erickson *et al.*, 1966; Falmagne, 1970); memory for hypotheses (Chumbley, 1969; Holstein & Premack, 1965; Nahinsky, 1968; Nahinsky & Slaymaker, 1969; Restle & Emmerich, 1966). The influence of this movement was an important source of the Zeitgeist, then, about 1970 when the first tentative applications of hypothesis theory to children's learning appeared (Eimas, 1969, 1970; Ingalls & Dickerson, 1969; Rieber, 1969).[2]

2. Some researchers talked about hypotheses in children during the 1960s, but did not adopt what were then standard methodolologies for studying them (Harter, 1965; Weir, 1964).

It is fair to say, however, that developmentalists, while certainly influenced by mathematical learning theory, were more directly affected by another movement that had stronger roots in the work of Krechevsky and Harlow. This involved attempts to detect hypotheses directly by studying response patterns. Mathematical theorists simply assumed that their subjects, usually college students, tested hypotheses and explored the implications. Developmentalists, however, were more cautious: They wanted techniques that permitted them to directly observe the child's hypotheses.[3] Marvin Levine developed and validated such techniques in research with college students during the 1960s (Levine, 1963, 1966; Levine, Leitenberg, & Richter, 1964; Levine *et al.*, 1967).

Levine

When, in his work with monkeys, Levine (1959) systematized error-factor analysis, he adopted the term "hypothesis" for each member of the class of all systematic response patterns (see Chapter 1). In this system, however, the frequency of individual hypotheses is detected only indirectly and relatively. Furthermore, the analysis itself is somewhat cumbersome. Thus, one goal of Levine's subsequent research, when he began working with college students in the early 1960s, was to find simpler and more direct techniques for detecting individual hypotheses during learning.

In his first attempts to accomplish these goals, Levine (1963) reported two experiments. In the first he applied a version of his earlier (1959) hypothesis model to the learning-set performance of college students in two-trial problems. The stimuli were pairs of syllables that were typed .5-inch apart on 3- × 5-inch cards. Different pairs were used for each problem. Two of his conditions will illustrate the general procedure. One condition involved standard learning-set problems in which the experimenter selected one of the two stimulus objects as the solution, that is, it was correct on both trials of the problem. In the second condition one stimulus object was designated correct on the first trial of the problem and the other one was correct on the second trial.

Levine also introduced an important modification to the standard learning-set procedure. Instead of providing feedback on every trial of every problem, the experimenter stopped the subject periodically and announced that the next few problems were tests and no feedback would be given following responses. He referred to the two types of problems as "outcome" and "nonoutcome," respectively. The results indicated that

3. This is not meant to imply that the mathematical approaches are not a legitimate means of studying hypothesis behavior.

the subjects showed essentially identical performance in the two: Subjects for whom the same stimulus object was correct on both trials in outcome problems chose the same object on both trials in nonoutcome problems, but, those for whom the correct stimulus changed from the first to the second trial in outcome problems shifted from one stimulus object on the first trial to the other one on the second trial in nonoutcome problems.

These findings, and others revealed by Levine's (1963) application of his hypothesis model were in stark contrast to results yielded by applications of the model to learning-set behavior in monkeys (Levine, 1959). The monkey's behavior, for example, was dominated by position-alternation and position-preference response patterns, but college students never showed them at all. Consequently, Levine (1963) introduced a distinction between two fundamentally different classes of hypotheses: *predictions* and *response sets*. The distinction between the two is behavioral. Prediction hypotheses are sensitive to disconfirmation, that is, if a prediction hypothesis is disconfirmed it is rejected and the subject resamples. Response-set hypotheses, however, are not sensitive to feedback consequences. They are frequently maintained for many trials despite repeated disconfirmation. Response-set hypotheses dominate the behavior of rats (Krechevsky, 1932a,b), chimpanzees (Schusterman, 1961), and monkeys (Harlow, 1950; Levine, 1959), but Levine's (1963) data indicated that college students show *only* prediction hypotheses.

In his second study Levine (1963, Expt. 2) generalized the model to more complex problems. He used four-trial problems of the kind illustrated in Figure 2.2. The stimuli differ on four specifiable dimensions: form (square versus circle), position (left side versus right side), size (large versus small), and color (black versus white). The stimulus sequence in the figure is constructed according to some special restrictions. Notice that each of the eight known cues has a unique representation in terms of left (L) and/or right (R) responses during the four trials illustrated in the figure. The pattern for "large" is LRRL, for example, and for the left side is LLLL, etc.

Levine presented subjects with a series of 24 problems of this type. Six nonoutcome problems were interspersed among 18 outcome problems. The size and position cues were the same in each problem, but each was constructed from a different pair of forms and colors. One group received nonoutcomes on problems 2, 6, 10, 14, 18, and 22 in the series; another group received them on problems 4, 8, 12, 16, 20, and 24. In the first half of the series a color was the solution in each outcome problem; in the remaining problems the solution to outcome problems was always one of the forms.

Levine postulated that at the outset of any problem the subject

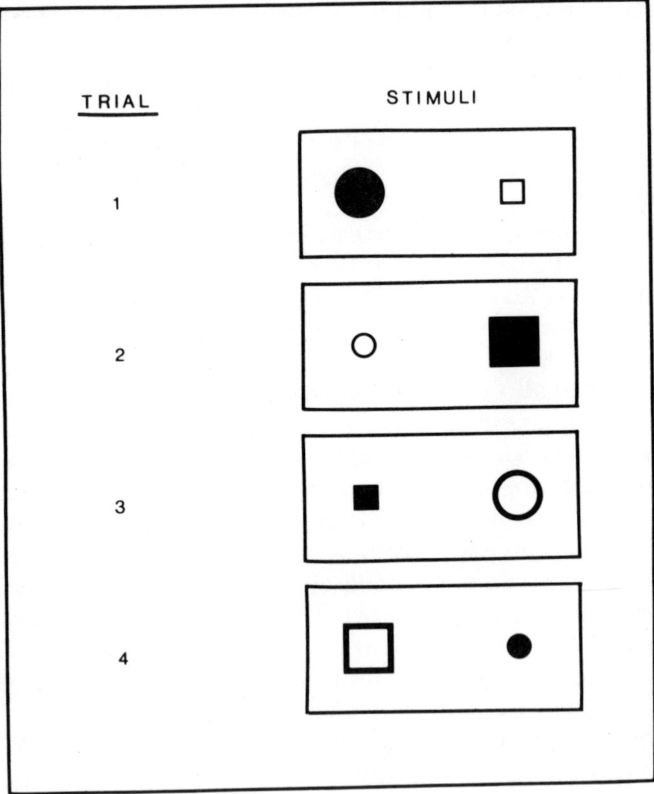

Figure 2.2. The four trials of a four-trial problem.

predicts that one value on one of the dimensions is the solution, and that this hypothesis determines the first response. In an outcome problem the subject retains this hypothesis if the first response is correct, but rejects it and selects a new hypothesis if the response is incorrect. In nonoutcome problems, however, the hypothesis selected at the outset determines the subject's choice response on each trial of the problem. Thus the subject's pattern of responses during nonoutcome problems would allow the experimenter to infer the hypothesis held by the subject at the outset.

The results of primary interest, then, concerned the hypotheses that were exhibited during nonoutcome problems. In the first half of the series there was consistent increase in the frequency with which color hypotheses were exhibited, reaching 80% by problem 12. The frequency of form hypotheses dropped to zero by the tenth problem. During the series

13–24, however, when forms served as solutions to outcome problems, the frequency of color hypotheses dropped precipitously. The frequency of form hypotheses showed a corresponding increase. Few hypotheses drawn from either the size or position dimensions were exhibited after the first few outcome problems. Levine applied his hypothesis model to the data and demonstrated that performance in outcome problems is accurately predicted by performance in nonoutcome problems.

In discussing his results, Levine elaborated further on the distinction between prediction hypotheses and response sets. In the model applied to learning set in monkeys (Levine, 1959), each "hypothesis" was defined as a systematic response pattern. In work with college students, however, a new definition was needed. Levine (1963, p. 271) argued that the "prediction hypothesis" is a mediating process which *determines* the behavior, or response pattern, that the subject exhibits. It follows that the unit of behavior most suited to analysis is the hypothesis, a mediating process, and not the subject's choice response or sequence of choice responses.

Levine next investigated the generality of his assumption that in nonoutcome problems the hypothesis selected at the outset determines the subject's choice response on each trial (Levine *et al.*, 1964). The addition of this assumption meant that there are *two* conditions under which the subject retains an hypothesis: when the experimenter says "correct" after a response, and when no feedback is given. Thus, the implication is that the subject should behave as though the experimenter said "correct" on each trial in nonoutcome problems. Levine *et al.* put this assumption to the test in four different experimental tasks: contingent discrimination, two-trial learning set, double alternation, and probability learning.

In each task college students received a large number of short problems. On prearranged problems in the series the experimenter announced to half the subjects that the next problem was a test and no feedback would follow responses. For the remaining subjects the series was not interrupted; instead, the experimenter simply said "correct," no matter which response was made, during all trials of the particular problem. The performance of the two groups on the selected problems was then compared. Essentially identical findings were obtained in all four tasks: The behavior of subjects in nonoutcome problems matched almost perfectly the behavior of subjects in problems in which the experimenter said "correct" following each response. Levine *et al.* (1964, p. 94) concluded, therefore, that positive feedback and no feedback are equivalent in their effects on behavior.[4] They labeled this equivalence "the blank trials law."

4. Subjects can, of course, be taught to interpret no feedback differently. Barringer and Gholson (1979) reviewed these issues.

Hereafter, any trial on which the subject received no feedback was dubbed a "blank trial."

From the current perspective, the important result of Levine's (1963; Levine *et al.*, 1964) early work with college students was his demonstration that a series of blank trials could be used as a probe for the subject's hypothesis. The next step was to use the probe systematically to explore these dynamics (1966, 1969, 1970, 1971; Levine *et al.*, 1967; Levine, Yoder, years Levine reported a series of experiments in which he investigated these dynamics (1966, 1969, 1970, 1971; Levine *et al.*, 1967; Levine, Yoder, Kleinberg, & Rosenberg, 1968). Sets of blank trials of the type illustrated in Figure 2.3 were used as probes for hypotheses.

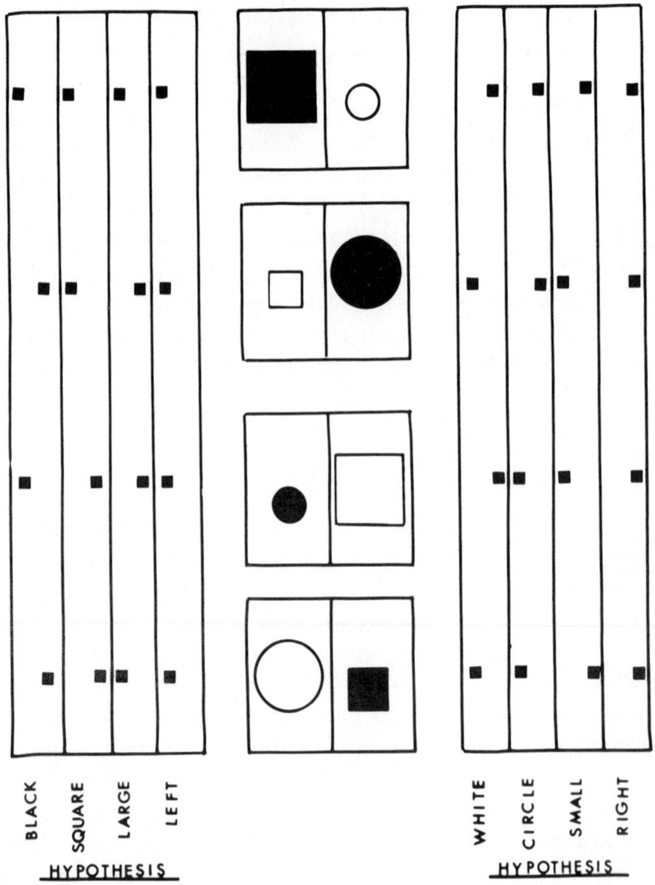

Figure 2.3. Eight patterns of choice responses that uniquely correspond to the eight hypotheses when the four stimulus pairs are presented on consecutive blank trials.

Several features of this four-trial probe are noteworthy. First, each of the eight cues specified as possible solutions corresponds to a unique pattern of left and right responses during the four trials. Second, the subject would be said to hold an hypothesis only if the response pattern exhibited during the four trials involved two responses to one side of the stimulus complex and two to the other, or all four responses to one side (2 : 2 or 4 : 0 response patterns). There are, of course, eight other response patterns, each involving 3 : 1 pattern of responses, that subjects could manifest during the probe. This feature provides a built-in null hypothesis to assess the validity of the procedure. If responding is haphazard during sets of blank trials, then the proportion of probes in which subjects show response patterns that correspond to simple hypotheses should approximate .50.

The first experiment in the series (Levine, 1966) will clarify the general procedure and demonstrate its value in detecting details of the learning process. Levine presented 80 college students with problems containing blank-trial probes of the type illustrated in Figure 2.3. A four-trial probe was inserted between feedback trials. In order to insure that the subjects sampled only among the eight specified hypotheses, four pretraining problems preceded the main experiment. The subject was instructed concerning the eight possible solutions, and blank trials were introduced as "test trials" during the pretraining.

Following pretraining each subject received a series of 16 16-trial problems in which feedback was presented on the first, sixth, and eleventh trials. On the sixteenth trial, the last trial of the problem, the subject was told "correct" in half the problems and given no feedback (blank) in the other half. The structure of a 16-trial problem is illustrated in Figure 2.4.

The stimulus sequence for blank-trial probes and feedback trials was constructed according to what Levine called an "internal orthogonality" criterion. In a four-dimensional bivalued problem there are exactly eight different stimulus pairs possible. These are divided into two sets of four pairs each. In both sets each value on every dimension appears exactly twice with each value of all other dimensions. One set was used to construct the blank-trial probes, and the other for the feedback trials of each problem. Thus different pairs of stimuli were presented on feedback trials and blank trials. The stimulus pairs were ordered so that three consecutive feedback trials logically specified the solution. Each of the eight hypotheses, of course, corresponded to a unique 2 : 2 or 4 : 0 response pattern in each probe.

A total of 3840 blank-trial probes were presented during the experiment. In 3550 (92.4%) the subjects showed response patterns that corres-

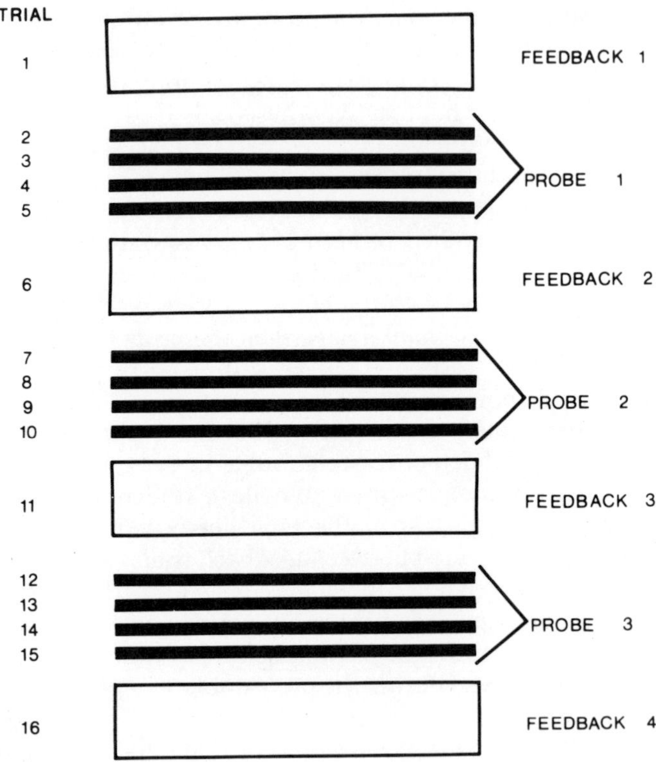

Figure 2.4. A schematic of the 16-trial problem showing how blank-trial probes are inserted between feedback trials.

ponded to simple hypotheses. This value is, of course, significantly higher than the 50% expected if subjects responded haphazardly on blank trials. There remained, however, the problem of explaining the 7.6% of the probes in which nonhypothesis (3:1) patterns were exhibited. Levine suggested that these patterns occur because the subject has a certain small, but constant, probability of accidentally choosing the stimulus complex not dictated by the hypothesis being tested. A subject who predicts that the left side is the solution might, for example, perhaps due to a lapse in attention, choose the right side on some trial. Levine (1969) labeled these responses "oops" errors.

The validity of the "oops" error assumption is easily tested. Although this simplifies the issue a bit (see Levine, 1969), the general idea is that if the subject shows nonhypothesis patterns in .076 of their probes, then the probability of choosing inconsistently with the hypothesis held on any one trial of the four-trial probe is about 25% of .076, or .02. It follows that this probability of choosing inconsistently with the hypothesis held should also hold on any given feedback trial. Thus, to test the assumption, one need only determine which hypothesis was held in each probe and see how often the subject failed to choose consistently with that hypothesis on the following feedback trial. If the hypothesis "left side" is inferred from the response sequence during the first probe in Figure 2.4, for example, the subject should accidentally choose the right-hand stimulus complex on the following feedback trial, Trial 6, with probability .02. The prediction was tested using the 3550 interpretable probes and the feedback-trial response that immediately followed each. Subjects chose inconsistently with their hypothesis 89 times, or .025. The prediction, then, was very accurate.

It will be recalled that Restle (1962) and Trabasso and Bower (1968) agreed that when the subject receives positive feedback the hypothesis that dictated the response is retained; when feedback is negative the hypothesis is rejected and the subject resamples. It was not necessary, however, for Levine to make any assumptions concerning the role of feedback during learning. Instead, he directly determined feedback effects by comparing the hypotheses exhibited before and after each feedback trial. This could be done, of course, only in the cases in which the subject showed hypotheses in two consecutive probes (the first and second and/or second and third) and chose consistent with the first hypothesis on the intervening feedback trial. Levine's subjects maintained confirmed hypotheses 95% of the time (based upon 1112 cases). Disconfirmed hypotheses were replaced 98% of the time (1027 cases).

These findings are, to some extent, at odds with the assumptions made by Trabasso and Bower and by Restle. In both models it is assumed that confirmed hypotheses are always retained (cf. Levine's 95%). The models made different predictions, however, concerning the probability that a disconfirmed hypothesis is immediately resampled, that is, that two consecutive hypotheses are identical when the intervening feedback is negative. Because the subject knows there are exactly eight hypotheses that are potential solutions, the zero-memory model (Restle, 1962) implies that a just-disconfirmed hypothesis will be immediately resampled with probability .125 (one time in eight). Levine's obtained value, .02, is closer to .00, which is implied by the local-consistency rule adopted by Trabasso and Bower.

Levine's procedure also provided a direct means of estimating the size of the hypothesis set from which subjects resampled following each error. When bivalued four-dimensional stimuli are used, Restle's model implies that the size of the set is fixed at eight hypotheses. The local-consistency rule fixes the set at four hypotheses. Levine's hunch was, however, that the size of the set is not fixed at some particular value, but changes from trial to trial. Thus he estimated the size of the set following errors on Trials 1, 2, and 3. There are actually two different procedures that may be used to obtain these estimates (Levine, 1966, 1967), but because one is simpler, and more general than the other, it is described here (Levine, 1967).

The estimate is simply the reciprocal of the conditional probability that the criterion run of correct responses begins following any particular error. If, for example, each subject's set contained four hypotheses after some error and each selected one of these at random, then with probability .25 (25% of the time) the one selected would be the correct hypothesis. Conversely, if among those subjects who make an error on a given trial the probability of obtaining the solution is .25, then we infer that the average size of the set from which they resampled was four hypotheses.

Levine's estimates of the size of this set following errors on Trials 1, 2, and 3 are presented in Figure 2.5. Each data point was based upon about

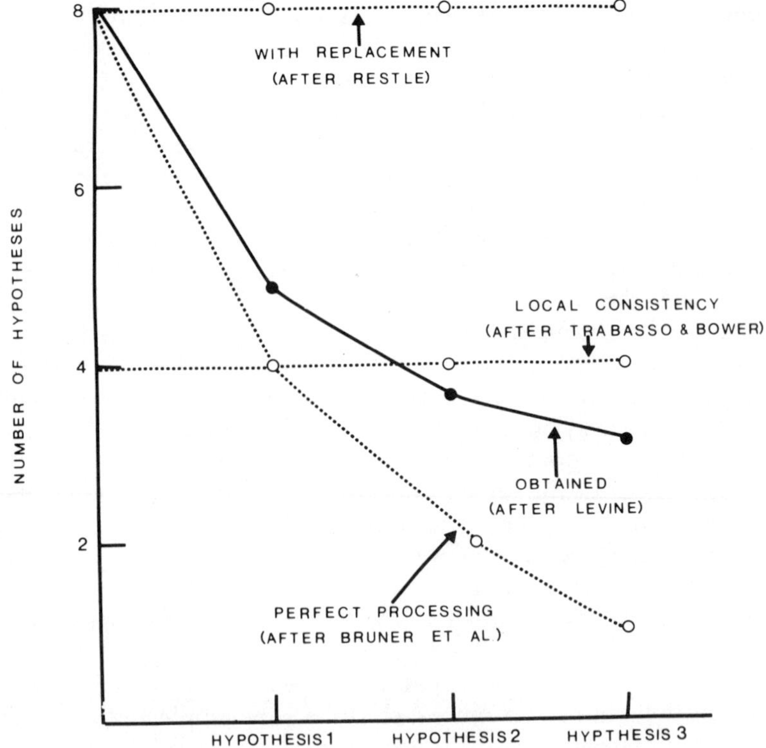

Figure 2.5. The size of the hypothesis set from which subjects resampled following negative feedback on each of the first three feedback trials (after Levine, 1975).

600 observations. The figure contrasts the obtained values with predictions derived from other models (Bruner *et al.*, 1956; Restle, 1962; Trabasso & Bower, 1968). Although the subjects were by no means perfect processors, the set from which they resampled was not of fixed size either. Instead, the size of the set showed a steady reduction across the three trials.

To complete his preliminary evaluation of hypothesis-testing dynamics during learning, Levine (1966) also provided a detailed analysis of the subjects' performance on feedback trials in which they made correct responses. The models presented by Restle and by Trabasso and Bower assumed that subjects learn only on error trials. In effect, these models propose that when any response is in error the subject forgets everything that happened previously and begins the problem anew. The findings reported by Bruner *et al.* (1956), however, indicated that things are more complicated than this. The subject attempts to store information on each feedback trial of the problem, whether the response is correct or incorrect, and collates that information in attempt to achieve solution. Because the process of storing and collating information would be more difficult following errors, when the subject must retrieve hypotheses, than following correct responses, Levine proposed that subjects might actually learn more on trials in which they are told "correct" than on error trials.

His means of evaluating this assumption was straightforeward. Because problems were constructed according to an internal orthogonality criterion, the solution to each was logically determined following the third feedback trial. In Levine's (1966) study feedback was always negative on this trial, so the proportion of solution hypotheses exhibited in the probe following the third feedback trial provided a good index of how efficiently the subjects processed information during the *entire* problem. Four patterns of correct (+) and incorrect (−)responses are possible, given that the response is in error on the third feedback trial: two correct (+ + −), one correct (+ − −, − + −), none correct (− − −). The likelihood of solution was closely correlated with the number of correct responses on these trials. When both were correct (+ + −) subjects solved almost 45% of their problems. When both were wrong (− − −) they solved only 25%, and when one was correct they solved about 32%. It seems clear, then, that subjects do learn, in the sense of eliminating hypotheses from any further consideration, on trials in which they make correct responses. In fact, they learn more on these trials than on error trials.

In addition to identifying the specific hypotheses subjects tested while attempting to attain solution, then, Levine's procedures permitted him to present a fine-grained analysis of the learning process. Results of these analyses revealed that during problem solving the subject is more flexible, vigorous, and ever changing than is implied by various mathematical theories. Thus it was not surprising that Levine's procedures were influential among developmentalists in their early, tentative applications of hypothesis theory to children's learning.

Early Applications to Children

Beginning in 1969, a series of experiments were reported in which Levine's (1966) exact procedures were applied to children of various ages (Eimas, 1969, 1970; Foreit, 1974; Ingalls & Dickerson, 1969; Nuessle, 1972; Weisz & Achenbach, 1975; B. R. Williams, 1974). Even though the research involved children as subjects, it is appropriate to present it here rather than in a later chapter. This is because Levine's (1966) procedures entail serious methodological shortcomings that sometimes lead to artifactual findings when they are applied, in unmodified form, to the behavior of young children. Thus findings obtained in some of the research in which these techniques were used with children are dramatically inconsistent with those obtained in subsequent research in which the methodological problems were avoided.

In addition, this early research with children mostly addressed issues then current among theorists concerned with learning in college students, rather than developmental issues, which are treated in the remaining chapters of this monograph. To preserve continuity, then, and in order to avoid confusion later, one study, the first in the series (Eimas, 1969), will be described in enough detail to illustrate the problems. The methodological shortcomings will then be identified and their empirical consequences demonstrated.

Eimas presented problems containing hypothesis probes of the kind shown in Figure 2.3 to children in Grades 2, 4, 6, and 8. He also included college students, but because the findings closely replicated Levine's results, and the procedures he used present no problem when used with this subject population, they will not be described here. Each child was presented with four pretraining problems and these were followed by eight 16-trial problems structured like the one illustrated in Figure 2.4. The children showed response patterns that corresponded to hypotheses (2:2 and 4:0 patterns) in 71, 73, 77, and 79% of their blank-trial probes, in order of increasing age. If these children always held an hypothesis, Levine's "oops" error assumption would imply that they chose the stimulus complex not dictated by the hypothesis being tested with probabilities ranging from about .05 to .07 on each blank trial and, of course, that they should show similar "oops" error probabilities on feedback trials. However, when Eimas tested this prediction by looking at the feedback-trial response that followed each hypothesis, he found that the children failed to choose consistently with probability .26, .33, .22, and .12 in order of increasing age. Thus comparison of the predicted to the obtained values revealed a large discrepancy, particularly among the three younger age groups.

Eimas (1969, p. 165) suggested that the reason for this discrepancy is that younger children tend to forget from trial to trial which hypothesis they are testing. His other findings seemed to support this conclusion. The second graders, for example, only maintained a confirmed hypothesis 60% of the time (cf. Levine's 95% among college students), and they immediately resampled, or retained, a disconfirmed hypothesis 18% of the time. In addition, when he estimated the size of the hypothesis set from which the children resampled following errors on feedback Trials 1, 2, and 3, he found that among the two younger age groups the size of the set actually showed a consistent increase, growing from about six hypotheses following the first feedback trial to between seven and eight following the third. The sixth and eighth graders showed no discernable pattern; the number of hypotheses in the set varied from four to six. It is clear, then, why Eimas concluded that young children have poor memories.

Difficulties with the Approach

Careful examination of the blank-trial probe illustrated in Figure 2.3 suggests, however, a different explanation for Eimas' findings. The response patterns that correspond to two of the cues (black and white) involve position alternation (LRLR, RLRL). In addition, the problems are constructed so that, in general, different cues, for example, large and small, would alternate positions in the next blank-trial probe. Furthermore, position hypotheses (left and right side) are specified as relevant to solution in each problem. It is well-known, though, that children frequently display position-alternation and position-preference response sets spontaneously, particularly in two-choice tasks, and that these are fairly resistant to feedback consequences (Berlyne, 1960; Fellows, 1968; Gollin & Saravo, 1970; Rieber, 1966, 1969; Schusterman, 1963; Weir, 1964). If these response sets occurred in Eimas' study, they were misinterpreted as legitimate hypotheses and, of course, this would add unknown sources of error that inflated scores obtained on some dependent measures and deflated scores on others. Consider, for example, the protocols of a child who exhibited a position-alternation response set throughout a given problem. First, the alternation patterns would be misinterpreted as cue-determined hypotheses in each probe. Second, on feedback trials the child would show a response consistent with the "hypothesis" inferred during the preceding blank-trial probe only at chance level (50%). Finally, whether feedback was positive or negative, the "hypothesis" that followed would be consistent with those feedback consequences only at chance level.

Levine (1975) and his colleagues (Gholson *et al.*, 1972) identified the confounding and suggested that blank-trial probes constructed according to different criteria should be used in research with children. An example of one such probe is presented in Figure 2.6. In this blank-trial probe, the

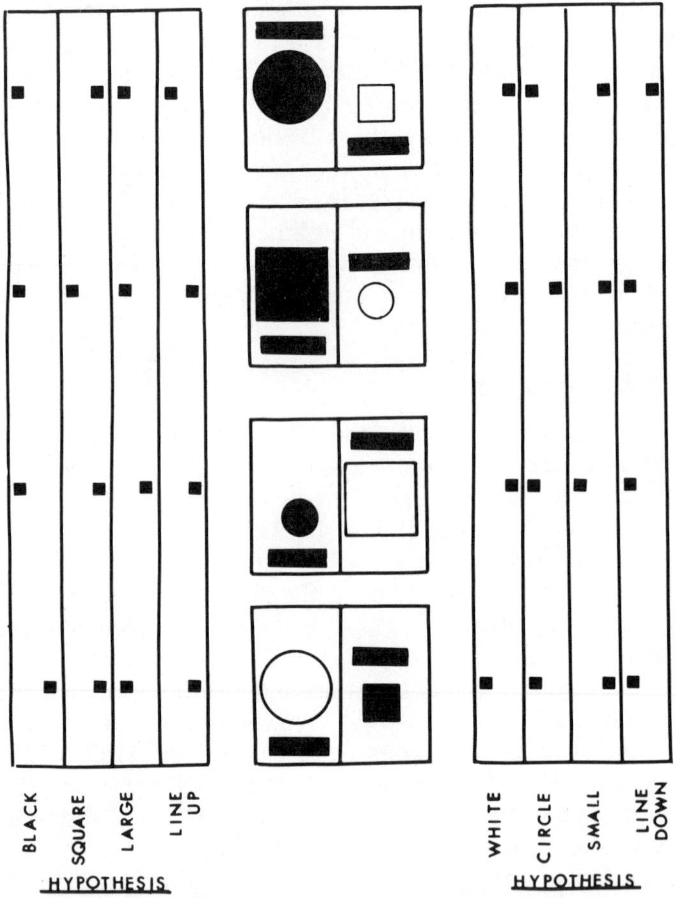

Figure 2.6. A stimulus sequence that permits inference of eight simple hypotheses, each from a unique pattern of three responses to one side and one response to the other side. Probes of this type also permit the unique identification of response patterns dictated by position-oriented response-set hypotheses (position alternation, position preference).

manifestation of each simple hypothesis corresponds to a unique 3:1 pattern of responses. In addition, when this probe is used, the position dimension is explicitly omitted from the set of possible solutions through appropriate pretraining.

Two experiments (Schuepfer & Gholson, 1978; Weisz, 1977) that were directly concerned with these methodological issues will demonstrate the importance of using probes that do not confound position-oriented response sets with legitimate hypotheses in research involving young children. Weisz and Achenbach (1975) used confounded four-dimensional probes (Figure 2.3) to investigate IQ (70, 100, 130) and mental age (MA) effects in children of MA 5:6 (5 years 6 months), 7:6, and 9:6. They obtained no differences in these problems due to MA level, a finding that is out of line with both earlier and later research in which unconfounded probes were used (this research is reviewed in Chapters 3 and 4). In addition, they reported that children of IQ 70 showed poorer performance on several dependent measures than did children of higher IQ levels.

In his doctoral dissertation, however, Weisz (1977) replicated the experiment, using unconfounded hypothesis probes of the type illustrated in Figure 2.6. Results of the study were the exact opposite of the earlier one. MA level produced significant effects on most dependent measures, but IQ produced no effects at all. Thus Weisz (1977) rejected his earlier findings (Weisz & Achenbach, 1975), attributing them to "the influence of specific methodological factors [p. 108]," that is, the confounding of position-oriented response sets with cues specified as possible solutions.

In a related study, Schuepfer and Gholson (1978) directly assessed the effects of the two kinds of blank-trial procedures. They studied normal and retarded children of MA levels 5:6 and 7:6. A transfer design was used in which half the children in each group received a block of problems containing confounded probes followed by a block of problems with unconfounded probes. The remaining children in each group received the problem blocks in reverse order. The problem type (confounded versus unconfounded) produced one main effect and entered into numerous interactions. The findings were otherwise similar to those obtained by Weisz (1977). MA produced significant effects on most performance measures, but IQ did not. IQ did enter into two higher-order interactions, but these indicated that the lower IQ group showed, if anything, better performance [Schuepfer & Gholson, 1978, p. 424]. The transfer data served to underscore the importance of using unconfounded probes. Children of both MA levels showed significantly more position-oriented response sets in unconfounded probes when these probes were preceded by confounded probes, than when unconfounded probes were presented first in the problem sequence. Thus the confounding strengthened both the establishment and transfer of position-oriented response sets. For this reason research in which confounded probes were used with young children must be viewed cautiously.

Conclusions

An associationistic framework dominated mainstream learning theory for about 20 years prior to the 1960s. During that decade, however, the framework was supplanted by hypothesis theory. This theory was constructed, for the most part (cf. Restle, 1962), to account for the behavior of college students. The version of hypothesis theory that resulted, with its restricted scope and procedures, was, of necessity, current when developmentalists began applying hypothesis-testing procedures to children's learning. The early research with children, although generally open to the kinds of criticisms described in the last few pages, evidenced promise for adapting a general hypothesis-theory conception to children of various ages. It was also clear that the procedures, and the theory, required refinement if the approach was to further our understanding of developmental processes. As will be seen in the next two chapters, these refinements were not long in coming.

3

Hypothesis Theory: A Developmental Theory of Human Learning

After 1970 there was a steady increase in the number of scientists who adopted hypothesis theory as a framework for evaluating developmental processes. Conceptual and theoretical advances moved quickly, as issues that seemed settled, or of little interest within the associationistic framework, were reopened or attracted new attention, sometimes with startling results. One purpose of this and the next chapter, then, is to review these developments. Our real goal, however, is to organize this and related literature around a general model of developmental learning. It should be made clear, though, that this statement is qualified by two important considerations. First, the theoretical account is concerned only with individuals older than about two years of age: Infant learning is presently beyond its scope. Second, the model is not presented in a precise quantitative language, although this is a distant goal of mine.

This chapter and the next are organized into four sections, and, because the third section will sometimes take us far afield, it will be useful to index the four at the outset. First, a few previously published experiments will be described in order to illustrate the fruitfulness of hypothesis theory as a conceptual framework for evaluating developmental processes, and to provide some basic data. Second, the assumptions of the model will be outlined, and those implications that must be addressed in a review of the literature will be explicitly stated. Third, the theoretical conception will be elaborated in the context of an extensive review of the relevant literature. Finally, the model will be restated in summary form vis-à-vis the literature review. New research that bears on the strengths and weaknesses of the conception will be presented in subsequent chapters (5, 6, and 7).

Some Basic Data

Gholson *et al.* (1972) reported two experiments in which bivalued four-dimensional problems were presented to children of various ages, and college students. Each problem contained blank-trial probes of the type illustrated in Figure 2.6. These were inserted between consecutive feedback trials in each problem. The stimulus sequences were constructed according to an internal orthogonality criterion, so the subject never encountered a specific stimulus pair on a blank trial that was presented on a feedback trial. Any three consecutive feedback trials logically specified the solution in each problem, and only 3:1 patterns of response corresponded to hypotheses in blank-trial probes. Stimuli were rear-projected onto two adjacent screens that served as response manipulanda. Mounted directly above each screen was a red light. On feedback trials the light located above the correct stimulus flashed on for three seconds, and the stimuli remained in view during this period.

In the first experiment the subjects were 50 second graders, mean calendar age (CA) 7 years 6 months (7:6), 50 fourth graders (CA = 9:7), 50 sixth graders (CA = 11:6), and 50 college students (range 17–24 years). Each subject, tested individually, was first presented with four pretraining problems that were used to introduce task demands: relevant dimensions, response requirements, blank trials, etc. Following pretraining, a series of six 76-trial problems of the kind illustrated in Figure 3.1 were presented. The relevant dimensions were color (black versus white), size (large versus small), letter (e.g., X versus T), and line position (line under versus line over the letter). Each problem was constructed from a different pair of letters, but values on the other dimensions were the same in each. Any problem in the series was terminated when the subject met a solution criterion of five consecutive correct feedback-trial responses.

Results revealed that the mean percentage of response patterns which corresponded to hypotheses during blank-trial probes for Grades 2, 4, 6, and college students were 88.4, 89.3, 92.4, and 92.8, respectively. These scores did not differ from each other, but each was significantly different from 50%, the score expected if responding is haphazard during probes. The children maintained confirmed hypotheses, that is, two consecutive hypotheses were identical when feedback was positive on the intervening feedback trial, with probabilities ranging from .93 to .97. The score for college students was .99. The probability that two successive hypotheses were identical when intervening feedback was negative

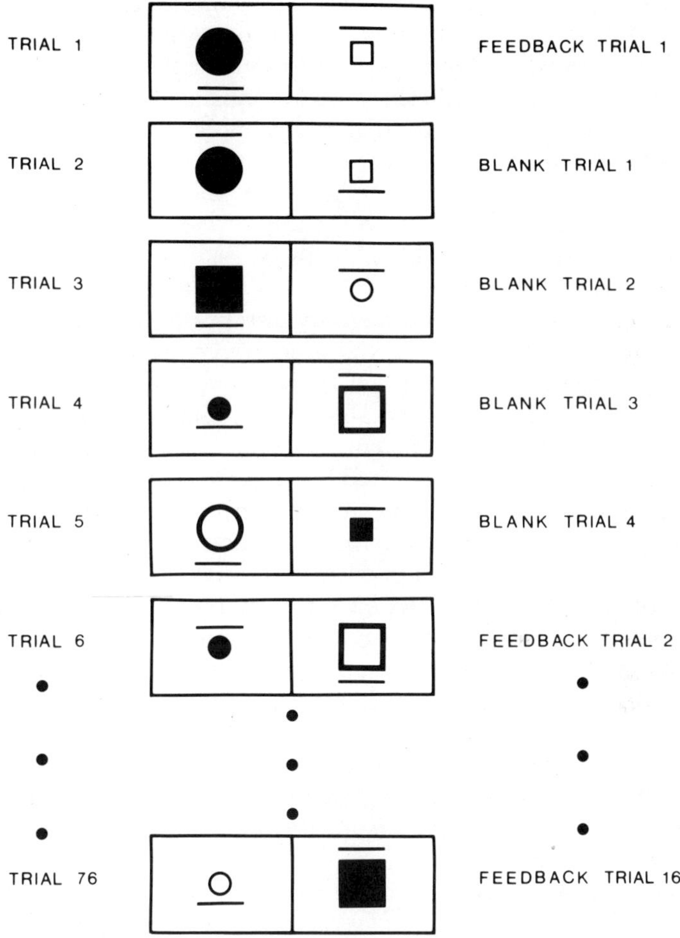

Figure 3.1. A schematic of the 76-trial problem showing how blank-trial probes are inserted between consecutive feedback trials.

ranged from .07 to .10 among the children, but was .01 for the college students. The children differed significantly from the adults but not from each other. Offenbach (1974) has reported similar findings among first, third, and fifth graders.

The high probabilities of immediately repeating disconfirmed hypotheses suggested that children of elementary-school age might tend to resample with replacement following errors (Restle, 1962), that is, show *zero memory*. Because the children's hypotheses were known, though, the appropriateness of the zero-memory assumption could be evaluated by a second datum. Consider, for example, a feedback trial on which the child chooses a stimulus complex containing "small, white T, line up." When feedback is negative, all four of these hypotheses are logically disconfirmed. If children sample according to a *local-consistency* rule (Trabasso & Bower, 1968), they will sample only from among the four hypotheses that are still logically viable, that is, "large, black X, line down." If they show zero memory, however, the hypotheses observed following negative feedback will be locally consistent only 50% of the time. The observed percentages of locally consistent hypotheses following errors were 89, 88, and 91 for Grades 2, 4, and 6, respectively.

Thus, evaluation of the zero-memory assumption using two different dependent measures led to two contradictory conclusions. On the one hand, the children appeared to forget which hypothesis was just tried and disconfirmed, resampling it with about the frequency expected if they randomly resampled with replacement. On the other hand, they eliminated all four logically disconfirmed hypotheses about 90% of the time following negative feedback. Thus it was necessary to explain the tendency to immediately repeat disconfirmed hypotheses in some way other than zero memory. Examination of the data revealed that a few of the children who adopted a primitive style of responding that Harlow (1950) dubbed "stimulus preference," accounted for most of the instances in which disconfirmed hypotheses were immediately repeated. Among the 150 children, 20 accounted for 60% of the cases. At the other extreme, 72 children *never* repeated a just-disconfirmed hypothesis, and 32 children did so only once. A few children at each grade level, whose responses were determined by a stimulus-preference response set accounted, then, when averaged with the remaining data, for the apparent applicability of the zero-memory resampling rule.

Backward learning curves and hypothesis curves were obtained for each age group. The TLE (trial of last error, see Chapter 2) was taken as Trial 0, the feedback trial preceding it was −1, the next preceding trial was −2, etc. The proportion of correct responses on these trials (after TLE the response is by definition correct) for each age group is plotted in Figure 3.2. Clearly, the children showed stationarity before TLE and none-to-all learning, as did the adults. The proportion of the times for each age group that the correct hypothesis occurred during a blank-trial probe before and after the TLE is also plotted in the figure. In general, the probabilities that correct hypotheses appeared before TLE ranged from about .03 to .05. After the TLE, the probabilities ranged from .95 to .99. Thus both children and adults rarely hold the correct hypothesis prior to the TLE, but nearly always hold it after TLE.

These results provided strong support for the conclusion that hypothesis theory provides a useful description of the behavior of

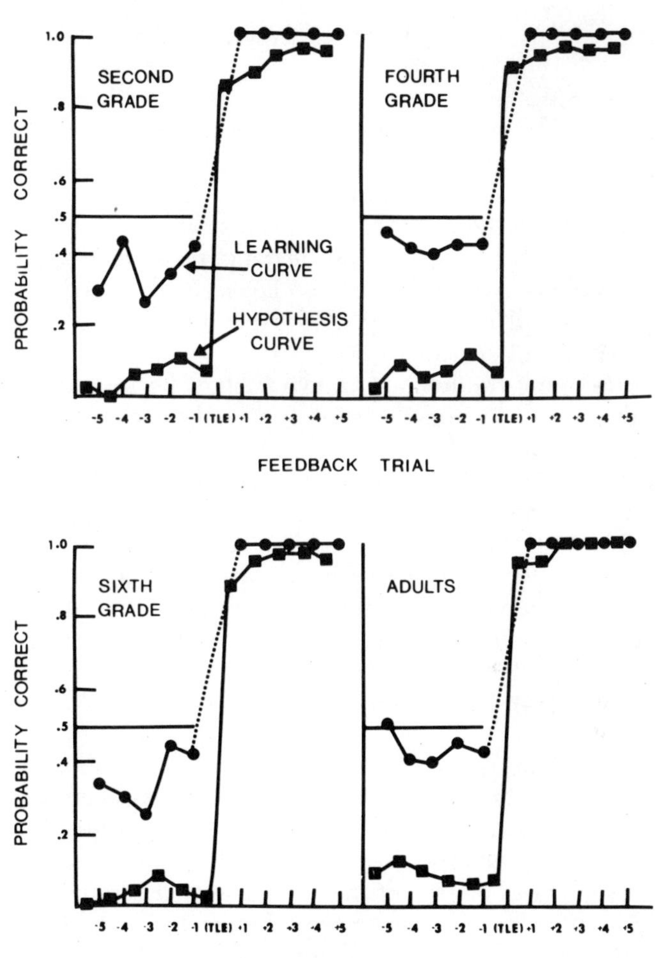

Figure 3.2. Learning curves (the proportion of responses that were correct on each feedback trial) and hypothesis curves (the proportion of solution hypotheses exhibited) plotted around the feedback trial of last error (TLE).

elementary-school children, as well as adults in concept-learning problems. Thus, in order to explore further the theory's range of applicability, a second experiment was conducted (Gholson *et al.*, 1972, Expt. 2) that included even younger children. The subjects were 48 kindergarten children (CA = 5:4) and 48 second graders (CA = 7:4). The details of the study were similar to the first experiment, except that the problems were shorter (25 trials), and in addition to inserting probes between consecutive feedback trials, a probe was also presented before the first feedback trial.

Data from the second graders were similar in all respects to those obtained in Experiment 1, so they will not be described. The kindergarten children showed dramatically different performance. They were presented with 2160 blank-trial probes, but showed consistent hypotheses (3:1) patterns in only 906 (42%) of them. This score was significantly *below* chance expectation (50%). In those instances in which these children showed legitimate hypotheses in two consecutive probes, they maintained disconfirmed hypotheses 45.6% of the time and rejected confirmed hypotheses 21.2% of the time.

Because young children are known to show position-preference and position-alternation response sets frequently, the response patterns exhibited in blank-trial probes were analyzed further. There are, of course, eight patterns of left (L) and right (R) responses that do not correspond to legitimate hypotheses: Half correspond to position-oriented response sets, LLLL, RRRR, LRLR, RLRL; and half do not, RLLR, LRRL, LLRR, RRLL. If the children responded haphazardly during probes in which consistent hypothesis patterns were not exhibited, half of these probes should fall in each category. Taken together, however, position-preference and position-alternation response sets accounted for 84.2% of them (1056 of 1254). The two remaining response patterns accounted for only 15.8%.

It seemed clear, then, that young children, like nonhuman primates (Harlow, 1950; Levine, 1959), frequently exhibit response sets. Thus, in order to provide a developmental account, the theory would need to incorporate both prediction hypotheses and response sets. In addition, even a cursory examination of the protocols of the individual children indicated that the sequences of hypotheses they exhibited from one blank-trial probe to the next were not a haphazard affair. Qualitatively different processes seemed to be operating. This led to an expansion of the theory along the lines suggested by Bruner *et al.* (1956).

Hypothesis Sampling Systems

The expansion was based upon the notion that the sequences of hypotheses generated by subjects during learning are determined by hypothesis-sampling systems: A *system* is a plan or general determinate that regulates the sequence in which hypotheses are manifested (Gholson *et al.*, 1972). Two kinds of systems are distinguished: *Strategies*, which involve systematic sequences of prediction hypotheses that always lead, if followed perfectly, to problem solution; and *stereotypes*, which entail long sequences of responses dictated by a particular response-set hypothesis that is held despite disconfirmation. Stereotypes, in principle, never lead to solution, except in the trivial case in which the child begins the problem with a stimulus-preference response set that happens to correspond to the cue designated as the solution. Six systems, three strategies, and three stereotypes have been delineated.

Before the means of detecting each of the systems in the subjects' protocols is illustrated, some qualifications should be noted. First, it must be assumed that the subject begins the problem with a particular system that dictates the mode in which hypotheses are sampled at the outset and following errors. Second, it is assumed that the system dictates the sequence of hypotheses that is manifested within the problem, at least long enough for it to be detected. In general, the sequence of hypotheses and feedback trials should be long enough to permit the various systems to be disentangled and short enough to minimize the probability that the subject changes systems within a problem. In bivalued four-dimensional problems of the kind used by Gholson *et al.* (1972), a sequence of three hypotheses, each preceded by a feedback trial, meets these criteria.

In describing each of the six systems, discussion is confined to bivalued four-dimensional problems, and it is assumed for *illustrative* purposes that:

1. The stimulus pairs presented on consecutive feedback trials are arranged according to an internal orthogonality criterion so that the first three such trials logically specify the solution.
2. The subject always receives positive feedback on the first feedback trial and negative feedback on the second and third (with orthogonal stimuli the third feedback trial must be negative, but given this restriction any feedback sequence may result in a classifiable problem).[1]
3. Following each feedback trial the subject's hypothesis is known to the experimenter through the insertion of a blank-trial probe.

Other kinds of hypothesis probe techniques, including single blank trials, introtacts (verbal statements), and subject-selected tokens (component stimulus cues), have also been used (e.g., Cole, 1976; Karpf & Levine, 1971; Kemler, 1972, 1978; Kornreich, 1968; Offenbach, 1974; Phillips & Levine, 1975; Spiker & Cantor, 1977).

In general, any probe that detects the subject's hypothesis following each feedback trial provides the data necessary for a systems analysis. In those cases in which comparisons between various kinds of hypothesis probes were possible (i.e., similar subject populations and treatment

1. If stimulus sequences are not internally orthogonal on feedback trials, the systems analysis becomes more tedious in that each sequence of stimulus pairs, feedbacks, and hypotheses must be treated individually.

conditions), they have yielded reasonably comparable results (cf. Karpf & Levine, 1971; Kornreich, 1968; Offenbach, 1974; Phillips & Levine, 1975). An important advantage of the blank-trial probe used by Gholson *et al.* (1972) is that it permits the unambiguous detection of both position-oriented response sets and legitimate hypotheses dictated by stimulus cues relevant to solution.

It should be explicitly stated, however, that all the various hypothesis probe techniques that have been used in research with children embody potential problems. The use of these probes assumes that the child holds one, and only one, hypothesis at any given time, *and* this hypothesis determines the choice response that is made. Research reviewed later in this chapter and the next, in which standard hypothesis-testing methodology was used, provides strong support for this assumption; but other research in which the reversal–extradimensional shift task was used suggests that children's responses are sometimes determined by different compound cues on successive trials of a problem (Cole, 1976; House, 1979; T. J. Tighe & L. S. Tighe, 1972; Zeaman & House, 1974). Standard hypothesis probes provide no means of detecting compound cues, if they occur. This issue is treated in more detail in Chapter 5.

A second problem is that, in general, research to date has been based upon the assumption that hypotheses, both predictions and response sets, emerge full-blown in the repertoire of the child. If, however, hypotheses are actually consolidated out of smaller, component units, standard hypothesis-probing methodologies provide no means of detecting and tracking the time course of these components. This issue is addressed in more detail later in this chapter and in the next, and research bearing directly upon it is presented in Chapter 5.

The three strategy systems are called *focusing, dimension checking*, and *hypothesis checking*. Only problems in which hypothesis sampling is locally consistent following errors are considered for these categories. The individual using the focusing strategy begins the problem by monitoring *all* eight hypotheses, then eliminates the four logically incorrect hypotheses from this set following the first feedback trial. Two more are eliminated following the second, and the final incorrect hypothesis is eliminated from this set following the third feedback trial. Each hypothesis exhibited is globally consistent (Gregg & Simon, 1967): The first is consistent with stimulus information from the first feedback trial, the second is consistent with information from both the first and second feedbacks, and the third hypothesis that is exhibited is the solution. The last is the only hypothesis consistent with information from all three feedback trials. When such a sequence of hypotheses is observed, one infers a focusing strategy. Table 3.1 contains the name, a brief description and an example of each of the six systems. Focusing is illustrated in the first row of the table.

TABLE 3.1

The Hypothesis Sampling Systems, Their Definitions, and an Example of Their Manifestations [a]

System	Definition	Example of manifestation							
		F_1	H_1	F_2	H_2	F_3	H_3	F_4	H_4
Focusing	The subject eliminates all logically disconfirmed hypotheses on each feedback trial	+	Large	–	White	–	Square (solution)		
Dimension checking	The subject checks all four dimensions systematically, one dimension at a time	+	Large	–	White	–	Line down (not solution)	–	Square
Hypothesis checking	The subject checks all eight hypotheses systematically, one hypothesis at a time	+	Large	–	Small	–	White	–	Black
Stimulus preference	The subject stays with one hypothesis, despite disconfirmation	+	Large	–	Large	–	Large	–	Large
Position alternation	The subject alternates from one side of the card to the other throughout each probe	+	LRLR	–	RLRL	–	LRLR	–	RLRL
Position preference	The subject chooses the same side of the card on each trial throughout each probe	+	LLLL (or) RRRR	–	LLLL (or) RRRR	–	LLLL (or) RRRR	–	LLLL (or) RRRR

[a] F_1 = Feedback Trial 1; H_1 = Hypothesis 1.

Dimension checking is the next most efficient system. When this strategy is manifested, it is assumed that the subject appropriately orders the two hypotheses onto each of the four dimensions, and then proceeds through the list, checking one dimension at a time. Because the subject recognizes that its complement was logically disconfirmed at the time of selection, only one hypothesis per dimension (locally consistent at the time of selection) is exhibited. The subject might, for example, try a locally consistent hypothesis from the size dimension, then if it is disconfirmed, reject the size dimension as containing the solution and sample a locally consistent hypothesis from the color dimension, etc.

Hypothesis checking is still less efficient. When this strategy is observed, it is again assumed that the subject orders the hypotheses into pairs on each dimension and then goes through the dimensions systematically. When this strategy is employed, however, both hypotheses on each dimension are exhibited, one after the other. The subject might, for example, try "large," then if it is disconfirmed try "small" before rejecting the size dimension as containing the solution. An hypothesis from a second dimension would be tried next, then its complement, etc.

Before the detection of the three stereotypes is described, some minor complications concerning the classification of problems involving strategies should be made explicit. In principle, how to decide which system the subject exhibits in a given problem is simple. By inspecting the first three hypotheses one decides which system determined the sequence exhibited. There is, however, occasional overlap in the manifestations of two systems. A subject who is following the dimension-checking strategy might, for example, when resampling after the third feedback trial, select the dimension that contains the solution and, of course, because the hypothesis is locally consistent, manifest the solution hypothesis. The resulting hypothesis sequence might be identical, then, to one shown by a subject who uses the focusing strategy. Such confounding requires special statistical techniques for arriving at valid estimates of the frequencies with which each of the various systems occur. These techniques, which vary somewhat with each of several types of confounding, have, along with their rationale, been published elsewhere (Levine, 1975, his Appendix). The specific correction for each feedback sequence and type of confounding is presented in Table 3.2.

The three stereotype systems are labeled *stimulus preference, position alternation,* and *position preference.* Each of these is based upon a sequence of responses dictated by a specific response-set hypothesis. When stimulus preference is manifested, an hypothesis dictated by a particular stimulus cue follows each feedback trial despite its repeated disconfirmation. It is as though the child "likes" a particular stimulus cue, and, regardless of the feedback consequences, always chooses the stimulus complex that contains it.

TABLE 3.2
The Corrections That Are Required to Obtain Estimates of the Real Frequencies (f) of Focusing (Fo), Dimension Checking (D-ch), and Hypothesis Checking (H-ch)[a] from the Observed Frequencies (Fo', D-ch', and H-ch') for Each Feedback (F) Sequence

Feedback sequence	Correction required
$F_1 = +,\ F_2 = +,\ F_3 = -$	f(D-ch) = f(D-ch') + ½f(D-ch')
	f(Fo) = f(Fo') − ½f(D-ch')
$F_1 = +,\ F_2 = -,\ F_3 = -$	f(D-ch) = f(D-ch') + ³/₅f(D-ch')
	f(Fo) = f(Fo') − ³/₅f(D-ch')
$F_1 = -,\ F_2 = -,\ F_3 = -$	f(D-ch) = f(D-ch') + ½f(D-ch')
	f(Fo) = f(Fo') − ½f(D-ch')
$F_1 = -,\ F_2 = +,\ F_3 = -$	f(H-ch) = f(H-ch') + ½f(H-ch')
	f(D-ch) = f(D-ch') + ½f(D-ch')
	f(Fo) = f(Fo') − [½f(H-ch') + ½f(D-ch')]

[a] Only the last feedback sequence in the table requires any correction for H-ch, and only when the hypothesis following F_3 is from a different dimension than the one shown following F_1 and F_2. In this case the hypothesis following F_4 determines whether the problem is classified as H-ch' or D-ch'.

The two remaining stereotypes involve response-set hypotheses which indicate that the child ignores the stimulus features specified as possible solutions to the problem at hand. The child who manifests position alternation chooses one side of the stimulus array and then the other throughout each blank-trial probe in the problem, for example, right side, left side, right side, etc. Similarly, position preference involves response to a single position throughout each of a series of probes, right side, right side, right side, etc. It is necessary, of course, to use blank-trial probes in which each of the eight simple hypotheses corresponds to a 3:1 pattern of responses in order to detect these position-oriented stereotypes.

In addition to hypothesis sequences that may be classified as resulting from one of the systems, subjects sometimes manifest hypotheses in *unsystematic* sequences. Because unsystematic sequences occur frequently under certain experimental conditions, brief consideration of them is in order. Consider again a problem in which feedback is positive on the first feedback trial and negative on the second and third, etc. If, for example, the hypothesis sequence "large, red, small" was manifested, the problem would be categorized as unsystematic, because the child tried one dimension (size) and rejected it, then a second (color), and then returned to the first (size) again. Similarly, the sequence "large, large, red" would be classified unsystematic because the subject first retained a disconfirmed hypothesis, then rejected it. This sequence appears to include some mixture of a stereotype and another approach, perhaps a strategy. In fact, only about 50% of the hypothesis sequences that subjects

TABLE 3.3

Examples of Each of the Unsystematic Hypothesis Sequences That Are Possible [a]

Feedback sequence $F_1 = +, F_2 = -, F_3 = -$	Feedback sequence $F_1 = -, F_2 = -, F_3 = -$
Black, black, large	Circle, circle, line up
Black, large, large	Circle, line up, line up
Black, white, white	Circle, square, square
Black, black, white	Circle, circle, square
Black, white, black	Circle, square, circle
Black, large, black	Circle, line up, circle
Black, large, white	Circle, line up, square
Black, large, small	

[a] F = Feedback trial.

could manifest in four-dimensional problems, if hypothesis sampling were haphazard, correspond to any system category. Examples of each of the sequences included in this unsystematic category are illustrated in Table 3.3. While unsystematic hypothesis sequences undoubtedly reflect a more sophisticated approach to the task than does stereotypic responding, how they should be considered in relation to the strategies is presently unclear. As will be seen in the next chapter, both subject and task variables can dramatically alter their frequency of occurrence.

Results of the Gholson *et al.* (1972, Expt. 1) systems analysis performed on the data of the elementary-school children and college students are presented in Figure 3.3. The two position-oriented stereotypes are not included in the figure because they occurred very infrequently, and only among the youngest children. The college students exhibited focusing in about 45% of their problems and dimension checking in most of the remainder. They showed a few unsystematic hypothesis sequences (about 2%), but the college students *never* showed a stereotype.

The modal strategy of the elementary-school children was dimension checking. They showed strategies in about 80% of their problems, and the remainder were about evenly divided between the stimulus-preference and unsystematic categories. The different data configurations generated by college students as compared to elementary-school children hinted, at the time, that qualitatively different processes might be operating.

Figure 3.4 contains the relative frequencies in each of the six system categories for the kindergarten and second-grade children of Experiment 2 (Gholson *et al.*, 1972). The abscissa of the figure may be thought of as a continuum of system sophistication, ranging from the most sophisticated strategy, focusing, to the least sophisticated position-oriented

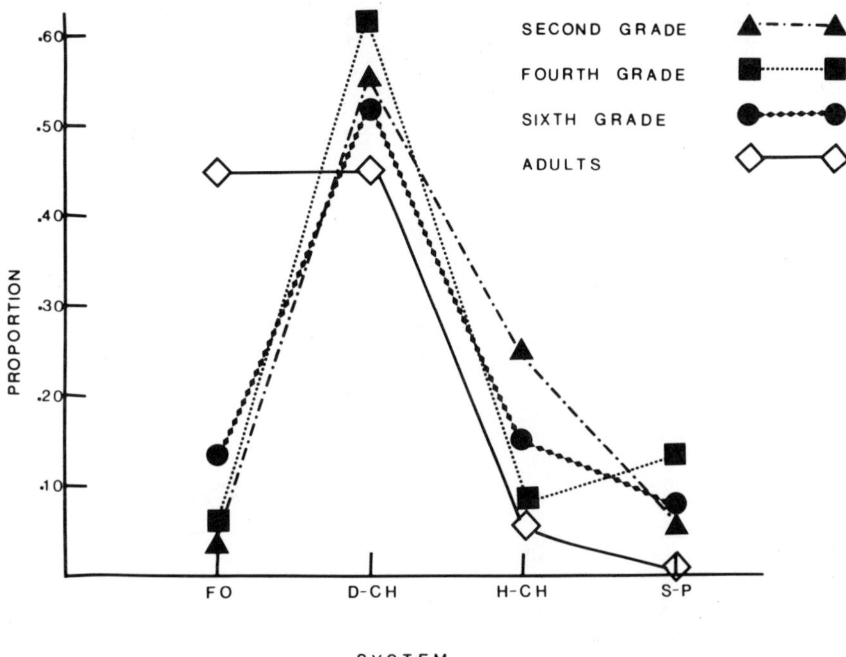

Figure 3.3. The relative frequencies of focusing (Fo), dimension checking (D-ch), hypothesis checking (H-ch), and stimulus preference (S-P).

stereotypes. The chief finding was, of course, that the distributions scarcely overlap at all. The second graders showed about the same distribution as the corresponding group in Experiment 1, that is, mostly dimension checking, little focusing, and a few stereotypes. The kindergarten children appeared to approach these problems in a very different fashion. They showed stereotypic responding in 94% of their problems.

The data from these experiments suggested, then, that qualitatively different processes might be operating when kindergarteners are compared with elementary-school children, and possibly even when college students are contrasted with the latter. These processes will be elaborated in considerable detail in the next section of this chapter and in Chapter 4, but it will be useful to describe one other experiment before outlining the general assumptions of the model. Minimally, most would probably agree that the systems data indicated there is one major characteristic that distinguishes among kindergarten, elementary-school, and college students: the efficiency with which information is processed during problem solving.

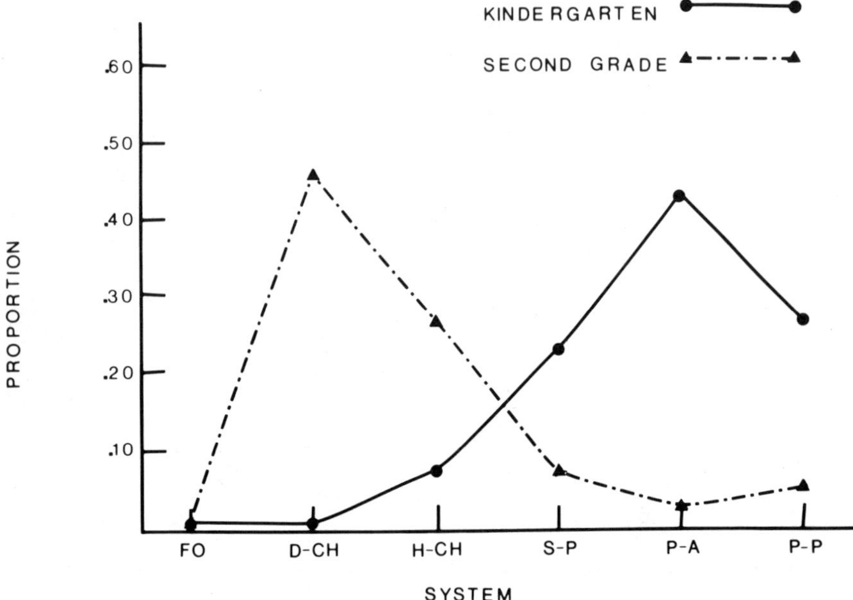

Figure 3.4. The relative frequencies of focusing (Fo), dimension checking (D-ch), hypothesis checking (H-ch), stimulus preference (S-P), position alternation (P-A), and position preference (P-P).

Cognitive Subprocesses

One possible reason for differences that are obtained on global measures of information-processing efficiency, such as the systems that are exhibited, is that there are deficiencies in one or more cognitive subprocesses that underlie the global behavior. According to this view (Bower, 1975; Eimas, 1970; Levine, 1966), a number of cognitive subprocesses must be considered in any attempt to evaluate performance. When the subject is presented with a stimulus array at the outset, one or more of the available stimulus cues is coded (Glanzer & Clark, 1964; H. H. Kendler & T. S. Kendler, 1962). If the indicated response receives positive feedback, then the subject stores the hypothesis, or hypotheses. When feedback is negative, however, the subject must eliminate the just-coded cues from storage and attempt to recode information consistent with feedback.

The coded (or recoded) stimulus information then dictates the response on the next trial. The subject employs similar processes of coding and recoding on the second feedback trial, as dictated by the feedback contingencies. To process efficiently, however, several other processes must be operative at this point. First, information stored after the first feedback trial must be retained and retrieved. Second, the retrieved information must be collated with the information gained at the second feedback trial. Finally, some form of logical inference must be applied that has the effect of reducing the total amount of information that must be considered on subsequent trials (Newell & Simon, 1972). This type of routine is followed, with greater or lesser efficiency, until the problem is solved. According to this view, then, defective functioning in any one of the cognitive subprocesses may produce a deficiency in the more global measures of performance that are directly obtained from the protocols.

With this conception in mind, Gholson, Phillips, and Levine (1973) explored the systems exhibited by second graders (CA = 7:4) and college students (range 17–24 years) under conditions assumed to manipulate the coding demands of the task. Coding demands were studied by manipulating the relationship between feedback and stimulus information. The general procedure was similar to that used by Gholson *et al.* (1972), which was described earlier in this chapter (see Figure 3.1). Four pretraining problems were followed by nine 36-trial problems that contained blank-trial probes between consecutive feedback trials. Stimuli were rear-projected onto panels that the subject pushed to indicate choice responses. Red feedback lamps were mounted above each panel.

Three conditions varying the temporal relationship between stimulus information and feedback were investigated. These conditions, schematized in Figure 3.5, were labeled /+3, /0, and /−3. In condition /+3 the feedback lamp was illuminated immediately after the subject's response and remained lit with the stimulus in view for 3 seconds. Thus it was possible for the subject to code or recode directly from the correct stimulus array after feedback was delivered. In condition /0 the 3-second feedback interval began immediately at the subject's response, but the stimuli were extinguished at the onset of this interval. Thus it was necessary for the subject to code the stimulus of choice prior to response and, when wrong, recode in the absence of the visual stimulus. In condition /−3 the stimuli were extinguished immediately when the subject responded, but there was a 3-second delay before the onset of the 3-second feedback interval. In this condition it was necessary for the subject to code before responding, hold the coded cues in storage for 3 seconds before feedback was delivered, and, when necessary, recode in the absence of the visual stimulus. Under all three conditions the next trial began one second after the end of the feedback interval.

The college students showed consistent hypotheses in 93, 92, and 90% of their probes in conditions /+3, /0, and /−3, respectively. The corresponding percentages for second graders were 88, 82, and 89. The probabilities that two consecutive hypotheses were identical when inter-

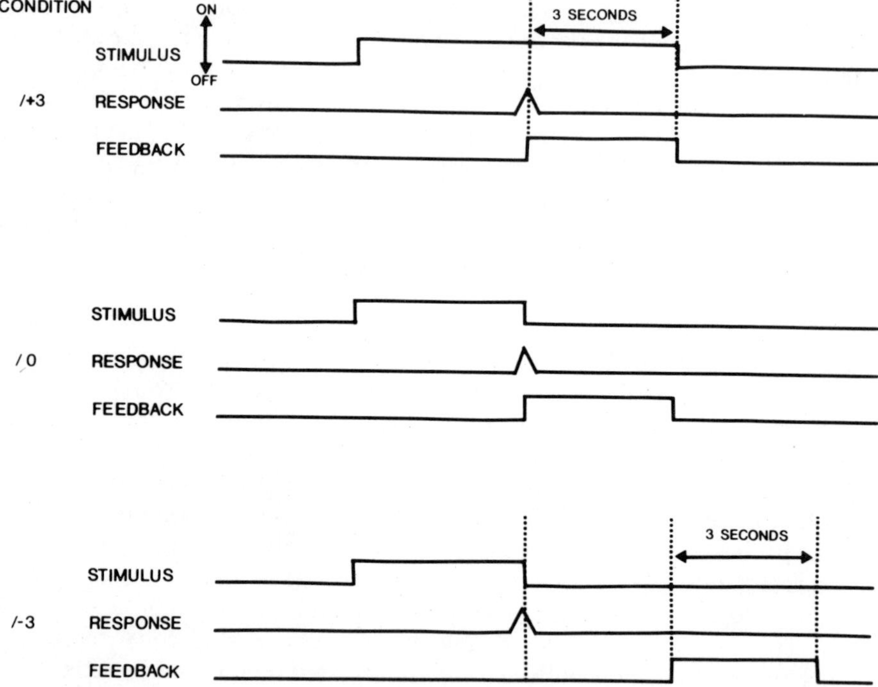

Figure 3.5. A schematic diagram of the temporal relationship between stimulus information, the subject's response, and feedback under each of the three conditions investigated.

vening feedback was positive, or negative, and the frequencies with which subjects resampled according to a local-consistency rule following negative feedback are presented in Table 3.4. In general, the coding demands of the task had little effect on the college students, but produced large effects on the children's performance.

The systems data for each age level and coding condition are presented in Figure 3.6. The two position-oriented stereotypes are omitted from the figure because they failed to occur (one child showed position alternation in one problem in condition /0). As was true with the other measures, the college students were largely unaffected by the different coding demands. They exhibited focusing in about 50% of their problems and dimension checking in most of the remainder.

In contrast, the distribution for the children shifted in direct correspondence to the coding demands of the task. The curve for condition /+3 was unimodal, peaking at dimension checking, and the three strategies accounted for most of the data. In particular, these children showed dimension checking in half their problems and stimulus preference in

TABLE 3.4
The Probabilities That Two Hypotheses Were Identical When Intervening Feedback Was Positive ($F_i = +$) or Negative ($F_i = -$), and the Local Consistency Data (LC)

Group	$F_i = +$ Interval			$F_i = -$ Interval			LC Interval		
	/+3	/0	/−3	/+3	/0	/−3	/+3	/0	/−3
Grade Two	.97	.93	.97	.10	.21	.23	.87	.67	.67
College Students	.99	.99	.99	.02	.01	.04	.96	.89	.86

only about 10%. This replicates almost perfectly data obtained by Gholson *et al.* (1972, Expt. 1) under the same /+3 conditions. The curve for condition /0 was bimodal, with the children exhibiting dimension checking in 40% of their problems and stimulus preference in 30%. In condition /−3 the curve was again unimodal, but the peak was at the stereotype, stimulus preference. Furthermore, children in this condition showed hypothesis checking, the least efficient of the strategies, slightly more frequently than dimension checking. Once again (cf. Gholson *et al.*, 1972), the children showed very few instances of the focusing strategy.

These results indicate that college students simply alter their manner of coding to meet the demands of the task, that is, if stimulus information must be coded prior to response, or both coded and rehearsed for a few seconds, college students simply adjust their behavior accordingly. Children, however, have not yet acquired this kind of sophisticated control over their own coding and rehearsal processes (cf. A. L. Brown, 1975, 1978). Consequently, children are at the mercy of laboratory manipulations that produce few, if any, effects among the more developmentally mature. It will be seen later that this holds for manipulations that affect other cognitive subprocesses—for example, memory and attention—as well as coding demands.

Assumptions and Issues

Most generally stated, our conception is that the individual in the learning situation brings to bear, with greater or lesser efficiency, a sequentially organized set of cognitive subprocesses in an attempt to solve the problem at hand (Gholson & Beilin, 1979). In our present state of understanding a complete list of these subprocesses would probably *include* the following: stimulus differentiation (Cohen, Weatherford, Lomenick, & Koeller, 1979; J. J. Gibson & E. F. Gibson, 1955; Siegel & White, 1975; L. S. Tighe & T. J. Tighe, 1965), directed attention (Adams & Shepp, 1975; Hohle, 1967; Neisser, 1967; Sperling, 1960; Trabasso &

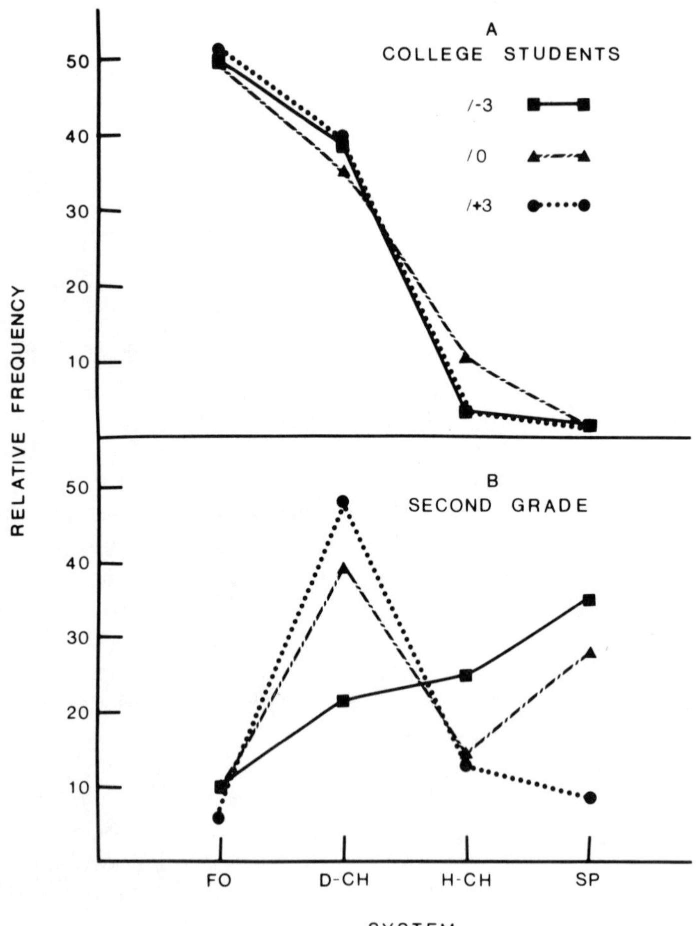

Figure 3.6. The relative frequencies of focusing (Fo), dimension checking (D-ch), hypothesis checking (H-ch), and stimulus preference (S-P).

Bower, 1968; Zeaman & House, 1963), verbal and nonverbal coding processes (Beilin, 1975; Glanzer & Clark, 1964; Glick, 1975; Haber, 1964; H. H. Kendler & T. S. Kendler, 1962; T. S. Kendler, 1979; Neisser, 1967; Paivio, 1972; Posner, 1973; Reese, 1970), memory storage (Hagen, 1972; Hale & Stevenson, 1974; Hoving, Morin, & Konick, 1974; Neimark, Slotnick, & Ulrich, 1971), and retrieval from memory (A. L. Brown, 1975, 1978; Neimark, 1976). It is also assumed that a *processor*, analogous to an executive system (Klahr & Siegler, 1978; Klahr & Wallace, 1976; Newell & H. A. Simon, 1972), integrates the various cognitive subprocesses. The processor, depending upon developmental level, permits the individual to construct and execute solution plans of varying sophistication through the application of forms of logical inference. The processor is seen as reflecting underlying cognitive capabilities (logical abilities) and changes *qualitatively* with development, both in the cognitive abilities available and in the ways they are organized. The nature of the processor becomes, then, the defining characteristic of each qualitatively distinct stage of development.

Several features of the processor require delineation. First, it is assumed that the processor consists of a set of logical operations and an interpreter that determines the sequence in which the logical operations are executed. Second, the integrating element in the processor is the cognitive *scheme*, which represents some form of regulating system of logical and related elements. Third, only information that reaches the processor is operated upon, transformed, and integrated into ongoing behavior by the activated schemes. Finally, as a first approximation, characteristics of the processor are identified with process implications of Piaget's descriptions of the cognitive operations available to preoperational (children about 2–6 years of age), concrete operational (about 6–12 years), and formal operational thought (children older than about 12); (Gholson & Beilin, 1979).

It is assumed that each of the sequentially organized cognitive subprocesses is available to the normally developing child older than about 2 years of age. The efficiency with which various of these subprocesses function, and the ease with which each is brought to bear on a given problem environment, however, changes *quantitatively* with development; *and* in some cases they are readily manipulable in the laboratory. Experimental manipulations that produce different effects on performance as functions of chronological age (or developmental level) may result from either (*a*) developmental changes in how efficiently the various cognitive subprocesses operate under particular task constraints, or (*b*) changes in the available logical abilities and their organization as reflected in the processor. Thus the model predicts two types of developmental effects: qualitative changes in the functioning of the processor, and quantitative changes in the functioning of the cognitive subprocesses that regulate a continuous flow of information to and from the processor.

Implications of the two types of effects may be considered in relation to the analysis of variance model. A qualitative change in the processor would be reflected in a developmental-level main effect, while differential functioning of the various cognitive subprocesses would lead to an interaction between developmental level and task variables. These implications receive support from a series of experiments that are reviewed in the next chapter.

The general conception is based, of course, upon the assumption that individuals approach problems by testing hypotheses (or rules) until one that results in solution is located. Thus the emergence of hypotheses in the child's repertoire is a fundamental conceptual issue. Because this cardinal point has received so very little attention previously (cf. Gholson & Schuepfer, 1979; Levinson & Reese, 1967), the first task will be to review the literature that bears on it. In order to unsnarl at least some of the questions raised by the general conception, it will be useful to consider them under four general headings.

1. *Hypothesis Formation*. What is the relationship between response sets and prediction hypotheses? Do both kinds of hypotheses emerge full-blown in the repertoire of the young child? If not, are the component units of various hypotheses acquired independently, at different rates, and over a protracted time period? How may the acquisition of hypotheses, or the component units out of which they are consolidated, be facilitated?

2. *The Processor*. What are the characteristics of the processor at each level of development? Is it useful to identify these characteristics with implications derives from Piaget's theory? Is it useful to conceptualize the processor as a set of logical operations and an interpreter that determines the sequence in which the operations are performed (i.e., in terms of a computer metaphor)? How do the cognitive operations reflected in the processor change during the transition from one developmental level to the next, that is, what induces transitions and what happens during those transitions? How resistant to training are the specific logical skills that are reflected in the processor at each level of development?

3. *The Cognitive Subprocesses*. Can individual subprocesses be unambiguously identified? What is the nature of the interactions among the various subprocesses under particular task constraints? How do the effects of various task manipulations change during development? A central question concerns what role the processor plays in organizing and integrating the various cognitive subprocesses. Does, or how does, this role change with developmental level?

4. *Empirical Issues*. Many task (and subject) variables that might be assumed (or have been shown) to influence performance during acquisition cannot be directly identified with a particular cognitive subprocess or the processor. Some of these manipulations are considered in later chapters. How does the general conception stack up when these variables are addressed?

Before proceeding to the next chapter and a review of the literature that bears on the issues raised by the general conception, it might be useful to explicitly state some virtues of the present model relative to strict information processing (e.g., Klahr & Siegler, 1978; Klahr & Wallace, 1976; H. A. Simon, 1972) and neo-Piagetian models (Case, 1974, 1978; Inhelder, Sinclair, & Bovet, 1974; Pascual-Leone, 1970). In general, information-processing models are very clear on the relationship between executive (logical) functions and performance, but provide no structural or operative basis for the executive functions. Thus these models are vague on the mechanisms that account for developmental change. The neo-Piagetian models are clear on the structural base for performance and therefore provide an account of development, but they are vague on the relationship between structures, operations, and performance. Thus they are not easily tested. It will be seen in the next chapter that the present model derives operations from structures and specifies the relationship between the operations embodied in the processor and performance. Thus the model is truly developmental and is, at the same time, easily tested.

4

Hypothesis Theory: Relevant Research

The distinction between response-set hypotheses and predictions, as was seen in the last chapter, has proven useful in work with young children (Cantor & Spiker, 1978; Gholson & Beilin, 1979; Morello, Turner, & Reed, 1977; Parrill-Burnstein, 1978; Phillips & Levine, 1975; Reese, 1977). The relationship between the two has not, however, been specified. A corollary issue, which has also received little attention (cf. Gholson & Schuepfer, 1979; T. S. Kendler, 1979), concerns the emergence of hypotheses in the repertoire of the young child. Thus a body of research bearing on these issues will be discussed before the hypothesis-testing literature itself is considered.

The Emergence of Hypotheses

Any hypothesis may be described in terms of the individual's behavior following correct and incorrect responses. Consider, for example, a feedback trial on which the child's response is determined by the prediction hypothesis "red." If feedback is positive the child maintains the hypothesis; thus the child may be said to "win–stay." Similarly, following negative feedback, when red is rejected and a new hypothesis is selected, the child is said to "lose–shift." Therefore, any hypothesis may be described in terms of the individual's stay and shift behavior following positive and negative feedback. Position alteration, for example, would be "win–shift, lose–shift" position, and stimulus preference would be "win–stay, lose–stay" on a particular stimulus cue. This kind of analysis is used to describe children's behavior throughout this section of the chapter.

We make the following proposals:

1. Prediction hypotheses do not emerge full-blown in the repertoire of the young child.
2. Instead, the component units of various hypotheses (e.g., win–stay, lose–shift, etc.) are acquired independently, at different rates, and possibly over a considerable time period.
3. The young child's behavior is, at first, dominated by response-set hypotheses.
4. The win and lose components of various response-set hypotheses must eventually be separated, evaluated, and coordinated with task-relevant information (stimulus cues, feedback) before the appropriate win and lose components are consolidated to yield prediction hypotheses.

Support for this analysis is derived from research concerned with position responses, object responses, and the acquisition of learning set.

Position Responses

Numerous researchers have reported that young children frequently exhibit position preference and alternation responses in two-choice spatial-learning problems. The kind of position response generated has been shown to be closely correlated with age (Gratch, 1964; Jeffrey & L. B. Cohen, 1965; W. Kessen & M. L. Kessen, 1961; Schusterman, 1963; White, 1965). In general, position preference precedes position alternation developmentally, and the change takes place sometime around age 4. Schusterman (1963), for example, reported that in a 100% feedback condition, children 3 years of age showed mostly win–stay position, but 5-year-olds showed mostly win–shift position. Ten-year-olds exhibited no significant trend toward either win–stay or win–shift.

Feedback schedules have been shown to affect the position responses of young children. Jeffrey and L. B. Cohen (1965) presented a simple two-choice problem with undiscriminable stimuli to 3- and 4½-year-old children. Three noncontingent feedback schedules were used: 100%, 50%, and 33%. Children who received 100% showed performance essentially identical to that reported by Schusterman. The older children exhibited strong win–shift position, while 3-year-olds showed mostly win–stay. Under the partial feedback conditions, the frequency of alternation responses dropped to chance level (50%) among the older children. In each case, however, the older children exhibited more alternation than the

3-year-olds, who showed mostly position preference (win–stay, lose–stay) in all three conditions. It seems reasonable to conclude, then, that the dominant action component changes from stay to shift sometime between the child's third and fifth year.

Rieber (1966), with a task similar to that used by Jeffrey and L. B. Cohen, demonstrated that the preference for alternation begins when the child is about 4 years old, remains—but to a lesser degree—through age 8, and drops to chance level by age 10. Rieber pointed out that the older children were more likely to shift their responses to the other position following an incorrect response than following a correct one. This difference in shift behavior was not found, though, in the youngest children. These findings indicate that the lose–shift position behavior obtained in young children may serve a different function from the same behavior in older (8 years and older) children. While the position responses of 4-year-olds are controlled by response sets (e.g., win–shift, lose–shift), the older child attempts to coordinate stay and shift components with feedback consequences and stimulus information (win–stay, lose–shift).

In conclusion, the research indicates that young children's position responses frequently involve the same action component (i.e., win–stay, lose–stay or win–shift, lose–shift) with the perseverative response preceding the alternation response. By about 8 years of age children begin to coordinate their stay and shift behavior with feedback consequences.

Object Responses

Those who have investigated developmental changes related to win–stay and lose–shift object responses (object refers to one or more nonposition stimulus cues) have frequently employed a modified learning-set procedure (Berman, 1971, 1973; Berman & J. Meyers, 1971; Berman, Rane, & Bahow, 1970; Cross & Vaughter, 1966). When this procedure is used, children are presented with a series of two-trial problems. On the first trial one stimulus object is presented; the response to this stimulus is either rewarded or nonrewarded. A test trial follows in which the previous stimulus object is paired with a new stimulus. The correct stimulus on the second trial is dependent upon the outcome of the first trial. If response on the first trial is rewarded, the child is required to respond according to a win–stay object principle, that is, choose the stimulus object that was present and rewarded on the first trial. If the Trial 1 response is not rewarded, then the newly introduced stimulus is correct on the second trial and the child must respond accordingly (i.e., lose–shift). In general, win–stay problems are more difficult than lose–shift problems for children between about 2 and 8 years of age (Berman,

1973; Berman *et al*., 1970; Cross & Vaughter, 1966). In fact, the probability of a correct Trial 2 response has rarely exceeded chance among young children in win–stay problems of this kind.

Because the stimulus introduced on the second trial is new, or novel (Berlyne, 1960), Berman (1971) investigated the role of this factor in win–stay and lose–shift object responses. She compared two different procedures for presenting stimuli on the first trial; either one stimulus object or two stimulus objects were presented. Each child received a series of two-trial win–stay and lose–shift problems. Berman predicted that if the superiority of performance in lose–shift problems resulted from children's preference for novel stimuli, then a significant interaction between problem type (i.e., win–stay versus lose–shift) and presentation method (one versus two stimulus objects on Trial 1) should be obtained. Win–stay problems would be more difficult in the one-stimulus condition, but lose–shift problems would be at least as difficult as win–stay problems when two stimulus objects were presented on both trials. No significant interaction was obtained. Instead, the single-stimulus procedure was more difficult than the two-stimulus procedure for both win–stay and lose–shift problems. In line with earlier findings, win–stay problems were more difficult than those with lose–shift solutions under both presentation methods. It should be noted, however, that a possible role of win and lose position responses in the two-stimulus procedure was not evaluated.

Berman *et al*. (1970) reported that children between 4 and 10 years of age show some improvement with practice on both win–stay and lose–shift problems. Ten-year-olds showed rapid improvements and reached criterion quickly in both. Performance of 4-year-olds was deterred by perseverative runs to position cues and to novel stimulus objects; practice produced more improvement in lose–shift than in win–stay problems. Six- and 8-year-old children showed about the same amount of improvement in problems of both types. In addition, Berman (1973) reported that the amount of improvement in win–stay performance was positively related to the number of win–stay problems experienced by the three younger age groups. Conversely, win–stay performance decreased with an increase in the number of lose–shift problems.

Cantor and Spiker (1977, 1978; Spiker & Cantor, 1977) have reported a series of experiments in which they used an hypothesis-testing procedure to investigate win–stay and lose–shift object components. One of their experiments (Cantor & Spiker, 1978) will illustrate their procedure and findings. They used a single nonspatial dimension (e.g., color). Four values on the dimension were arranged to form two artificial, or "pseudodimensions" (e.g., red–green and blue–yellow). The stimulus object that had red on it, for example, also contained blue or yellow on each trial, but it was never green. These stimulus materials were used to construct bivalued problems in which a value drawn from one pseudodimension was selected as the solution. The two values on the remaining pseudodimension were irrelevant.

The children were presented with two stimulus objects on each trial, and were required to state an "hypothesis," that is, name the color thought to be the solution, before picking one of the objects to indicate their choice responses. A marble was concealed under the correct object on each trial and the children moved the object (a block) to indicate their choice responses. Following pretraining, the children were divided into groups that received varying amounts of training in win–staying, lose–shifting, and in selecting new hypotheses that were never *explicitly* disconfirmed on a previous trial, that is, they were instructed to never select a hypothesis that had been previously stated and disconfirmed.

Their subjects, kindergarten children and first graders (range 67–91 months) were divided into three groups that received varying amounts of instruction in the demands of the task: no training, intermediate training, and extensive training. The children showed lose–shift hypotheses in 73%, 76%, and 88% of the trials when feedback was negative, in order of increasing training. The corresponding scores for win-stay hypotheses were 29%, 62%, and 89%. These results were clearly in line with those obtained using a modified learning-set procedure (Berman, 1973; Berman *et al*., 1970). The children exhibited hypotheses that had never been explicitly disconfirmed 33%, 56%, and 79% of the time.

In summary, the literature indicates that the young child's dominant position response is preference (win–stay, lose–stay position) until about age 4, then changes to alternation (win–shift, lose–shift position). By about age 8 or 10, neither is dominant. Instead, the child's behavior is largely determined by feedback consequences, that is, by prediction hypotheses. Lose–shift object precedes the development of win–stay object, which is weak or nonexistent in the repertoire of the young child. Furthermore, practice (limited) usually produces only a mild facilitative effect upon the win–stay object responses of preschoolers and young elementary-school children (cf. Cantor & Spiker, 1978). Young children, then, have clearly acquired the component units out of which prediction hypotheses are eventually consolidated. Learning-set research provides further confirmation for this conclusion and suggests how the consolidation process might be accomplished.

Learning Set

Before reviewing the learning-set research, it will be useful to review the task and describe the procedures that have been used to evaluate the data. A learning set is acquired through extensive practice on short problems that have a common type of solution. The learning set is said to be acquired when the solution to each new problem is immediate.

Usually, a different pair of stimulus objects is used for each problem with one object designated as correct (cf. Levine, 1963). The position of the correct object (i.e., right or left side) is randomly determined on each trial. The progressive acquisition of the learning set is observed in an increased percentage of correct responses across the problems. Thus the study of learning set provides measures of learning efficiency within a single problem, and measures of the cumulative improvement in performance across a large number of problems. When the learning set is acquired, the subject needs feedback information only from the outcome of the first trial of each new problem to obtain solution.

Harlow (1949, 1950), who conducted the earliest research on learning set, was interested in systematic response patterns (or error factors) shown by monkeys during a series of several hundred discrimination problems. Different error-producing factors appeared to determine response patterns during progressive phases of acquisition (Harlow & Hicks, 1957). The rate of learning increased across each phase, as different error factors were eliminated. Thus the acquisition of learning set may be viewed as the result of error-factor elimination, that is, the suppression of various incorrect response tendencies.

Levine's (1959, 1963) more systematic approach permitted the proportion of responses controlled by each hypothesis to be identified. In Levine's analysis the probability of any hypothesis is one-half the sum of the probabilities of the win and lose components that comprise it. He arranged the hypotheses into complementary pairs (e.g., position preference versus position alternation) and derived equations for calculating the relative frequencies of those in each pair. Levine's equations yield difference scores which range from −1.00 to +1.00. The resulting scores indicate the amount by which the proportion of responses resulting from one of the complementary pair of hypotheses exceeds the proportion of responses accounted for by the alternative hypothesis. Given the pair position preference-position alternation, for example, a score of +1.00 indicates that the position-preference hypothesis is completely dominant, while −1.00 indicates that position alternation dominated the pair. Any intermediate score reflects the extent to which one member of the pair was dominant over the other. Levine's equations are based upon the assumption that the probability of a correct response following a win is equal to the probability of a correct response following a loss, for example, win–stay object is equal in strength to lose–shift object.

Bowman (1963) questioned this latter assumption and modified Levine's analysis in order to estimate the relative strengths of each win and lose component separately (research on object responses indicates that Levine's assumption may not hold in young children). This modification permits the proportion of responses controlled by each of the component units (e.g., win–stay object, win–stay position) to be calculated. Bowman arranged the eight win and lose response components into the following complementary pairs: (*a*) win–stay object versus win–shift object; (*b*) win–stay position versus win–shift position; (*c*) lose–stay object versus lose–shift object; (*d*) lose–stay position versus lose–shift position. The equations then permitted him to calculate the proportion of responses by which one response component exceeded its complement (e.g., win–stay object versus win–shift object). The analyses indicate which component is dominant in each complementary pair.

Levine's and Bowman's models yield identical results if subjects' responses are only determined by hypotheses (response sets, predictions) or if the win and lose components of each hypothesis are equivalent in strength. However, the models differ if responses are determined by individual win and lose components that differ in strength or do not share a common cue referent (e.g., win–stay position combined with lose–shift object). Such combinations reflect "hypotheses" that are *impossible* in Levine's system and, therefore, cannot be assessed. Because each component unit is estimated separately in Bowman's model, such combinations present no problem. Thus, if Levine's hypotheses are acquired or function in a piecemeal fashion, then Bowman's analysis will yield more information about the process. Levine's hypotheses and Bowman's symbols for them are presented in Table 4.1. Details of the analyses are presented in Chapter 5.

Levinson and Reese (1967) applied Levine's and Bowman's models to learning-set data of preschool children (CA range 3–5:6 years), fifth graders (no age data were reported), college students, and the aged (68 to 85 years). Subjects were presented with a series of 10 four-trial problems per day until five consecutive problems were completed in which no more than one error occurred on Trials 2, 3, and 4 (approximately 93% correct). The stimuli were pairs of stereometric objects. For response, the subject moved the object to expose a well. The well under the stimulus object designated correct in the given problem was baited on each trial. As expected, the rate of learning-set acquisition was closely related to age. The median number of problems required to attain the criterion was 20.4, 10.8, and 6.7 for the preschoolers, fifth graders and college students, respectively. The aged, who were tested in seven different experiments, were extremely variable in their performance. The median was as low as about 40 problems and as high as several hundred.

Levinson and Reese used the criterion reference method to analyze their acquisition data (Hayes & Pereboom, 1959). When this method is used subjects' scores are grouped according to the day or problem on

TABLE 4.1
Levine's Descriptions and Names for His Hypotheses, and Bowman's Symbols for Them [a]

	Levine's description	Levine's name	Bowman's symbols
HYPOTHESIS 1:	The subject stays on the same object after a win, and shifts after a loss	Win–stay, lose–shift, with respect to object	WSt_o LSh_o
HYPOTHESIS 2:	The subject shifts to the alternate object after a win, and stays after a loss	Win–shift, lose–stay, with respect to object	WSh_o LSt_o
HYPOTHESIS 3:	The subject stays on the same position after a win, and shifts after a loss	Win–stay, lose–shift, with respect to position	WSt_p LSh_p
HYPOTHESIS 4:	The subject shifts position after a win, and stays after a loss	Win–shift, lose–stay, with respect to position	WSh_p LSt_p
HYPOTHESIS 5:	The subject stays on the same object each trial	Stimulus preference	WSt_o LSt_o
HYPOTHESIS 6:	The subject shifts object selected on each trial	Stimulus alternation	WSh_o LSh_o
HYPOTHESIS 7:	The subject stays on the same position each trial	Position preference (position habit)	WSt_p LSt_p
HYPOTHESIS 8:	The subject shifts position on each trial	Position alternation	WSh_p LSh_p

[a] Adapted from Levine (1963) and Bowman (1963).

which criterion is attained. The shapes of the acquisition curves yielded by this technique were very similar across the four age levels. The curves exhibited two distinct phases. The first phase showed little or no improvement in performance; this was followed by rapid acquisition in the second phase. The duration of the first phase was related to age level. This phase became progressively shorter in going from preschoolers to college students, and then lengthened dramatically in the elderly.

The preschool children were divided into five criterion reference groups, based upon the day they reached criterion. Improvements in performance were assessed by an analysis of performance in blocks of 10 problems. Performance of all groups, except those who met criterion on the first day, rose significantly above chance level on at least one precriterion day. Others have obtained similar results in learning-set research with young children (Harter, 1965, 1967; Hill, 1965; Koch & Meyer, 1959; Kuenne, 1946; Stevenson & Swartz, 1958), and some have assumed that this portion of the learning curve reflects associative learning processes (T. S. Kendler, 1979).

Application of Levine's and Bowman's analyses, however, revealed an alternative explanation for the precriterion improvements in performance. Most of the preschoolers (37 of 53) showed dominant position habits during the first 20 or 30 problems. Many showed strong win–stay position responding early in training; this was sometimes combined with a lose–stay or a lose–shift position component, but it also combined with lose–shift object. As one would predict from research on object responses, in all cases lose–shift object was acquired earlier than win–stay object. (The solution was an object cue, so the two components had to be combined to yield the correct hypothesis and, of course, criterial learning.) Levinson and Reese suggested that the different acquisition rates of lose–shift object and win–stay object, along with the difficulty preschoolers have inhibiting other responses, such as win–stay position, are important determinants of learning efficiency.

According to Levinson and Reese, chance levels of performance during the initial phase of acquisition reflect the dominance of response sets such as position alternation or an incorrect object (e.g., win–shift, lose–stay object). The gradual rise in performance prior to criterion occurred because lose–shift object was combined with either win–stay position or with win–shift position. Performance can reach a maximum of 75% correct (in two-choice tasks of the type used) prior to criterion when such combinations occur. The rationale is that responses will always be correct (100%) following errors, when the child shows lose–shift object. In addition, the child will be correct 50% of the time following correct responses when win–stay or win–shift position is shown. The two values are then simply averaged to produce the maximum of 75%. It should be noted that all preschool groups, with the exception of those who achieved criterion on the first day, showed a gradual rise in performance before the learning set was acquired. Bowman's model revealed that during this gradual increase, the children had combined a win–position component with lose–shift object.

Among the fifth graders, hypotheses usually determined behavior rather than smaller component units. Also, object hypotheses were dominant over position hypotheses, but position hypotheses did occur and influenced the rate at which the learning set was acquired. Among the slower learners (18 of 53), lose–shift object appeared earlier than win–stay object, but there was no detectable difference among the faster learners. In addition, in comparing the criterion reference groups, only the slower-learning fifth graders showed a gradual rise in performance prior to criterion (the three fastest groups showed no rise in performance prior to the criterion phase).

The acquisition curves of college students were saltatory, but the curves never rose above chance level prior to the criterion phase for any group. The college students' responses were controlled entirely by prediction hypotheses; hence, Levine's and Bowman's models yielded essentially identical findings and interpretations. Further, the only incorrect hypotheses shown by college students involved position hypotheses (predictions) and these occurred only in the slowest-learning groups. Lose–shift object occurred only in combination with win–stay object or win–shift object. Thus performance did not rise above chance level prior to criterial learning.

Generalizations concerning the aged subjects are difficult due to the extreme variability associated with institutional factors, amount of formal education, and variations in the procedures that were used in the different experiments. Their performance, like the preschoolers', showed two phases during acquisition: slow improvements in the first phase, followed by rapid acquisition during the criterion phase. Position responses tended to dominate their behavior early in training and frequently persisted for prolonged periods. Unlike the preschoolers, however, win–stay object and lose–shift object tended to emerge simultaneously, if at all, in the aged subjects. Thus the gradual rise in performance prior to criterion was not due to some combination of object and position components. Offenbach (1974, p. 487) has suggested that the aged have great difficulty recognizing when they have adopted the correct hypothesis. In short problems they are as likely to reject the correct hypothesis (win–shift object) as they are to retain it (51.5% versus 49.5%).

In general, results of the Levinson and Reese studies indicate that there is a shift in the mode of response sometime between preschool and the fifth grade. The shift does not appear to be a sudden change from response sets to information-contingent responding (prediction hypotheses). Instead, the child appears to evaluate the effects of different response components (e.g., win–stay position, win–stay object) in the problem-solving situation. Young children (the preschoolers) appeared restricted in the manner by which each win and lose component was tested. That is, each component unit was assessed individually until the correct win and lose components were combined into the appropriate response scheme (or rule). Generally, the fifth graders and college students evaluated each win and lose combination as an integrated response unit, that is, as a prediction hypothesis. The aged subjects evaluated combinations as integrated units, but their behavior was frequently dominated by predictions about the position of the correct object, and they may have had difficulty recognizing when they had selected the correct hypothesis.

The transition from response-set hypotheses to prediction hypotheses may also be assessed in a study reported by Harter (1967). She applied Levine's model to the learning-set performance of children at two mental age (MA) levels (5:6, 8:6) and three levels of IQ (65, 100, 130). The acquisition curves were composed of two phases similar to those reported by Levinson and Reese. Differences associated with both IQ and MA were revealed in the precriterion period. Both MA and IQ influenced the duration of the initial phase (i.e., the number of problems required prior to the rapid acquisition that produced criterial learning).

The type of hypothesis manifested during the initial phase was a function of MA. Children of the lower MA level showed mostly response-set hypotheses (position alternation, position perseveration, stimulus alternation), while children of MA 8:6 employed hypotheses that were contingent on the outcome of the previous response (e.g., win–stay lose–shift position or object). There was no significant relationship between the type of hypothesis manifested and IQ. Instead, IQ appeared to affect only the duration of the precriterion phase. Children of 65 IQ required significantly more problems prior to the abrupt rise to criterion than did their MA-matched peers of higher IQ levels. Some of the precriterion curves rose above chance level in the lower MA group and in the lowest IQ group. Because Harter did not apply Bowman's model to her data, whether these curves reflected some combination of position and object components cannot be determined. The degree to which position components compete with win–stay object may be dependent upon IQ level, but Harter's analyses do not permit an assessment of this possibility.

In summary, then, research on position responses, object responses, and learning set in young children is reasonably consistent in suggesting that prediction hypotheses result from a three-tiered process. The very young child's behavior (2½ to about 6 years) is dominated by response-set hypotheses in which the win and lose components involve the same action (win–stay, lose–stay, or win–shift, lose–shift), at least at the outset of acquisition. Before the child can begin the process of consolidating prediction hypotheses that involve, for example, win–stay object combined with lose–shift object, the win and lose action components of various response sets must be separated. Once separated, these components can be evaluated, coordinated with task-relevant information (stimulus cues, feedback), and eventually reconsolidated into integrated response rules, or schemes, that yield prediction hypotheses. It seems likely that it is during this period of evaluation and coordination that object components are sometimes combined with position components (e.g., win–stay position combined with lose–shift object). In addition, the research indicates that the rate of acquisition of some component units may vary considerably (e.g., lose–shift object versus win–stay object).

Hypothesis Testing

Before reviewing the research concerned with children's hypothesis testing, an important qualification should be made explicit. In nearly all of this research (cf. Rieber, 1969), the children received a series of four or five pretraining problems prior to the main experiment which provided the data that were reported. The purpose of pretraining problems is to instruct the child concerning the task demands: possible solutions (hypotheses corresponding to stimulus cues) are enumerated before each problem, probes for hypotheses are introduced, feedback is demonstrated, etc. It has been implicitly assumed that this kind of pretraining simply facilitates the child's grasp of the problem environment, that is, that pretraining procedures shorten the time necessary to obtain asymptotic performance. Literature reviewed in the previous section suggests, however, that pretraining might facilitate the consolidation of hypotheses from component response units, particularly among younger children.

This section of the chapter is presented in three parts. First, the various system categories are related to Piaget's stages so that predictions may be derived from his theory. Second, research bearing on these predictions—that there are qualitative differences in the characteristics of the processor at each stage of development—is described. Finally, research is reviewed which bears on the assumption that there are quantitative changes, with development, in the ease with which various cognitive subprocesses, which regulate the flow of information to the processor, operate under diverse laboratory manipulations.

Stages and Systems

Preliminary research in which the protocols of subjects of various ages were classified according to the six system categories (Gholson *et al.*, 1972, 1973) revealed some interesting developmental differences: kindergarten children (mean CA = 5:4) manifested stereotypes in at least 90% of their problems; elementary-school children (grades two through six; CA = 7:4 to 11:6) showed mostly dimension checking and hypothesis checking (about 65–80%) and very little focusing (5–15%); college students manifested focusing in about half their problems, and no stereotypes. These differences in performance as functions of chronological age and educational experience led Gholson and McConville (1974) to posit several kinds of underlying mechanisms that might account for the observed changes in information-processing efficiency. One of these, which is directly related to characteristics of the processor, concerns the relationship between the system categories and Piaget's descriptions of the cognitive capabilities available to children at different stages of development (e.g., Inhelder & Piaget, 1958, 1964; Piaget, 1952, 1968, 1970). What is considered below is the relationship between the system categories and the catalogue of cognitive capabilities Piaget proposes is available to preoperational, concrete operational, and formal operational thought.

Discussion is confined to the relationship of Piaget's theory to performance during conventional concept-learning tasks involving problems of the type illustrated in Figure 3.1. Piaget's views on cognitive structure will not be examined.

Four distinct features characterize preoperational thought and should be reflected in the child's processor (Gholson & Beilin, 1979): (*a*) assimilation of external causes and effects to the child's own actions or schemes; (*b*) attentional centration; (*c*) thought involving a semilogical system of one-way dependencies; and (*d*) an ascending mode of classification.

1. According to Piaget, preoperational children do not view a problem to be solved as a set of causes and effects that are independent of their own activities. These children fail to distinguish between the physical events they observe and the effects of their own behavior; instead, external causation is assimilated to the child's own successive activities at the expense of the actual problem presented. In effect, the external environment is represented as a set of uncoordinated forces that are only partially differentiated from the child's own activities (e.g., Inhelder & Piaget, 1958, p. 184; Inhelder *et al.*, 1974, p. 12). Frequent observation of position-oriented stereotypes (win–stay, lose–stay and win–shift, lose–shift), in which the stimulus cues specified as possible solutions are assimilated to a systematic pattern of the child's own actions is not unexpected, then, according to Piaget's theory.

2. The preoperational child may center attention upon one striking feature of an object or salient cue in a problem, but then other features are neglected or ignored. The child does not decenter, that is, take account of other properties or dimensions of the problem at hand (Flavell, 1963; Piaget, 1952, 1963). Thus one might also expect to observe the stimulus preference stereotype (win-stay, lose-stay object) with some frequency among these children. The question is, does Piaget's theory imply that these are the most sophisticated systems preoperational children are capable of generating?

3. Piaget's answer to this question is easily discerned. Because preoperational thought involves only one-way dependencies, preoperational children cannot *think* their way from point x to point y and back to x (except as a matter of empirical return). Given a class or dimension, B, the preoperational child might be able to separate or compare two classes on that dimension, A and A', but then the larger class or dimension, B, ceases to exist. This child might intuitively grasp that B may be decomposed into A and A', but the inverse operation (logical subtraction) that $A = B - A'$ (e.g., Inhelder & Piaget, 1964, pp. 50, 106, 208) is not understood.

4. Similarly, the preoperational child does not comprehend the relation of class inclusion. Reasoning is from particular to particular, from one salient feature of an object or problem to another, but not in part-to-

whole (*A* to *B*) or whole-to-part (*B* to *A*) relations (e.g., Brainerd, 1978; Flavell, 1963; Inhelder & Piaget, 1964). Further, this child engages in an *ascending* mode of classification (Inhelder & Piaget, 1964, pp. 212–213). This means that if the child does eventually differentiate among some of the cues relevant to problem solution, it is accomplished through trial and error, and not because the child surveys the problem materials, anticipates all the possible solutions, and formulates a plan to systematically evaluate each possibility. Finally, preoperational children do not flexibly alter their choice criterion (take account of feedback) when the task demands it.

According to Piaget, then, preoperational children assimilate external physical events to their own actions, do not decenter, are capable of only semilogical thought that involves one-way dependencies, and show only an ascending mode of classification. These characteristics are, of course, reflected in the child's processor. Because the logical processes that are available are very restricted in preoperational children, there are clear limitations upon the kinds of systems they are capable of manifesting.

According to Piaget's theory the focusing system should not appear until the acquisition of formal operations is well underway; therefore, only dimension checking and hypothesis checking will be examined in relation to the characteristics of preoperational thought. In the description of the system categories it was pointed out that in order to manifest either dimension checking or hypothesis checking, the child must (*a*) order the two cues associated with each of the four dimensions appropriately (class inclusion and decentration), (*b*) recognize that when one value (hypothesis) is disconfirmed its complement remains (logical subtraction). and (*c*) be able to systematically eliminate from consideration the hypotheses and dimensions following disconfirmation (formulate a plan to systematically evaluate possible solutions). Piaget's assumption that all these characteristics are beyond the cognitive capabilities of preoperational children leads to the expectation that they will show only the three stereotypes, never strategies. However, because the preoperational child is assumed to have the capability to engage in an ascending mode of classification (i.e., to differentiate among various stimulus cues through a process of trial and error) the theory does allow that unsystematic hypothesis sequences might occasionally be observed. That is, prediction hypotheses might be exhibited, but the processor lacks the logical operations necessary to generate a systematic strategy for testing them.

Concrete operational children, unlike the preoperational, separate environmental contingencies from their own actions, decenter, show logical reversibility (which means this child has no difficulty with logical subtraction), logically grasp the nature of class inclusion, show a descending mode of classification (see below), and can formulate a systematic plan and carry it through (e.g., Flavell, 1963, pp. 164–201; Inhelder & Piaget, 1964, pp. 100–150, 212–213). As was shown above, a processor with these characteristics is requisite to the manifestation of either dimension checking or hypothesis checking. This change in the properties of the processor is due, according to Piaget, to the acquisition of several groupings of logical operations, each of which involves an organized *system* of cognitive operations (e.g., Flavell, 1963, p. 171). For present purposes the properties of the various "groupings" need not be explicated, because they have in common the characterisitcs of decentration, logical subtraction, etc. (see Flavell, 1963, pp. 164–173).

Despite this considerable advance over preoperational thought, the concrete operational child is limited to a mode of processing that involves a serial ordering and evaluating of experiential data associated principally with the world of tangible objects (Inhelder & Piaget, 1958, pp. 212, 298). More specifically, concrete operational children manifest a *descending* mode of classification. That is, they locate the general classes (or dimensions) of the problem at hand, then subdivide them into specific properties or cues (hypotheses). These children systematically survey the problem materials and formulate a systematic plan that anticipates possible classes and subclasses. Choice criteria are flexibly altered (taking account of feedback) when the task demands such alteration (Inhelder & Piaget, 1958, pp. 208–231). Thus the cognitive capabilities necessary to manifest both dimension checking and hypothesis checking strategies are embodied in this child's processor. However, the focusing strategy requires even more complex functioning.

The individual who manifests the focusing strategy begins the problem by monitoring all eight hypotheses and eliminates from consideration the maximum shown to be logically inconsistent with all previous stimulus information after each feedback trial. But the concrete operational child is limited to a mode of processing that brings classes together by a class inclusion that moves from one element (or cue) to the next (i.e., a descending mode). This child is limited, then, to an orderly subtraction of a single class (hypothesis or dimension) or the adding of classes to form a single larger class (Inhelder & Piaget, 1958, p. 274).

"Unlike the concrete operational child, the adolescent begins his consideration of the problem at hand by trying to envisage all possible relations which could hold true in the data and then attempts, through a combination of experimental and logical analysis, to find out which of these possible relations, in fact, do hold true [Flavell, 1963, p. 204]." This individual has the logical capabilities necessary to simultaneously consider the entire set of possible solutions and make logical deductions from them. Formal operational children (may) start the problem with a set of hypotheses that includes all the possibilities in the situation, and apply such logical operations as intersection and deduction in an attempt to achieve solution (Inhelder & Piaget, 1958, p. 253). These activities are, of course, precisely the ones required by the focusing strategy. That is, in order for subjects to focus they must consider the entire set of possible solutions (hypotheses) at the outset of a problem and logically deduce which ones are still viable following each feedback trial until solution is achieved. This change from concrete to formal operational thought is due to the acquisition of a complete combinatorial scheme and the INRC group of transformations (Flavell, 1963, p. 212; Inhelder & Piaget, 1958, pp. 273–278; Neimark, 1975a, pp. 548–554). The differences between the cognitive structures of concrete and formal thought have many implications for theory construction (Neimark, 1975b), but for present purposes it will suffice to note that if Piaget's characterization of the cognitive structures of the two stages of development is accurate, the processor of the formal operational individual, but not the concrete operational, should reflect the cognitive capabilities necessary to exhibit perfect processing in complex problems. Thus only formal operational individuals should exhibit the focusing system.

The preliminary findings described above indicated that kindergarten children exhibited nearly all stereotypes, elementary-school children showed mostly dimension checking and hypothesis checking, and college students showed focusing in about half their problems. These findings are clearly in line with implications derived from Piaget's descriptions of the characteristics of preoperational, concrete operational, and formal operational thought. Gholson and McConville (1974), however, obtained discrepant findings. They gave kindergarten children (mean CA = 5:5) extensive stimulus-differentiation training (24 problems) with feedback following each response, and then gave a series of problems containing probes for hypotheses. The children manifested strategy systems (dimension checking and hypothesis checking) in 50% of their problems, and stereotypes in only about 20%. They showed unsystematic hypothesis sequences in almost 30%. Another group who received the differentiation training without feedback showed stereotypes in more than 90% of their problems and no strategies.

It appeared, then, that extensive differentiation training with feedback might lead kindergarten children to manifest strategies regardless of their Piagetian stage. There was also the puzzling finding, however, that they manifested almost 30% unsystematic hypothesis sequences. Previous research had revealed such sequences no more than about 10% of the time among subjects ranging from kindergarten to college age. This discrepancy suggested, in retrospect, that the sample of children used in the experiment might have included a mix of preoperational and concrete operational children.

PREOPERATIONAL VERSUS CONCRETE OPERATIONAL PERFORMANCE

The finding, while obviously inconclusive, did indicate the need for more precisely designed experiments. Ideally, this research would involve children who differed in Piagetian stage, but who were equated for age, amount of formal schooling, SES level, etc. Several experiments approximating these criteria have been reported. In two of them preoperational children were compared with concrete operational children (Gholson, O'Connor, & Stern, 1976; Morello *et al.*, 1977) in problem-solving tasks. In both, the child's cognitive status was assessed according to Piagetian criteria prior to the experiment proper. Gholson *et al.* used two conservation tasks for this assessment: number and continuous quantity. Morello *et al.* included, in addition, area conservation. For descriptions of these tasks see Beilin (1965, 1969, 1976), Gelman (1969), or Piaget (1952, 1968). Children who completely failed all parts of each task were considered preoperational, those who were correct on all parts of each were classified concrete operational; any child who showed intermediate performance was considered "transitional." Both judgments and explanations were obtained from the children (Brainerd, 1978; Miller, 1976).[1]

Gholson *et al.* (1976) selected kindergarten children (mean CA = 5:5–5:7) as a subject population for several reasons: First, it is well known that the transition from preoperational to concrete operational thought frequently occurs in the age range 5 to 7 years; second, as was indicated earlier, it is desirable for the chronological ages, educational experiences, etc., of children assigned to the various groups to be as comparable as possible; finally, earlier research indicated that without special training, unselected kindergarten children almost always exhibit either position-oriented stereotypes or stimulus preference (e.g., Gholson *et al.*, 1972; Gholson & McConville, 1974; Rieber, 1969; Weisz, 1977).[2]

Groups of preoperational and concrete operational children (transitional children were excluded) received stimulus differentiation training

1. Although labeled transitional here, this group might have included some décalage children as well (Reese, 1977).

2. Children of this age range and even younger do, of course, solve even complex problems eventually. What is considered here is how the children use information in attempt to achieve solution.

identical to that administered by Gholson and McConville (1974). All children were presented with 24 stimulus-differentiation problems during a first session. Half the children at each cognitive level received feedback following each response (experimental groups) and half did not (control groups). During a second daily session all subjects received pretraining and were then given a series of six standard four-dimensional problems that included blank-trial probes for hypotheses. Although the error rates among all groups were relatively low during stimulus-differentiation training (.9–5.8%), the concrete operational children exhibited significantly better performance than the preoperational on six dependent measures derived from the hypothesis-testing protocols: Concrete operational children (*a*) solved more problems, (*b*) showed more consistent hypotheses during probes, (*c*) showed fewer position-oriented response sets during probes, (*d*) were more likely to reject a disconfirmed hypothesis, (*e*) sampled more locally consistent hypotheses following errors, and (*f*) showed more strategies.

The results of the systems analysis are presented in Figure 4.1. Concrete operational children showed strategies in about 75% of their problems under the experimental condition and 45% under the control condition, while the preoperational children exhibited about 90% stereotypes under both conditions. Data from individual subjects reinforce these findings (see Cantor & Spiker, 1978, p. 343). Of 30 children in each group, 21 contributed classifiable problems in the preoperational control and the concrete operational experimental conditions; 22 children contributed classifiable problems in each of the remaining conditions. Among the preoperational groups, 5 of the 43 children exhibited one strategy each. Among the 43 concrete operational children who contributed problems to the systems analysis, 27 contributed at least one strategy. The difference is highly significant.

The findings were clearly in line with predictions derived from Piaget's theory, but it had been expected on the basis of previous work involving conservation training (e.g., Beilin, 1969, 1976), that preoperational children assigned to the experimental condition would show unsystematic hypothesis sequences in a large proportion of their problems. They did not and there was, therefore, no explanation for the 30% unsystematic sequences reported by Gholson and McConville (1974) among kindergarten children who were not assessed according to Piaget's criteria, but were trained under the same conditions used in the later study. This failure to replicate suggested that transitional children, who were specifically excluded in the research presented in Figure 4.1, may have been responsible for the large proportion of unsystematic hypothesis sequences observed in the earlier study.

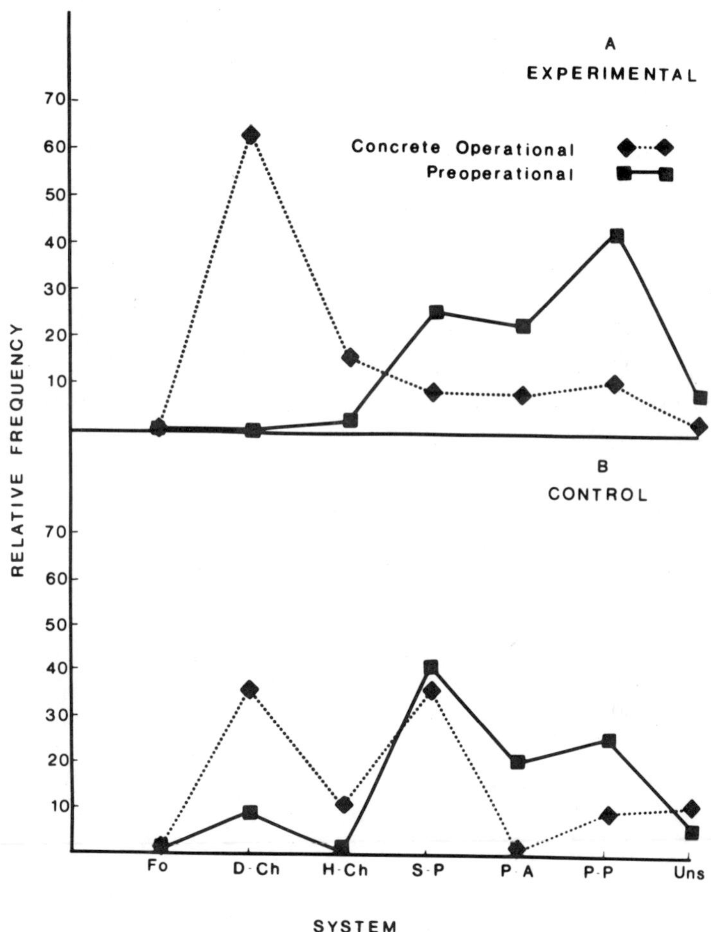

Figure 4.1. The relative frequencies of focusing (Fo), dimension checking (D-ch), hypothesis checking (H-ch), stimulus preference (S-P), position alternation (P-A), position preference (P-P), and unsystematic hypothesis sequences (Uns).

Therefore a second experiment was conducted (Gholson *et al*., 1976, p. 73) using exactly the same conditions described above, but only transitional children were included. The performance of children assigned to the experimental condition was generally intermediate between that of the preoperational and concrete operational children on each dependent measure examined. The transitional children in the control condition, however, performed almost identically to the preoperational children. The systems analysis revealed that children in the control condition manifested stereotypes in 86% of their problems, and unsystematic hypothesis sequences in 14%. They showed no strategies. The experimental group, however, exhibited stereotypes in 47%, strategies in 13%, and unsystematic sequences in 40% of their problems. The number of children in this latter study was small, 12 per group, so the findings were viewed as tentative, but the overall pattern of results from the two studies indicated that transitional children were probably responsible for the large proportion of unsystematic hypothesis sequences obtained by Gholson and McConville.

The research provided preliminary support, then, for identifying the logical characteristics of the processor with the cognitive schemes available to children of the two stages (Inhelder & Piaget, 1958, 1964; Piaget, 1970). It should be explicitly stated, though, that implications of Piaget's theory for the performance of transitional children are unclear. Piaget's theory predicts, of course, that concrete operational children will show better performance than those who are preoperational in complex problem-solving tasks. In other tasks, however, the theory implies that preoperational children might surpass those who are concrete.

Morello *et al.* (1977) used a task of this latter kind: A three-choice task in which the child's response to the position of one of three identical stimulus objects was rewarded on a response-contingent 66% random schedule. Responses to the remaining stimulus objects were never rewarded. Sixty children were divided into three basic groups of 20 each: preoperational, transitional, and concrete operational (mean CA = 6:2–8:1). Each child received 90 trials on the three-choice task. The response measure of interest was the frequency with which the children chose the rewarded position. Data were reported in blocks of 10 trials.

Morello *et al.* obtained a significant Cognitive-level × Trial-blocks interaction. The three groups showed very similar performance during the first three trial blocks. In the first block they showed chance performance (about 33% correct), but improved somewhat during the second and third. In every block after the third (i.e., Blocks 4–9), however, the preoperational children showed better performance than either the transitional or concrete operational children, who did not differ appreciably from each other.

What the child was required to do in order to maximize rewards (66%), was to win–stay, lose–stay on the rewarded position. Morello *et al.* predicted—and trial-by-trial analysis of the children's protocols confirmed—that both the transitional children and those who were concrete operational would generate complex hypotheses during the task. In particular, these children would be more likely to combine lose–shift position with win–stay position than would the preoperational children. Following Piaget, they reasoned that preoperational children fail to "distinguish between external physical events and the effects of their own actions" and thus "view a nonreinforced response as an event beyond their control, rather than one which can be controlled" by choosing a stimulus object located in another position (Morello *et al.*, 1977, p. 83). The more advanced children, however, suppressed maximizing responses, because they generated more complex hypotheses that tended to include lose–shift as one response component.

CONCRETE VERSUS FORMAL OPERATIONAL PERFORMANCE

The two experiments (Gholson *et al.*, 1976; Morello *et al.*, 1977), then, provided some support for identifying gross characteristics of the processor with the cognitive capabilities of preoperational and concrete operational thought (corresponding findings are reported in Chapters 5 and 6). Related research bearing on the transition from concrete to formal thought has been reported by Richman (1975, 1976; Richman & Gholson, 1978) and by Saarni (1973).

According to Piaget (1970; Inhelder & Piaget, 1958), many children begin the transition from concrete to formal thought during the age range 12–13 years, that is, at about the time the average child is in the sixth grade (Inhelder & Piaget, 1964; Neimark, 1975b). It is known (Gholson *et al.*, 1972; Gholson & Danziger, 1975; Kemler, 1978), though, that such children show mostly dimension checking and little focusing—the strategy that according to the theory should occur only among formal operational individuals. Others, using different kinds of analyses, have also reported that children of this age range usually fail to show the perfect processing implied by the focusing strategy (Eimas, 1969; Ingalls & Dickerson, 1969; Nuessle, 1972).

Richman and Gholson (1978), however, reported a study in which sixth-grade children exhibited a focusing strategy in more than half their problems. As part of a larger study, second-grade (CA = 7:8) and sixth-grade children (CA = 11:9) were exposed to an observational learning procedure in which the operations involved in the use of the focusing strategy were demonstrated and a summary rule was provided. Following exposure to this observational procedure, the sixth graders exhibited performances very similar to those typically observed among college students on each dependent measure examined (e.g., about 55% focusing). The second-grade children, however, following exposure to the same modeling procedure, showed much poorer performances than typically are observed among children of this age range (e.g., only about 75% of their probes yielded hypotheses), and little focusing (6%).

An interpretation of these data which is consistent with the conception presented here is that many of the sixth-grade children were either formal operational or were transitional from concrete to formal thought, and exposure to the focusing model elicited (Bandura & Walters, 1963; D. R. Denney, 1972) the strategy because the requisite cognitive skills were available to them. The second-grade children, however, were probably concrete operational. Following exposure to the modeling procedure they may have attempted to implement a focusing strategy, but because they lacked the logical skills necessary to do so, they not only failed to focus, but also showed a considerable decrement in performance relative to a control group that was not exposed to the modeling procedure, or compared to the performance typically observed among second graders (cf. Gholson *et al.*, 1972; Kemler, 1978; Phillips & Levine, 1975).

Reasoning similarly, Richman (1976; Richman, Shaheen, & Montgomery, 1978) assessed eighth graders (mean CA = 13:8) as either concrete operational, transitional from concrete to formal operations, or formal operational.[3] She used three tasks for this assessment: number conservation, volume conservation, and the oscillating pendulum problem. Those who passed only the first were classified concrete operational. Because volume conservation is taken to indicate that the transition is underway (Inhelder & Piaget, 1958; Neimark, 1975a, p. 559), those who passed this task in addition to number conservation were considered transitional. Only those children who satisfied Inhelder and Piaget's (1958) criteria for correct performance on the pendulum problem were considered formal operational (these criteria are detailed in Chapter 6). Several observational learning procedures were used, one of which involved the focusing system. The data indicated that the formal operational and transitional children showed focusing in about 55% of their problems, and dimension checking in the remainder. The concrete operational children exposed to the focusing model, however, showed focusing in only about 15% of their problems. They showed dimension checking in about 50%, with hypothesis checking and unsystematic sequences in the remainder.

Saarni (1973) has reported convergent findings in a study in which she assessed sixth-, seventh-, eighth-, and ninth-grade children (mean CA = 10:9–15:1) as either concrete operational, transitional to formal operations, or formal operational. Each child was administered two problem-solving tasks developed by Covington, Cruchfield, and Daves (1966):

3. Data from Richman's first study (1975) were collected in New York City. In piloting the second experiment in the same location she obtained a mix of concrete operational, transitional, and formal operational children among sixth-grade populations. In rural Georgia, where the second study was actually conducted, however, it was necessary to use eighth graders to obtain the same mix.

"The Missing Jewel," and "The Old Black House." These are detective-type mystery stories in which certain clues and contradictions are provided to the subject. Saarni ascertained that the cognitive operations needed to solve the mystery problems "coincide with the cognitive requirements for solving Inhelder's and Piaget's formal operational problems [1973, p. 340]."

Performance on each problem was scored in four categories: (*a*) the number of discrepant cues and relevant cues noticed, (*b*) the number of correct analytic choices, (*c*) the number of plausible ideas for solution, and (*d*) speed and adequacy of the solution offered. In general, her predictions were confirmed by the data. The formal operational and transitional children showed very similar and very good performance in each category. The concrete operational children's performance was considerably depressed.

These findings, then, like those obtained in research contrasting preoperational and concrete operational children, were in line with a conception of the processor as reflecting underlying cognitive capabilities that expand at some points in development and lead to qualitative changes (or main effects of developmental level) in the child's strategic approach to problem solving. Thus the findings support a stage conception of development. Critics of stage conceptions (e.g., Brainerd, 1977, 1978; W. Kessen, 1962; Rosenthal & Zimmerman, 1978) have legitimately stressed that any theory which postulates a sequence of qualitatively distinct stages must ultimately be subjected to four canons: It must specify (*a*) the behavioral characteristics of each stage, (*b*) the changes that are to be expected within each stage, (*c*) the rules that govern movement from one stage to the next, and (*d*) the behavioral implications of each transition period. The research comparing preoperational, concrete operational, and formal operational children indicated that the first criterion can be met, and provided some data bearing on the third and fourth. Research that addressed the second criterion, mostly concerned with developments during the concrete operational period, is described next.

WITHIN-STAGE CHANGES

Johnson and Scholnick (1979) used a false-recognition paradigm to investigate semantic integration in third- and fourth-grade children (mean CA = 9:6). The children were divided into four subgroups on the basis of an assessment of their class-inclusion and transitive-inference skills. The class-inclusion assessment took the form: "There are seven cokes and two iced teas. Are there more cokes or more things to drink?"

The form of the transitive-inference task was as follows: "There are more lawyers than teachers, and more teachers than doctors. Are there more lawyers or more doctors?" The four groups were (*a*) high-inclusion and high-inference skills, (*b*) high-inclusion but low-inference skills, (*c*) low-inclusion but high-inference skills, and (*d*) low-inclusion and low-inference skills.

They used a conventional semantic-integration task in which the children heard a series of stories, each containing premises, and later, during a recognition task, were asked to identify those they had previously heard (Barclay & Reid, 1974; Bransford & Franks, 1971; Paris & Landauer, 1977). The stories contained implicit class inclusions and implicit transitive inferences. The recognition task included true premises (heard previously), false premises, true inferences, and false inferences. If the child integrates semantic information, then during the recognition task the implicit inferences would be "recognized" as having been heard previously. The rationale, derived from Piaget's theory, was that if semantic integration reflects the degree to which children have mastered specific logical operations, they should integrate *that* semantic information, and only that, which taps the specific, logical knowledge possessed. In part, the prediction was confirmed.

The children with high transitive-inference skills "recognized" true transitive inferences (never heard) as often as true premises (heard before), but did not recognize false premises or false inferences; their scores on true inferences exceeded those of children low in inference skills, but the two groups did not differ in the recognition of true premises. In addition, children low in transitive-inference skills recognized true premises much more frequently than true inferences, and they recognized true inferences no more often than false premises or false inferences. Thus the children's transitive-inference skills did not predict how they rated true premises, false premises, or false inferences, but did predict how they rated true transitive inferences.

The children with high-inclusion skills, however, frequently failed to recognize true class-inclusion inferences; in fact, they did so just as often as did those who were low in these skills. Johnson and Scholnick (1979) suggested that this was because these children had not yet consolidated their class-inclusion skills and were, therefore, unable to apply them to semantic information (Flavell & Wohlwill, 1969). While this latter result was disappointing, the research does indicate that during the period of concrete operations the child consolidates a skill, transitive inference, which regulates how certain semantic information is coded into memory. In a related study, Prawat and Cancelli (1976) reported that first graders who conserved (mean CA = 6:6) "recognized" more true transitive inferences than did those who did not conserve (CA = 6:5). The difference was not large, less than 20%, but was significant.

Tomlinson-Keasey, Crawford, and Miser (1975) obtained corresponding findings in an experiment in which they investigated the relationship between class-inclusion skills and memory organization among kindergarten and first-grade children. Each child received two classification tasks described by Kofsky (1966). The first task involved two blue triangles, four blue squares, and three red triangles. The child was asked whether there were (*a*) more blues or squares, (*b*) more reds or triangles, and (*c*) more triangles or blues? The second task involved dogs and cats. The children were asked three questions concerning the superordinate category (i.e., animals).

Children who gave correct judgments and explanations to four or more of the six questions were placed in the classifier group. Nonclassifiers received scores of zero or one. The two groups did not differ significantly in mean age (6:5 versus 6:4). Half the children in each group served in a free-recall condition, the remainder were given category cues. Classifiers exhibited significantly more category clustering (Robinson, 1966) than nonclassifiers. They did so in both the free-recall and the cued-recall conditions. The classifiers also recalled more items than the nonclassifiers.

Haynes and Kulhavy (1976) addressed an allied issue, the relationship between level of concrete operational development and category clustering, in two experiments. Three conservation tasks were used to assess cognitive level: mass, weight, and volume. These were chosen because children usually acquire the three in a standard sequence (Inhelder & Piaget, 1958, 1964; Neimark, 1975a). Mass is generally conserved by about age 7, weight at about age 9, and volume at around age 11. According to Piaget's theory (1952, 1968, 1970; Inhelder & Piaget, 1958), though, the child who conserves volume is, strictly speaking, transitional to formal operations, rather than concrete operational. Because Haynes and Kulhavy did not assess for formal operations, whether the children who conserved volume were transitional or formal operational cannot be determined. In addition, no age data were reported; just that the children were enrolled in elementary and junior-high schools (p. 180).

In the first experiment the children in each conservation-level group learned a 16-item list containing four items in each of four conceptual categories. Two lists were constructed: one list maximized associative relatedness among the items in each conceptual category; the other list minimized it. Both recall data and clustering scores (Cole, Frankel, & Sharp, 1971) for the two lists revealed ordered differences. Children who conserved volume produced significantly better performance than weight conservers, who showed better performance than children who conserved only mass.

In their second experiment Haynes and Kulhavy investigated the kind of organizational devices preferred by children of the two conservation levels. The children were presented with a 16-item word list and allowed to select a mnemonic device (circle one of four items that would help them remember). Once again recall scores were ordered by conservation level: volume > weight > mass. The children who conserved volume chose the most sophisticated mnemonic aid (class inclusion) significantly more frequently than did the children of the lower conservation levels. Conversely, volume conservers were much less likely to choose an unrelated, and presumably useless, word as a mnemonic than were the children who conserved only mass. The weight conservers showed intermediate performance.

E. W. Simon and Bohannon (1978), however, failed to obtain differences in clustering when they compared conservers with nonconservers. The subjects, kindergarten (mean CA = 5:8), first-grade (mean CA = 6:7), and second-grade children (mean CA = 7:10), were classified according to their performance in a continuous quantity conservation problem. The scoring procedure was not given, but appeared to be based only on judgments (p. 428). The children then received a 24-item free-recall task. The conservers recalled more items than the nonconservers, but the two groups did not differ significantly in the amount of category clustering they exhibited. Unfortunately, direct comparisons with Tomlinson-Keasey *et al.* and Haynes and Kulhavy are not possible, because Simon and Bohannon did not specify their clustering index.

In another related study, Hartman (1977) investigated the relationship between the acquisition of classification skills, semantic memory organization, and reading achievement. The subjects were second- and fourth-grade children (age data were not reported), all of whom were concrete operational. Hartman adopted the criteria proposed by Inhelder and Piaget (1958, 1964) to score the child's level of classification development. He used additive and multiplicative classification tasks (Inhelder & Piager, 1964).

The analysis of semantic memory was based upon a model presented by Collins and Quillian (1972). This model proposes that in the adult subject, or college student, concepts in memory are like "hooks or nodes in a network from which many different properties hang [p. 314]." This network is said to be arranged on the basis of set–superset relations, that is, a class-inclusion hierarchy. A set of properties surrounds each concept, arranged in a hierarchy. Because certain properties are more central to the meaning of a given concept, they are closer together in the hierarchy. Therefore, not all properties are equally accessible. Yellow is a more central property of canary, for example, than is skin. Thus, in a verification task of the form "A ____ is (has) ____," the model predicts that the closer the property is to the central concept in a class hierarchy, the faster will be the verification time.

Hartman used the Collins and Quillian (1972) model along with their verification procedure to assess semantic memory organization. His hypothesis was that there would be a close relationship between the child's classification skills and the extent to which semantic memory was organized hierarchically. His hunch was, also, that the two would be closely correlated with reading achievement scores.

In each case, Hartman's predictions were confirmed. Children with sophisticated classification skills showed the expected differences in their verification times, that is, verification times for object–property relations differed according to their proximity in the hierarchy of semantic memory as predicted by the model. The relationship also held, in part, for children with intermediate classification skills, but not as strongly. Among the children with low classification skills, however, there was no relationship at all between concept–property proximity and verification times. Hartman concluded that these latter children's memories were not yet fully organized into hierarchically arranged semantic networks. This is because they had not yet acquired the sophisticated classification skills necessary to produce this kind of organization.

In addition, Hartman administered three reading-achievement tests, and then intercorrelated the scores obtained on each. He also correlated the children's classification skills with their scores on each achievement test. It was not surprising to learn that performance on one reading test was a good predictor of performance on another. It was surprising, though, that the child's level of classification development correlated *just* as highly with reading achievement scores on the various tests as the reading scores did with each other (about .61–.72).

The findings, taken together, indicate that the consolidation of certain logical skills during the concrete operational period has an important bearing on how the child processes information. These skills influence how information is coded into memory, and, in addition, they appear to regulate how semantic memory itself is organized. Whether the consolidation of these and other logical skills during the concrete operational period, or any period, produce comparable effects upon other cognitive subprocesses remains to be determined by future research. There are preliminary data which indicate that quest will not be fruitless:

Fitzgerald (1977), for example, has reported a close relationship between preschool children's (preoperational) classification skills and their ability to use verbal labels during learning.

These findings (Hartman, 1977; Haynes & Kulhavy, 1976; Johnson & Scholnick, 1979; Prawat & Cancelli, 1976; E. W. Simon & Bohannon, 1978; Tomlinson-Keasey *et al*., 1975) have important implications for a question raised earlier. This concerns the role of the processor in organizing and integrating the various cognitive subprocesses. Clearly, the answer is that at least some of the logical skills embodied in the processor play a *crucial* role in governing both how semantic information is coded into memory and how semantic memory is organized. This statement is qualified, however, because not all the predicted relationships held (cf. Johnson & Scholnick findings on class inclusion and semantic inference), and the data bear directly only on the concrete operational processor.

The literature reveals findings that are generally in line, then, with the conception of the processor described earlier. The processor embodies logical capabilities that expand at some points in development and lead to qualitative changes (or main effects of developmental level) in the child's strategic approach to problem solving. The effects of these wholesale modifications upon the organization and integration of the various cognitive subprocesses remain to be determined (cf. A. L. Brown, 1975, 1978; Wright & Vlietstra, 1975). The consolidation of some logical skills embodied by the concrete operational processor, however, was shown to regulate how semantic information is coded into memory and how memory is organized. Thus the more pervasive changes in the processor—those associated with stage changes—may be expected to produce corresponding effects in the organization of the subprocesses. The processor permits the child to generate solution plans of varying sophistication and to apply cognitive transformations involving forms of logical inference to stimulus information presented for processing from either short-term or long-term memory (Atkinson & Shiffrin, 1968; Newell & Simon, 1972). Obviously, then, only information that reaches the processor may be operated upon and integrated into ongoing behavior.

Cognitive Subprocesses

Next, some research involving task manipulations that (presumably) altered the amount of information reaching the processor will be considered. Specific information reaching the processor from moment to moment would depend, of course, upon the particular solution plan in use. But it would also depend upon how efficiently each of the cognitive subprocesses involved in the flow of information to the processor was able to function under the prevailing task constraints. As was indicated earlier, quantitative changes in the child's ability to control the functioning of the various subprocesses would be expected to produce *interactions* between developmental level and task manipulations.

Unfortunately, at present it is not possible to specify exactly *how* each subprocess is involved in processing information in any given task environment (Bower, 1975; Klahr & Siegler, 1978; Newell & Simon, 1972). Previous research and theory do provide some guidance, though, concerning *which* cognitive subprocesses should be considered in a typical problem-solving task: The individual must differentiate the relevant stimulus information in the task environment (R. Cohen *et al.*, 1979; J. J. Gibson & E. J. Gibson, 1955; Kemler, 1978; L. S. Tighe & T. J. Tighe, 1966), selectively attend to some of this information from trial to trial (Adams & Shepp, 1975; Hohle, 1967; Sperling, 1960; Zeaman & House, 1963), code appropriate information as determined by the solution plan in use (Beilin, 1975; H. H. Kendler & T. S. Kendler, 1962; T. S. Kendler, 1972, 1979; Posner, 1973), and both store and retrieve information from moment to moment during the attempt to achieve solution (Atkinson & Shiffrin, 1968; A. L. Brown, 1975, 1978; Hagen, 1972; Hoving *et al.*, 1974; Neimark, 1976). Research reviewed in the previous section indicates that the processor plays a role in organizing these subprocesses, but so does the child's ability to adjust the functioning of a given subprocess when task demands are altered (Gholson *et al.*, 1973). In general, the child's ability to adjust to varying task constraints is expected to improve continuously with development; perhaps declining in old age. Unfortunately, relatively little developmental research has been aimed at isolating and manipulating the performance of the various cognitive subprocesses during problem solving. Findings obtained in a series of experiments conducted within the framework of hypothesis theory, however, provide support for this part of the general conception. (Other experiments are reported in Chapter 7.)

In these experiments the predicted interactions between developmental level and task variables were usually obtained. Subjects of different age ranges (or cognitive levels) were exposed to experimental manipulations involving two or more levels of one independent variable that might reasonably be assumed to produce differential constraints upon the performance of a particular subprocess (or processes). In fact, several experiments described earlier involved such manipulations. Stimulus-differentiation training, for example, which is usually assumed to increase perceptual learning (J. J. Gibson & E. J. Gibson, 1955; L. S. Tighe & T. J. Tighe, 1966), when combined with feedback led concrete operational kindergarten children to generate strategies in 75% of their problems. When feedback was omitted during this training, concrete operational children exhibited strategies in only 45%. The preoperational children, however, showed stereotypes in about 90% of their problems under both conditions (Gholson *et al.*, 1976). Because the concrete operational children who received feedback during training learned more about the relevant cues in the task environment than did their peers not given feedback, more relevant information presumably made its way to the processor. Among the preoperational children, in contrast, the manipulation produced no effect at all; these children lacked the cognitive capabilities necessary to generate any strategy, that is, stimulus information that did reach the processor was not operated upon and integrated into ongoing behavior. Gholson and McConville (1974) obtained convergent findings among kindergarten children whose stage was not assessed.

CODING DEMANDS

Parallel findings were obtained by Gholson *et al*. (1973) when they manipulated coding demands among second graders and college students. The effect on the children was profound; they showed almost all strategies under the easiest coding condition (/+3), but under the most difficult condition (/−3) more problems involved the stimulus-preference stereotype than any other system category. The college students, however, were essentially unaffected by the manipulation (see Figure 3.6). They showed focusing in about 55% of their problems under all three conditions. The college students adjusted their approach to correspond to the demands of the task. The second graders did not have this type of sophisticated control of their own functioning. Consequently, when the task demands increased, their coding processes frequently malfunctioned and the required stimulus information failed to reach the processor.

Schonebaum (1973) reported a related experiment in which he investigated coding processes in third- (mean CA = 8:9), fifth- (mean CA = 11:0) and seventh-grade children (mean CA = 8:9), and college students (mean CA = 23:0). Each subject was presented with a series of two-trial problems in which the first stimulus pair in each problem varied on either three, four, or six bivalued dimensions. Twenty-four problems of each type were presented to each subject. In 12 of these, the first stimulus pair remained in view for four seconds following response and feedback (the experimenter said "correct" or "wrong"); in the remainder the stimulus was terminated immediately following response and feedback. Thus when feedback was negative the subject was forced to recode in the absence of stimulus information in half the problems, but the stimuli persisted in the other half. A few seconds after offset of the first stimulus pair, a test pair was presented. The test pair varied on only one of the relevant dimensions.

Schonebaum reasoned that if subjects coded (or recoded) appropriate stimulus information on the first trial, this should be revealed by their exhibiting hypotheses consistent with this stimulus information on the test trial. When stimuli persisted for four seconds following response, the third- and fifth-grade children showed more logically consistent hypotheses following both positive and negative feedback. Stimulus persistence aided the seventh graders only following negative feedback, when they were forced to recode. As one would predict from the results of the Gholson *et al.* (1973) study, college students showed equally good performance whether the stimuli persisted or not, following both positive and negative feedback.

The conception presented here, which predicts interactions between task variables and developmental level, indicates that there should be interactions between grade level and stimulus persistence, and between grade level and stimulus complexity. Schonebaum reported that the predicted interaction between grade level and stimulus persistence was significant (1973, p. 421), but he did not publish results of the grade level by complexity analysis. More recently, however, he communicated the following: "Incidentally, the interaction between grade and complexity on transformed proportions of errors was statistically significant in my 1973 study, $F(6, 1254) = 3.36, p < .01$, MSE = .22. The statistical test was not reported because it was not a primary concern of the study [personal correspondence from Schonebaum, dated September 19, 1975]."

Nuessle (1972) investigated the relationship between reflective and impulsive styles and problem solving among fifth- (mean CA = 10:4) and ninth-grade (mean CA = 14:4) children. He used Kagan's (1965) reflection–impulsivity selection device, the Matching Familiar Figures Test, to select subjects: Reflectives exhibited long response latencies and low error rates; impulsives showed short latencies and high error rates on the selection test. The experimental task involved conventional bivalued four-dimensional problems of the kind described by Levine (1966). Blank-trial probes were inserted between consecutive feedback trials in 16-trial problems (see Figures 2.3 and 2.4).

Nuessle reasoned that impulsive children would fail to use their coding, recoding, and retrieval processes as efficiently as the reflective children. He examined these predictions by evaluating the size of the hypothesis set from which the children sampled following errors, and their latency data during problem solving. Although Nuessle did not report that the Age × Reflective–impulsive interaction reached significance, his data, presented in Figure 4.2, hinted at an interaction.

He reported analyses of two latency measures: total average time required to complete problems, and the latency between feedback-trial response and the response on the following blank trial. In both analyses

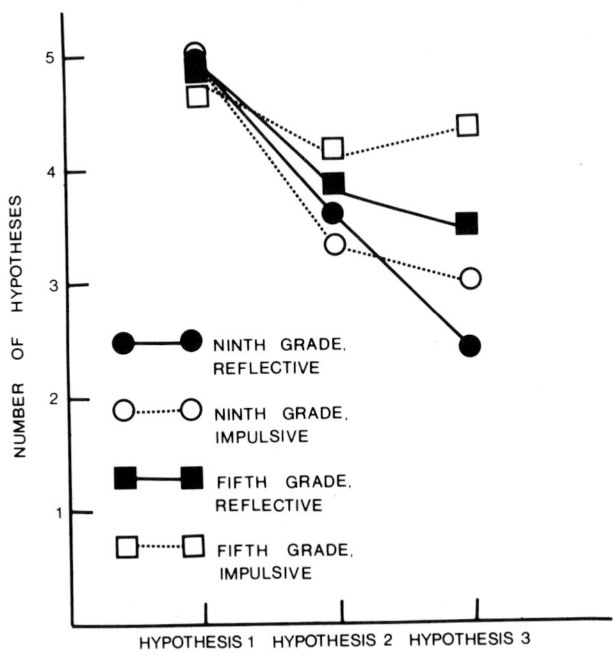

Figure 4.2. The size of the hypothesis set from which subjects resampled following negative feedback on each of the first three feedback trials (after Nuessle, 1972).

the Grade-level × Reflective–impulsive interactions were significant. Ninth-grade reflectives took, on average, 69.6 seconds per problem, but the other groups each took about 50 seconds (range 49.2–51.3 seconds). A similar pattern obtained in the latencies between feedback and the child's next response. The ninth-grade reflective children took 4.5 seconds between feedback and their next response. The ninth-grade impulsives took 3.0, the fifth-grade reflectives 2.9, and the fifth-grade impulsives took 2.6 seconds before they made their next response. Nuessle concluded that the reflective children employed their retrieval and recoding processes more efficiently than did the impulsives, but that this interacted with grade level: The ninth-grade impulsives performed at about the same level as the fifth-grade reflectives on several dependent measures.

MEMORY DEMANDS

Eimas (1970) used blank-trial probes of the kind illustrated in Figure 2.3 in an experiment in which he provided second-grade children (mean CA = 7:6) with memory aids of various kinds.[4] His results showed that

4. Some of Eimas' memory aids may have facilitated a kind of perceptual processing in which the child simply located common cues in the available stimulus objects.

some aids produced greater improvements in information processing than did others, but in each case performance was much improved over a control condition in which no memory aids were provided. Eimas did not perform a systems analysis on his data, but instead used Levine's (1966, 1967) trial-by-trial estimate of the size of the hypothesis set from which the children resampled following errors (see Figure 2.5). The results of this analysis indicated that the number of hypotheses eliminated from the set from which the children resampled was closely related to the specific memory aids provided. The memory aids, then, permitted the child to eliminate logically irrelevant information from consideration, that is, they reduced the total demands placed on the processor.

In a related, developmental study, Gholson and Danziger (1975) presented second- and sixth-grade children (mean CA = 7:10 and 11:10) with an alternating series of four- and eight-dimensional problems. (Eighth-dimensional problems are illustrated in Chapter 7.) While some decrements in performance were found among children of both age levels in the more complex problems, the systems analysis revealed a substantial interaction between age and stimulus complexity (see Figure 3.6). Consistent with some previous findings (e.g., Gholson *et al.*, 1972), children of the two age groups showed essentially identical performance in the less complex problems (about 75% strategies, 10–15% unsystematic hypothesis sequences). In the eight-dimensional problems sixth graders continued to perform at the same level, but second graders showed unsystematic hypothesis sequences in about 40% of their problems, and strategies in only 35%. The findings from the four-dimensional problems indicated that the second- and sixth-grade children had available to them similar underlying cognitive skills as reflected in the processor, but findings from the eight-dimensional task suggested that their memory capacities differed. This is qualified, though, because cognitive level was not assessed.

The memory organization required by the eight-dimensional problems was presumably too great for the second graders to be able to keep track of the hypotheses and dimensions that had been previously disconfirmed (or conversely, were yet to be evaluated) and, consequently, the processor essentially malfunctioned. Sixth-grade children, however, had achieved more sophisticated memory organization, and the processor continued to function in its characteristic way. Memory researchers (e.g., A. L. Brown, 1975, 1978; Hagen, Jongward, & Kail, 1975; Neimark, 1976; Neimark *et al.*, 1971) have reported increases in children's memory capabilities during the elementary-school years that support the plausibility of this interpretation, and Byrd (1979) has recently provided supporting data.

Byrd used 24 pictures that could be categorized into four classes (Neimark *et al.*, 1971) to assess the memory capabilities of fourth-grade children. She told the children they could do anything they wanted to with the pictures that would help them remember (e.g., move the pictures around). They were then given a three-minute study period followed by a recall task. Children who formed four exhaustive categories or formed partial categories and met a recall criterion were classified as organizers. The remaining children were classified as nonorganizers. The children of each group then received a series of eight-dimensional problems of the kind used by Gholson and Danziger. The organizers exhibited strategies in about 66% of their problems, unsystematic sequences in 26%, and stimulus preference in 8%. The nonorganizers, however, showed only 27% strategies, along with 45% unsystematic sequences and 28% stimulus preference. Although Byrd's organizers showed about 10% more unsystematic hypothesis sequences than the sixth graders depicted in Figure 4.3, they showed only 5% fewer strategies (66% versus 71%). Her fourth-grade nonorganizers performed at about the same level as the second graders in eight-dimensional problems (Figure 4.3).

OTHER RESEARCH

Parrill-Burnstein (1978, 1979) has reported research in which she presented four-dimensional problems containing blank-trial probes to groups of young children. Her first experiment will illustrate the procedure and findings. She analyzed the problem-solving task into four sequentially dependent units. Each of these units was said to correspond to a particular cognitive subprocess or series of subprocesses. Groups of kindergarten children (mean CA = 5:5) were given successively greater amounts of training on the units. The training sequence was designed to teach the child the individual processes that are required to solve the problems.

Three colored strips were mounted on a large magnetic chalkboard. The strips, going from the child's left side, were green, yellow, and red. The stimuli were presented in a card holder located at the top of the board. Each problem was 46 trials in length, with blank-trial probes inserted between consecutive feedback trials. Each hypothesis corresponded to a unique 3:1 pattern of responses during probes.

The experiment was conducted in four phases: pretraining, pretest, training, posttest. Parrill-Burnstein used the standard four-problem pretraining procedure. The pretest consisted of three problems. The children received nine training problems, with varying amounts of instruction, and these were followed by a three-problem posttest.

Children in Condition 1 were required to enumerate the cues (hypotheses) contained in the stimulus complex that was designated correct on the first feedback trial of each training problem (this was called "stimulus differentiation"). In addition, children in Condition 2 were

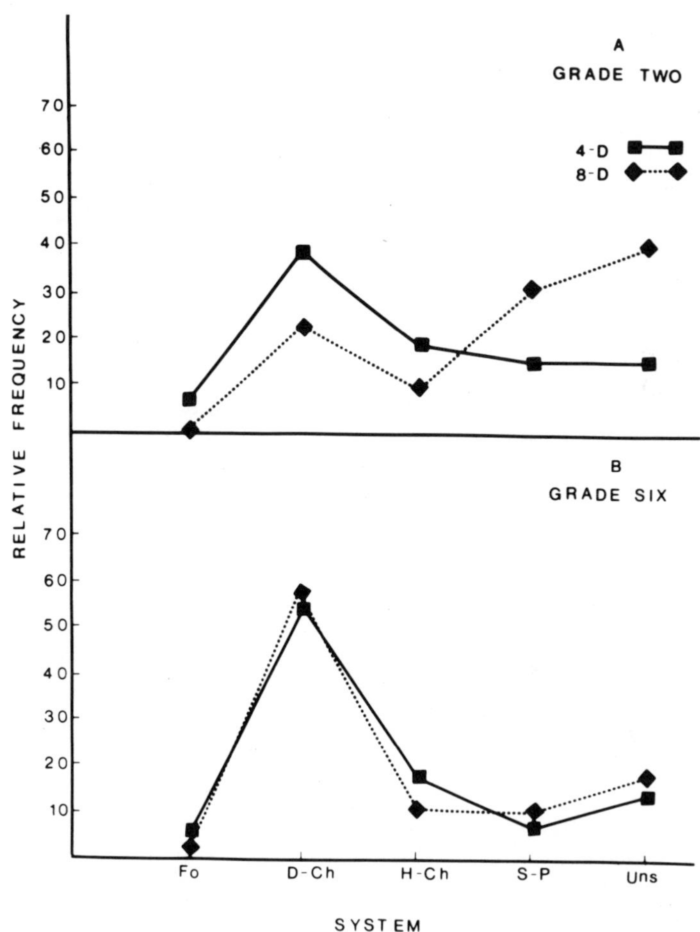

Figure 4.3. The relative frequencies of focusing (Fo), dimension checking (D-ch), hypothesis checking (H-ch), stimulus preference (S-P), and unsystematic hypothesis sequences (Uns).

provided with magnetic representations (squares) of each of the hypotheses relevant to solution. Eight squares, each designating a particular stimulus cue (i.e., one was orange, one was blue, etc.), were placed before the child. As the children enumerated each hypothesis contained in the correct stimulus complex, they located the corresponding magnetic block and placed it on the green strip (called "memory training").

In addition to the training given the first two groups, children in Condition 3 were taught to selectively attend to one of the four cues at the outset of each problem ("selective attention"). The child was instructed to move one of the magnetic squares, representing one hypothesis to the yellow strip, and to name this hypothesis on each trial of the first blank-trial probe. No additional instruction was provided.

The children in Condition 4 were taught, in addition, to manipulate hypotheses in response to positive and negative feedback (this was designated "feedback training"). That is, they were taught to maintain confirmed hypotheses and to reject those that were disconfirmed. The children were instructed that following a disconfirmation the cue on the yellow strip was to be moved to the red strip. Once on the red strip, the cue was to be excluded from further consideration. The child then selected a new cue from the green strip and moved it to the yellow strip. This cue then dictated choice responses. If feedback was positive the child was instructed to leave the cue on the yellow strip and continue to make corresponding choice responses. All the materials remained available to children in Conditions 2, 3, and 4 during posttest, but the instructions were discontinued.

Results indicated that the effects of the various training procedures were, in part, cumulative. In pretraining the children in all groups solved, on average, about 10% of their problems. In posttest children in Conditions 1, 2, 3, and 4 solved 30, 36, 56, and 100% of their problems, respectively. Performance was ordered this way on most dependent measures. In pretest they showed consistent hypotheses in 44–56% of their probes; in posttest between 62 and 97%. The children maintained confirmed hypotheses with probabilities ranging from .41 to .55 in pretest and .52 to .94 in posttest.

In pretest the children maintained disconfirmed hypotheses with probabilities ranging from .30 to .41. In posttest children in Conditions 1, 2, 3, and 4 maintained disconfirmed hypotheses with probabilities .21, .31, .52, and .025, respectively. The children in Condition 3 actually showed significantly worse performance on this measure in posttest than in pretest, probably because the cue that corresponded to their first hypothesis remained on the yellow strip throughout the entire problem. Those in Condition 4, of course, showed the reverse pattern. Similar findings were obtained on a measure of local consistency.

Clearly, the training produced marked improvements in the performance of children in Condition 4. Unfortunately, however, it is not possible to specify exactly what was responsible for the improvements. This is because no posttest was administered in which the children were required to solve problems in the absence of the magnetic blocks that were manipulated from the green to the yellow to the red strip. Thus, while the children in Condition 4 learned the task as presented, whether memory, selective attention, or some other subprocess was actually improved by the training is not known. The approach taken by Parrill-Burnstein is certainly exciting (1978, 1979), but in the absence of further data, the effects of the training on the child's information-processing capabilities cannot be determined.

While not conclusive, the research to date is certainly congenial to the broad theoretical conception proposed here. Other findings, reported in Chapters 5, 6, and 7 are also generally in line with the conception. Before turning to those findings, however, it will be useful to restate the conception vis-à-vis the research reviewed in this chapter.

Summary and Conclusions

The model proposes that prediction hypotheses per se do not underlie the behavior of young children, at least at the outset of acquisition. Rather, their behavior is determined by individual response components (e.g., win–stay position, win–shift object), out of which prediction hypotheses are eventually consolidated. In children younger than about 6 years of age, the win and lose components frequently involve the same action (e.g., win–stay, lose–stay position) at the outset of acquisition. Levine (1963) called these combinations "response-set" hypotheses. Position-oriented response sets appear to dominate over object responses (object refers to one or more nonspatial cue) in young children, and position preference (win–stay, lose–stay) precedes position alternation (win–shift, lose–shift) developmentally. In addition, the rate of acquisition of the component units out of which prediction hypotheses are eventually consolidated appears to vary. Lose–shift object, for example, is acquired earlier than win–stay object. In addition, object components may, at times, combine with position components; for example, win–stay position has been shown to combine with lose–shift object (Levinson & Reese, 1967) during the course of acquisition.

Eventually, the various win and lose action components of response-set hypotheses are separated from each other, coordinated with task-relevant information (stimulus cues, feedback) and combined into integrated response rules or schemes (e.g., win–stay, lose–shift object). By the early elementary-school years, children show little difficulty in exhibiting these integrated rules, which Levine (1963) calls "prediction" hypotheses. For younger children, however, this process appears to be more troublesome. Once prediction hypotheses *are* consolidated, the manner in which they are processed during problem solving depends upon the child's developmental level.

The conception involves a processor that operates upon information which is processed, transformed, and integrated into ongoing behavior by activated logical schemes, and an organized set of cognitive subprocesses that regulate a continuous flow of information to (and from) the processor. The processor, the characteristics of which undergo qualitative changes with development, embodies the underlying cognitive (logical) operations available to the child at each level of development. These capabilities determine the kinds of solution plans the child may generate and execute and, consequently, they are reflected in the efficiency with which information is processed. Although the research is sparse, the processor may play an important role in organizing and integrating the cognitive subprocesses. Characteristics of the processor appear to determine how some information is coded into semantic memory, and how semantic memory itself is organized. The logical skills reflected in the processor are identified with Piaget's description of the catalogue of cognitive operations available to preoperational, concrete operational, and formal operational thought.

The cognitive subprocesses probably include differentiating cues in the task environment, selective attention, verbal and nonverbal coding processes, memory storage, and retrieval from memory. Like the logical operations embodied in the processor, the functioning of the various cognitive subprocesses is reflected in the child's performance. How efficiently the subprocesses function changes continuously with development. In addition, it appears that the efficiency with which they operate is readily manipulable in the laboratory, at least among children. When task demands make it difficult for the child, for example, to attend to, code, or remember information concerning cues yet to be tested or already tested, decrements in information processing result.

The model predicts that qualitative changes in the processor lead to developmental-level main effects in analysis of variance designs. The literature to date appears to confirm this prediction. Quantitative changes in the child's ability to adjust to altered task demands were predicted to produce interaction between developmental level and task variables. Again, the literature to date is congenial to this assumption. The emergence of hypotheses, effects of developmental level, and the manipulation of various cognitive subprocesses are explored further in the next three chapters.

II
RESEARCH ON THE ACQUISITION AND USE OF HYPOTHESES

This part is divided into three chapters. Each chapter contains research that was designed to investigate one facet of the model presented in Chapters 3 and 4: the emergence of hypotheses, the processor, and the cognitive subprocesses. In Chapter 5 two experiments are reported that bear on the emergence of hypotheses in the repertoire of the young child. In the first experiment procedures were devised to monitor the time course of the individual component units out of which prediction hypotheses are consolidated. The subjects were preschool children and second graders. In the second experiment preschool children were trained to generate prediction hypotheses in order to explore whether they would then test them systematically, that is, exhibit strategies.

Two experiments concerned with characteristics of the processor are presented in Chapter 6. The first involved kindergarten children who were preoperational, transitional to concrete operations, or concrete operational. The children were exposed to modeling procedures designed to induce systematic hypothesis testing. The second experiment involved young, middle-aged, and elderly adults who were transitional to formal operations or were formal operational.

Chapter 7 contains four experiments that are concerned with the effects of various task manipulations upon the functioning of individual cognitive subprocesses. In one experiment children who normally show poor voluntary attentional control were taught to switch their visual attention from a disconfirmed stimulus object to one that contained the solution. The effects of material and verbal feedback upon attentional processes were evaluated in a second study. In the third experiment a procedure (Kornreich, 1968) that permitted the evaluation of memory processes as well as coding and recoding was used to monitor hypotheses in children and adults. The abilities of normal and underachieving readers to selectively disembed stimulus information under various conditions was studied in the final experiment.

5

The Acquisition of Hypotheses: Research with Preschool Children

Although Levine's (1963) distinction between prediction hypotheses and response sets has proven quite useful in work with young children (e.g., Bessemer & Stollnitz, 1971; Cantor & Spiker, 1978; Gholson & Beilin, 1979; Gholson *et al*., 1976; Levine, 1975; Phillips & Levine, 1975; Reese, 1977; Rieber, 1969), the relationship between the two has not been specified. Research on position responses, object responses, and learning set indicates that response-set hypotheses initially dominate the young child's behavior. In Chapters 3 and 4 it was suggested that the various win and lose action components of response sets must be separated and then individually coordinated with task-relevant information before they can be reconsolidated into prediction hypotheses. Previous research provided some support for this analysis, but implications of the conception have not been directly evaluated. The first experiment in this chapter was designed to provide a preliminary exploration of some of these implications.

In the analysis presented in Chapter 4 it was shown that Piaget's theory implies preoperational children should be capable of generating prediction hypotheses, that is, hypotheses that are sensitive to feedback consequences through a trial-and-error process. The theory also implies that the logical capabilities of the preoperational processor are so restricted that these children are incapable of testing hypotheses systematically (e.g., Inhelder & Piaget, 1964; Inhelder *et al*., 1974). That is, these children's prediction hypotheses should be exhibited only in unsystematic sequences. In previous research (Gholson & Beilin, 1979; Gholson *et al*., 1976; Rieber, 1969; Schuepfer & Gholson, 1978) preoperational children have almost inevitably exhibited response-set hypotheses which, of course, yield only stereotypes when hypothesis sampling systems are analyzed. Thus, in order to provide a direct test of implications concerning the processor, procedures were devised to elicit prediction hypotheses from preoperational (preschool) children.

Experiment 1: The Acquisition and Consolidation of Prediction Hypotheses among Preschool Children and Second Graders[1]

THERESE SCHUEPFER AND BARRY GHOLSON

In previous chapters it was suggested that the emergence of prediction hypotheses in the repertoires of young children results from a three-tiered process. At the outset of acquisition their behavior is dominated by response-set hypotheses in which the win and lose components involve the same action (e.g., win–stay position, lose–stay position). These components must be separated from each other before the acquisition of prediction hypotheses may begin. It was also suggested that the individual response components may be acquired independently and at different rates. Lose–shift object, for example, is usually acquired earlier than win–stay object (cf. Levinson & Reese, 1967). If prediction hypotheses do result from the consolidation of individual response components, then it should be possible to directly monitor the time course of both the individual components and the consolidation process. The problem, of course, was to devise techniques that would permit this to be accomplished.

A combination of learning-set and hypothesis-probing methods was finally decided upon. The procedures permitted Bowman's (1963) equations to be used to estimate the relative dominance of each component unit in four complementary pairs: (*a*) win–stay object versus win–shift object; (*b*) win–stay position versus win–shift position; (*c*) lose–stay object versus lose–shift object; (*d*) lose–stay position versus lose–shift position. These estimates provided data bearing upon the acquisition of individual components and the various ways in which the components combined during the course of learning-set acquisition. Each feedback trial was followed by a blank-trial probe. These probes were designed to identify

1. This report is based upon a doctoral dissertation submitted to the faculty at Memphis State University by the first author as part of the requirements for the Ph.D degree. The second author directed the work.

each object, object-alternation, position, and position-alternation hypothesis that young children are known to exhibit. Thus the relative frequencies of occurrence of each kind of hypothesis could be directly determined from the data. In addition, conditional probabilities derived from hypotheses exhibited in consecutive probes provided a second measure of how the children combined individual components during the course of acquisition.

Method

SUBJECTS

The subjects were 71 preschool children with a mean age of 4:1 years (range 3:2–4:9), and 58 second graders 7:0–8:0 years of age (mean CA = 7:6). The younger children attended a private (Educare) preschool program in which the teaching of simple concepts is part of the curriculum. The second-grade children were drawn from a public school that serves mostly middle-class families.

GENERAL PROCEDURE

Each child was individually presented with a series of bivalued problems in which the stimulus materials were appended to 5- × 8-inch cards with lines down the vertical midline to separate the stimulus objects clearly. The children were given no pretraining and only minimal instructions. They were told there were two pictures on each card, that they were to point to the one they thought was correct, and that sometimes they would be told whether their response was correct or wrong. The experimenter also informed them that they should always try to be correct because she was marking it on her (data) sheet. On feedback trials the experimenter said "yes, this picture is correct," or "no, *this* picture is correct," and pointed to the correct stimulus object for about four seconds. On blank trials she simply turned the card to expose the next stimulus pair immediately following the child's response.

A series of 10 two-dimensional problems was presented in each daily session until a learning-set criterion was achieved. When the criterion was met the two-dimensional problem series was terminated and, beginning with the next daily session, a series of 10 four-dimensional problems was presented in each session until criterion was achieved on these problems. The two-dimensional problems were constructed from combinations of four nonspatial dimensions that were used in the four-dimensional problems: color, shape, size, and line position. All six of the possible combinations of two bivalued dimensions were presented one time in each consecutive series of six problems. Different combinations of colors and shapes were used in each problem that called for variation on these dimensions, but the sizes and line positions were constant across problems (i.e., 1.5 versus 3 inches; line over versus line under the shape). When a two-dimensional problem involved size and/or line position, the other dimensions were neutralized. Squares of the same color, for example, might be presented on each trial with appropriate variation on the relevant dimensions. Each of the four-dimensional problems contained variation on all four of the dimensions listed immediately above.

The two-dimensional problems were 17 trials in length with feedback delivered on Trials 1, 5, 9, and 13. The four-dimensional problems were 24 trials in length. Feedback was delivered on Trials 1, 7, 13, and 19. Probes for hypotheses followed each feedback trial in both kinds of problems. The criterion for the acquisition of learning set was derived from the last three feedback trials of five consecutive problems. The child was required to make no more than one error on these 15 trials (i.e., 14 of 15 correct; about 93%). If the child failed to meet this criterion within seven sessions (70 problems) in the two-dimensional problems, training was discontinued. Children who met the criterion were transferred to four-dimensional problems in the next daily session.

STIMULUS MATERIALS

The sequence of stimulus pairs presented in each problem was constructed according to specific criteria. These criteria were required because Bowman's (1963) model can be applied only to stimulus sequences that meet certain restrictions and because each simple cue and alternation pattern must correspond to a unique response sequence during each blank-trial probe if all possible hypotheses are to be directly identified. The first nine trials of a two-dimensional problem are illustrated in Figure 5.1. Each hypothesis and the response pattern that corresponded to it in the first probe (Trials 2–5) is identified in the figure.

Several features of this sequence of stimulus pairs require delineation. First, Bowman's model was devised for problems in which pairs of stereometric objects were used as stimuli. When his equations are applied, the only cues that may vary from one trial to the next are the positions of the rewarded and unrewarded objects. Second, the data to which Bowman applied his equations involved only the first two trials of each problem: the object chosen on each trial (same or different), the position chosen on each trial (same or different), and the feedback received on the first trial (positive or negative). Because it was desirable to apply Bowman's equations to each feedback trial and the (blank) trial that immediately followed it in the present experiment, it was necessary for the stimulus objects presented on each feedback trial and the blank trial that immediately followed it to be identical, except for the positions

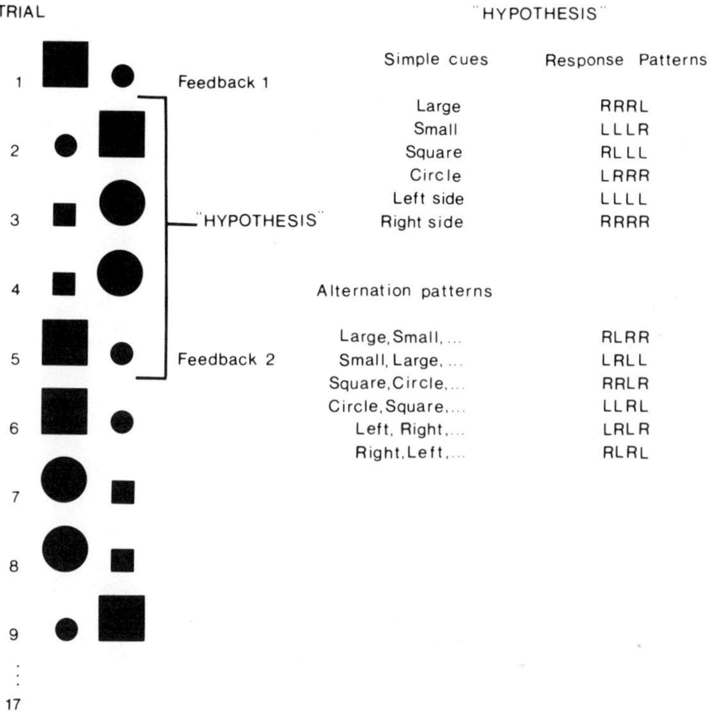

Figure 5.1. A stimulus sequence that permits the unique identification of each simple cue, simple-cue alternation, simple position, and simple-position alternation hypothesis from the response pattern exhibited on four consecutive trials.

of the objects, which varied "randomly." The stimulus objects presented on Trials 1–2 and 5–6 in Figure 5.1, for example, involve the cues *large–square* versus *small–circle* in each case. In general, Bowman's equations require that the object pairs presented in the two consecutive trials submitted to analysis occupy the same positions half the time and change positions half the time.

Trials 2–5, 6–9, 10–13, and 14–17 were used to infer the hypotheses that dictated responses in each two-dimensional problem. Even though the child received feedback on the last trial of each of the first three hypothesis probes, these data may be included along with the response data from the preceding trials of the probe, to infer the cue that dictated all responses during the probe. This was done, rather than adding another blank trial to each probe, in order to minimize the potential disruption caused by a long series of trials in which the child received no feedback. It will be seen below, however, that the caution was not necessary, because behavior was highly systematic throughout.

The middle trials of each probe (e.g., Trials 3–4, 7–8 in Figure 5.1) involved the second combination of two nonspatial dimensions that may be constructed from bivalued two-dimensional stimulus materials (i.e., small square versus large circle in the sequence illustrated). These stimulus objects were positioned in such a way that each simple cue and alternation pattern corresponded to a unique pattern of left and right responses during each probe; that is, during Trials 2–5, 6–9, etc.

Finally, there are exactly 16 different combinations of left and right responses that are possible during the four trials that constituted each hypothesis probe. Of the 16 combinations, 12 correspond to simple cues or alternations: 4 correspond to simple object cues, 4 to object-alternation cues, 2 to simple position cues, and 2 to position-alternation cues. Each of the 12 is illustrated in the insert in Figure 5.1, along with the response sequence that corresponded to it during the first probe (i.e., Trials 2–5).

The stimulus sequences used in four-dimensional problems were similar to those described above. The blank-trial probes were five trials in length, however, so 32 different combinations of left and right responses were possible during each. Of the 32 combinations, 20 corresponded to simple cues or alternations: 8 to simple object cues, 8 to object-alternation cues, 2 to simple positions, and 2 to position alternation. Another change that was introduced was that the five trials in the probe were all blank trials. This change was introduced because, despite the potential disruption introduced by the added blank trial, it was deemed important to assess the frequencies with which the children's responses on feedback Trials 7, 13, and 19 were consistent with the hypotheses exhibited in the immediately preceding probes. Actually, children of both age levels chose consistently about 98% of the time, so the caution was unnecessary.

Results

The results are presented in three sections: acquisition data, hypothesis data, and the components as estimated by Bowman's model. In each case, the data of preschoolers were pooled according to the daily session in which they achieved criterion in two-dimensional problems. This procedure is termed the "criterion reference method" (Hayes & Pereboom, 1959; Levinson & Reese, 1967). The data of children who did not meet criterion on the two-dimensional problems within the allotted seven sessions were separately pooled. Because no second grader required more than two sessions to meet criterion in the two-dimensional problems, these children's data were pooled according to the block of five problems in which they achieved criterion. That is, the children who met criterion in the first session were pooled into two groups according to whether they did so in the first five problems of the session or the second five, as were the children who met criterion in the second session.

ACQUISITION DATA

The preschool children who achieved criterion in the two-dimensional problems did so in one of the first 4 days: 45 in the first session, 12 in the second, 4 in the third, and 4 in the fourth session. Six preschoolers failed to achieve criterion. The data of each of these groups were pooled to yield five criterion reference groups, called Groups 1, 2, 3, 4, and 7, respectively. The number of second graders who met criterion in the first, second, third, and fourth blocks of five problems was 24, 24, 5, and 5, respectively. These groups are referred to as Groups 1A, 1B, 2A, and 2B. There was no relationship between age and criterion group among the children of either age level.

The acquisition curves for the four preschool groups that achieved criterion and the four second-grade groups are presented in Figure 5.2. The proportion correct responses on the second, third, and fourth feedback trials in the five problems in which the children achieved criterion is labeled "criterion" in the figure. The block of problems that preceded the criterion block is labeled "−1," etc. Most of the groups showed some improvement in performance prior to the criterion block, but in no case did performance exceed .70. In general, these acquisition data are consistent with findings obtained previously among children of these age levels (e.g., Harter, 1967; Levinson & Reese, 1967; Schusterman, 1963). The children who failed to achieve criterion (Group 7) showed chance performance throughout their 70 problems.

HYPOTHESIS DATA

In the two-dimensional problems, 12 of the 16 possible response patterns in each four-trial probe corresponded to hypotheses. Thus, if the children responded haphazardly, about 75% of their probes would be expected to yield consistent hypothesis patterns. The probabilities that probes yielded response patterns that corresponded to simple object cues, object-cue alternation, position cues, position alternation, and no hypothesis during each session for each criterion reference group among the preschool children are presented in Tables 5.1–5.5. Data from the four-dimensional problems are not presented by daily sessions. This is because only four children required more than one session to meet criterion in these problems: three in the first criterion group and one in the second. These children all met criterion in the second session. In fact, more than half the preschool children met criterion in the first five four-dimensional problems that were presented to them.

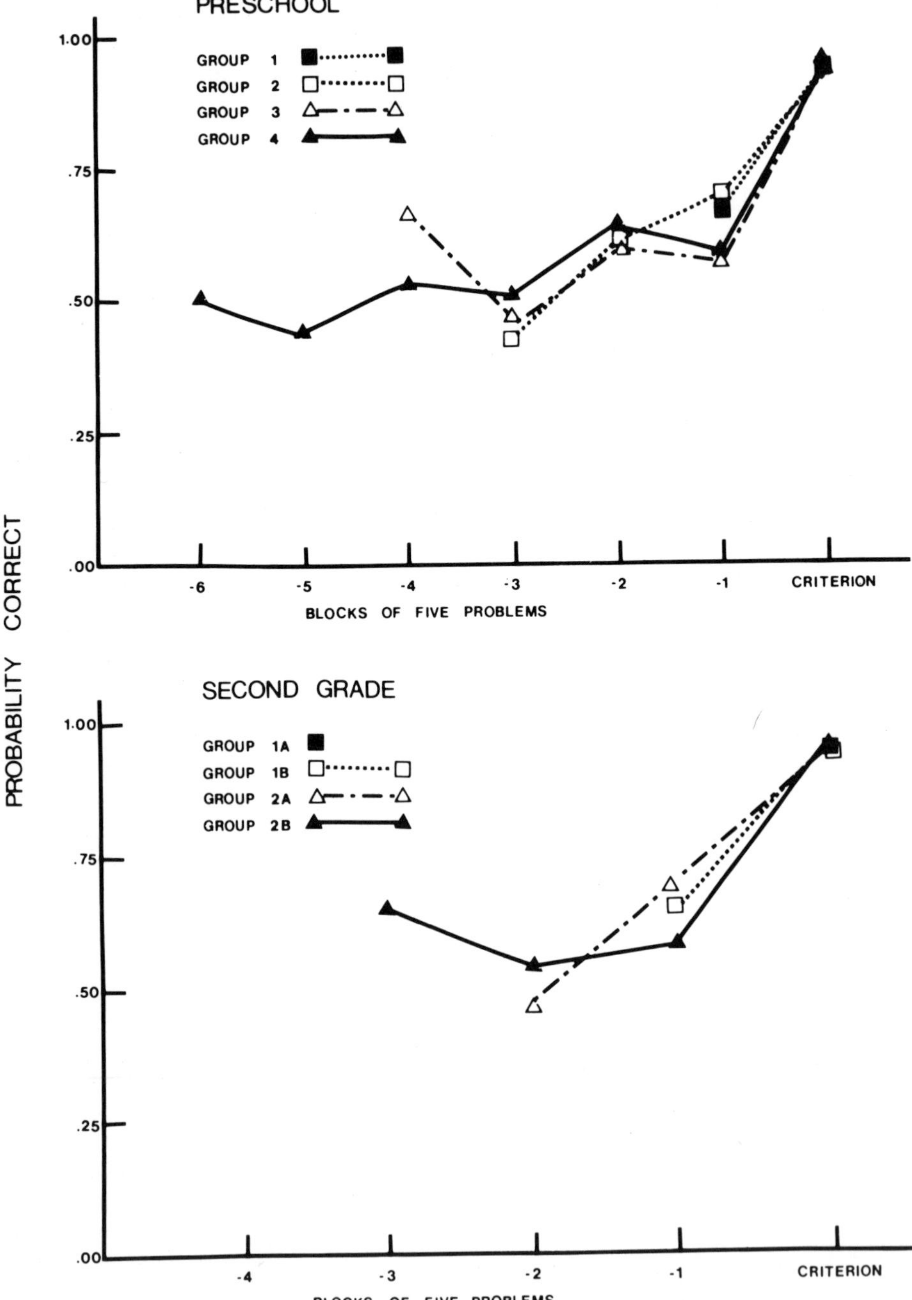

Figure 5.2. The probabilities of correct responses in blocks of five problems for each criterion reference group. "Criterion" represents the block of problems in which criterion was achieved, -1 the five-problem block that preceded it, -2 the five problems that preceded it, etc. Only the second, third, and fourth feedback trials of each problem were considered in computing these probabilities.

TABLE 5.1
Hypotheses Exhibited in Blank-Trial Probes in Daily Sessions by the 45 Preschool Children Who Achieved Criterion in the First Session in Two-Dimensional Problems

Hypothesis	Dimensions[a]	
	2	4
Simple object cue	.859	.813
Object cue alternation	.039	.052
Position preference	.056	.036
Position alternation	.020	.019
No hypothesis	.026	.081

[a] Ten problems per session.

TABLE 5.2
Hypotheses Exhibited in Blank-Trial Probes in Daily Sessions by the 12 Preschool Children Who Achieved Criterion in the Second Session in Two-Dimensional Problems

Hypothesis	Two dimensions		
	Session 1[a]	Session 2[a]	Four dimensions
Simple object cue	.554	.791	.743
Object cue alternation	.088	.032	.059
Position preference	.246	.136	.068
Position alternation	.058	.009	.006
No hypothesis	.054	.032	.124

[a] Ten problems per session.

TABLE 5.3
Hypotheses Exhibited in Blank-Trial Probes in Daily Sessions by the Four Preschool Children Who Achieved Criterion in the Third Session in Two-Dimensional Problems

Hypothesis	Two dimensions			
	Session 1[a]	Session 2[a]	Session 3[a]	Four dimensions
Simple object cue	.075	.400	.808	.800
Object cue alternation	.406	.206	.015	.050
Position preference	.050	.175	.074	.063
Position alternation	.363	.138	.029	.025
No hypothesis	.106	.081	.074	.063

[a] Ten problems per session.

TABLE 5.4
Hypotheses Exhibited in Blank-Trial Probes in Daily Sessions by the Four Preschool Children Who Achieved Criterion in the Fourth Session in Two-Dimensional Problems

	Two dimensions				
Hypothesis	Session 1[a]	Session 2[a]	Session 3[a]	Session 4[a]	Four dimensions
Simple object cue	.213	.145	.363	.847	.663
Object cue alternation	.231	.115	.108	.028	.013
Position preference	.238	.585	.229	.042	.086
Position alternation	.225	.075	.204	.028	.013
No hypothesis	.094	.080	.096	.056	.225

[a] Ten problems per session.

In the two-dimensional problems the probabilities that the response patterns exhibited in the probes corresponded to hypotheses ranged from about .89 to .98. Each of the scores was significantly higher than the .75 expected by chance. In four-dimensional problems the children would have been expected to show response patterns that corresponded to hypotheses with probability .625 (20 of 32) by chance alone. The scores ranged from about .78 to .94. Again, each of the scores was significantly above chance level.

The hypotheses exhibited in two-dimensional problems show a clear pattern among the children of each group that achieved criterion. On the criterion day they exhibited about 80% simple object hypotheses, with the remainder spread haphazardly over the four remaining categories. Among the groups who achieved criterion after the first day, the relative frequencies of response patterns that corresponded to simple object cues increased across sessions, while those corresponding to object alternation, position preference, position alternation, and no hypothesis decreased. Because the achievement of learning set required that the children learn to "win–stay, lose–shift object," it might appear that no other pattern could have obtained, given that they achieved criterion. This would not necessarily follow, however, because there is evidence from reversal–extradimensional shift research which has been taken to imply that preschool children's responses are frequently determined by compound cues (e.g., Cole, 1976; House, 1979; T. J. Tighe & L. S. Tighe, 1972; Zeaman & House, 1974).

Due to the way the stimulus pairs were sequenced, the present experiment provided data bearing directly on this possibility. If the children's responses were determined by compound cues, they would have been expected to show response patterns that corresponded to simple object cues at very depressed levels, especially on the criterion

TABLE 5.5

Hypotheses Exhibited in Blank-Trial Probes in Daily Sessions by the Six Preschool Children Who Failed to Reach Criterion in Seven Sessions in Two-Dimensional Problems [a]

Hypothesis	Session 1	Session 2	Session 3	Session 4	Session 5	Session 6	Session 7
Simple object cue	.279	.213	.188	.125	.129	.142	.204
Object cue alternation	.183	.042	.079	.079	.092	.100	.092
Position preference	.154	.379	.392	.517	.354	.438	.429
Position alternation	.308	.329	.283	.238	.329	.263	.208
No hypothesis	.079	.038	.058	.042	.096	.058	.067

[a] Ten problems per session in each of the seven sessions.

day. To see why this was the case, consider, for example, the first probe illustrated in Figure 5.1. Suppose the correct object on each feedback trial was the large circle. On the third and fourth trial of the first probe, large and circle split; that is, the circle was small and the large object was square. Thus, if the children held compound cues they would have chosen the large object, by chance, on half of these trials, and the object that was a circle on the other half during the criterion run. Had this occurred, they would have been expected to show response patterns that corresponded to circle 25% of the time, large 25% of the time, position alternation 25% of the time, and no hypothesis 25% of the time. Identical expectations held in each probe in all two-dimensional problems. It follows, then, that if the children's responses were determined by compound cues, the relative frequency of response patterns yielding simple object cues would approach .50 on the criterion day. Similarly, patterns corresponding to position alternation and no hypothesis would have accounted for about .50 of the data. These latter categories accounted, however, for less than 11% of the data on any criterion day, while simple object cues accounted for more than 79% in each case. It seems clear, then, that preschool children's responses are not usually determined by compound cues, at least in problems of the kind used here.

In precriterion sessions the children of the various groups exhibited somewhat different patterns of hypotheses. The children in Group 2 showed mostly position preference in those probes in which simple object cues were not manifested. Those who met criterion in the third session exhibited mostly position alternation and object-cue alternation in the first session, but little position preference. By the second session the relative frequencies of hypotheses in each of the three categories were roughly equivalent.

The children in Group 4 exhibited object-cue alternation, position alternation, and position preference with about equal frequencies on the first day. In the second session the amount of position preference more than doubled (24 to 58%), but both kinds of alternation patterns decreased by at least 50%. In the session preceding criterion the two kinds of position hypotheses each occurred twice as often as object alternation (about 20 versus 10%), and the frequency of simple object hypotheses increased from 14% to more than 35%.

The children who failed to achieve criterion showed little in the way of a discernable pattern, except that the frequency of position hypotheses increased from about 45% on the first day to more than 60% in each of the following sessions. The frequency of response patterns that corresponded to object cues (simple cues, alternations) actually dropped consistently across the first four sessions, and then increased only slightly. These children would, no doubt, eventually have reached criterion had training continued, but there was no hint that performance was improved after 70 problems.

The hypothesis data of the second-grade criterion groups are presented in Tables 5.6–5.9. No second grader failed to reach criterion in the four-dimensional problems in the first session. In general, these data parallel those obtained among the preschoolers (who reached criterion). That is, the frequencies of simple object hypotheses increased across blocks of problems, while the frequencies in other categories decreased. In precriterion blocks the second-grade groups, unlike the preschool groups, showed very similar patterns of performance. They exhibited mostly position alternation and object-cue alternation. Position preference hardly ever occurred among the second graders. One very surprising finding was that the second graders in Group 2A exhibited no-hypothesis patterns more frequently than any group of preschool children. They also exhibited fewer simple object hypotheses in each of their criterion blocks

TABLE 5.6
Hypotheses Exhibited in Blank-Trial Probes in Daily Sessions by the 25 Second-Grade Children Who Achieved Criterion in the First Five Two-Dimensional Problems

Hypothesis	Two dimensions Problems 1–5	Four dimensions
Simple object cue	.938	.894
Object cue alternation	.006	.012
Position preference	.010	.010
Position alternation	.025	.026
No hypothesis	.021	.057

TABLE 5.7
Hypotheses Exhibited in Blank-Trial Probes in Daily Sessions by the 24 Second-Grade Children Who Achieved Criterion in the Second Five Two-Dimensional Problems

	Two dimensional problems		
Hypothesis	1–5[a]	6–10	Four dimensional problems
Simple object cue	.523	.087	.808
Object cue alternation	.146	.023	.025
Position preference	.056	.009	.006
Position alternation	.165	.056	.042
No hypothesis	.100	.042	.119

[a] The first 5 of the 10 problems presented in the first session.

TABLE 5.8

Hypotheses Exhibited in Blank-Trial Probes in Daily Sessions by the Five Second-Grade Children Who Achieved Criterion in the First Five Problems of the Second Session in Two-Dimensional Problems

	Two dimensions, half sessions			
Hypothesis	1–5[a]	6–10	1–5	Four dimensions
Simple object cue	.220	.420	.650	.630
Object cue alternation	.280	.210	.113	.100
Position preference	.030	.040	.025	.040
Position alternation	.330	.210	.088	.080
No hypothesis	.140	.120	.125	.150

[a] The first 5 of the 10 problems presented in the first session.

TABLE 5.9

Hypotheses Exhibited in Blank-Trial Probes in Daily Sessions by the Five Second-Grade Children Who Achieved Criterion in the Second Five Problems of the Second Session in Two-Dimensional Problems

	Two dimensions, half sessions				
Hypothesis	1–5[a]	6–10	1–5	6–10	Four dimensions
Simple object cue	.220	.250	.680	.909	.820
Object cue alternation	.250	.280	.080	.000	.030
Position preference	.010	.030	.050	.000	.030
Position alternation	.400	.360	.110	.000	.020
No hypothesis	.120	.080	.080	.091	.100

[a] The first 5 of the 10 problems presented in the first session.

than did any group of preschoolers who met criterion. It was possible that some of the children in this group attempted to respond according to compound cues during the criterion blocks. One of the five children in this group showed very high frequencies of position alternation responses and no-hypothesis patterns throughout, even during the criterion block of problems. This was not the general pattern, however, among either the second graders or the preschoolers.

In order to evaluate the relative strengths of the win and lose components associated with each type of hypothesis, conditional probabilities were derived from the sequences of hypotheses the children exhibited. These data evaluated the same eight components that may be estimated using Bowman's (1963) procedures: win–stay object, win–shift object, win–stay position, win–shift position, lose–stay object, lose–shift object, lose–stay position, lose–shift position.

To understand how these probabilities were derived, consider the two-dimensional problems. Each problem contained four hypothesis probes, Trials 2–5, 6–9, 10–13, and 14–17. Assume, for illustrative purposes, that all protocols contained response patterns that corresponded to hypotheses in each probe. In the first probe the children could exhibit either object hypotheses or position hypotheses. The feedback that was delivered on Trial 5 could be positive (+) or negative (−). These combinations produce a fourfold matrix: object hypothesis +, object hypothesis −, position hypothesis +, position hypothesis −. Following the feedback on Trial 5, the children had three options (assuming a hypothesis was exhibited). They could maintain the same hypothesis, switch to another hypothesis of the same class (i.e., switch from one position hypothesis to another position hypothesis or from one object hypothesis to another object hypothesis), or they could switch to an hypothesis from the other class (position to object or vice versa).

Thus the conditional probabilities for each of the three events could be obtained for each hypothesis–feedback combination in the fourfold matrix. The probabilities of these events among the preschool children in each criterion group and daily session are presented in Tables 5.10–5.15. Only the two-dimensional problems are represented in the tables. This is because they met criterion very quickly in the four-dimensional problems and, consequently, win–stay object and lose–shift object were nearly always exhibited. The four-dimensional data, therefore, do not bear on the acquisition process. All instances in which hypotheses were exhibited in two consecutive probes were used in computing the data presented in the tables. Some cells in the tables are empty. This was because the estimates were misleading when the numbers of observations were small. Consider, for example, Criterion Group 4 in their fourth session. Among this group there were only two instances in which position hypotheses

TABLE 5.10
The Conditional Probabilities That Preschool Children Exhibited a Given Object Hypothesis in Two Consecutive Probes When Intervening Feedback Was Positive (Top), and Switched from One Object Hypothesis to a Different Object Hypothesis When Intervening Feedback Was Positive (Bottom)

	Daily sessions						
Criterion group	1	2	3	4	5	6	7
	Object Hypothesis + Same Object Hypothesis						
Day 1	.892						
Day 2	.683	.800					
Day 3	.455	.385	.778				
Day 4	.160	.060	.304	.875			
Day 7	.293	.224	.091	.025	.027	.051	.191
	Object Hypothesis + Different Object Hypothesis						
Day 1	.040						
Day 2	.110	.051					
Day 3	.127	.154	.067				
Day 4	.280	.164	.283	.042			
Day 7	.196	.132	.221	.215	.178	.177	.167

TABLE 5.11
The Conditional Probabilities That Preschool Children Exhibited a Given Position Hypothesis in Two Consecutive Probes When Intervening Feedback Was Positive (Top), and Switched from One Position Hypothesis to a Different One When Intervening Feedback Was Positive (Bottom)

	Daily sessions						
Criterion group	1	2	3	4	5	6	7
	Position Hypothesis + Same Position Hypothesis						
Day 1	.143						
Day 2	.692	.727					
Day 3	.733	.500	—				
Day 4	.555	.681	.444	—			
Day 7	.735	.766	.761	.828	.654	.769	.660
	Position Hypothesis + Different Position Hypothesis						
Day 1	.057						
Day 2	.026	.091					
Day 3	.200	.222	—				
Day 4	.050	.085	.111	—			
Day 7	.059	.149	.087	.086	.077	.054	.160

TABLE 5.12
The Conditional Probabilities That Preschool Children Switched from an Object to a Position Hypothesis When Intervening Feedback Was Positive (Top), and Switched from a Position to an Object Hypothesis When Intervening Feedback Was Positive (Bottom)

	Daily sessions						
Criterion group	1	2	3	4	5	6	7
	Object Hypothesis + Positive Hypothesis						
Day 1	.042						
Day 2	.133	.056					
Day 3	.175	.213	.071				
Day 4	.467	.550	.400	.043			
Day 7	.310	.345	.548	.810	.619	.609	.412
	Position Hypothesis + Object Hypothesis						
Day 1	.800						
Day 2	.282	.182					
Day 3	.067	.278	—				
Day 4	.400	.234	.444	—			
Day 7	.206	.085	.152	.086	.269	.179	.180

TABLE 5.13

The Conditional Probabilities That Preschool Children Exhibited the Same Object Hypothesis in Two Consecutive Probes When Intervening Feedback Was Negative (Top), and Switched from One Object Hypothesis to Another When Intervening Feedback was Negative (Bottom)

Criterion group	Daily sessions						
	1	2	3	4	5	6	7
	Object Hypothesis – Same Object Hypothesis						
Day 1	.136						
Day 2	.115	—					
Day 3	.273	.393	—				
Day 4	.000	.000	.118	—			
Day 7	.313	.063	.091	.095	.000	.000	.048
	Object Hypothesis – Different Object Hypothesis						
Day 1	.773						
Day 2	.615	—					
Day 3	.182	.357	—				
Day 4	.313	.364	.412	—			
Day 7	.375	.500	.136	.238	.429	.333	.238

TABLE 5.14
The Conditional Probabilities That Preschool Children Exhibited the Same Position Hypothesis in Two Consecutive Probes When Intervening Feedback Was Negative (Top), and Switched from One Position Hypothesis to Another When Intervening Feedback was Negative (Bottom)

Criterion group	Daily sessions						
	1	2	3	4	5	6	7
	Position Hypothesis – Same Position Hypothesis						
Day 1	.086						
Day 2	.306	.000					
Day 3	.577	.273	—				
Day 4	.333	.520	.543	—			
Day 7	.571	.597	.644	.587	.414	.545	.423
	Position Hypothesis – Different Position Hypothesis						
Day 1	.114						
Day 2	.292	.467					
Day 3	.000	.273	—				
Day 4	.167	.200	.130	—			
Day 7	.071	.236	.169	.222	.379	.242	.250

TABLE 5.15

The Conditional Probabilities That Preschool Children Switched from an Object Hypothesis to a Position Hypothesis When Intervening Feedback Was Negative (Top), and Switched from a Position to an Object Hypothesis When Intervening Feedback Was Negative (Bottom)

Criterion group	Daily sessions						
	1	2	3	4	5	6	7
	Object Hypothesis – Position Hypothesis						
Day 1	.091						
Day 2	.269	—					
Day 3	.545	.250	—				
Day 4	.687	.636	.471	—			
Day 7	.313	.438	.773	.667	.571	.667	.714
	Position Hypothesis – Object Hypothesis						
Day 1	.800						
Day 2	.403	.533					
Day 3	.423	.455	—				
Day 4	.500	.280	.326	—			
Day 7	.357	.167	.186	.190	.207	.212	.327

were exhibited during this session. In one case positive feedback followed the probe, and in the other negative feedback followed it. In both instances the child shifted from the position hypothesis to an object hypothesis. Thus the entries in the bottoms of Tables 5.12 and 5.15 would have been 1.0, based upon the single instance in each case. Correspondingly, .000 would have been entered into the tops and bottoms of Tables 5.11 and 5.14. Clearly, this would be misleading, because it does not represent the performance of this group or any other, either prior to criterion or on the criterion day. In order to avoid this problem of presenting misleading findings that were based upon small frequencies, any entry that yielded fewer than 10 observations in the basic fourfold matrix was deleted from the tables.

Table 5.10 reveals that win–stay object was very weak in Group 4 during their first two sessions, and it was fairly weak in Groups 2 and 3 in precriterion sessions. It never reached .30 among the children who failed to achieve criterion. In general, all groups showed comparably good win–stay object performance on the criterion day, but on average they showed it only about 35% of the time on precriterion days. The bottom of Table 5.10 and the top of Table 5.12 indicate that when the children shifted from a confirmed object hypothesis, they were much more likely to replace it with a position hypothesis than a new object hypothesis.

The top of Table 5.13 reveals that lose–shift object was strong among all criterion groups from the outset. The children showed lose–shift object responses about 90% of the time. In the precriterion sessions the children were about as likely to shift to a position cue as to a different object cue (Tables 5.13 and 5.15). Criterion performance, of course, required a combination of win–stay object and lose–shift object. It was necessary, then, for the children to strengthen the win–stay object component and to consolidate it with the lose–shift object component, which was already strong, before the learning-set criterion could be achieved. In addition, they had to replace disconfirmed object hypotheses with new object hypotheses rather than position hypotheses.

Table 5.11 shows that the win–stay position component was strong among Groups 2, 3, 4, and 7. When they did abandon a confirmed position hypothesis, however, they replaced it with an object hypothesis about twice as frequently as they switched to a different position hypothesis. These children also exhibited relatively weak lose–shift position responses. Groups 2, 3, and 4 showed lose–shift position only about 60% of the time in precriterion sessions, and Group 7 did so less than 50% of the time. Thus the lose–shift position component was weak in precriterion sessions—much weaker than lose–shift object.

The strength of win–stay position did not alter with practice. Lose–shift position, however, did show some strengthening, particularly in the frequencies with which the children replaced the disconfirmed position hypothesis with an object hypothesis (bottom of Table 5.15). Thus, as practice continued, the win–stay object component strengthened and, to a lesser extent, so did the lose–shift position component. One result of the strengthening was that fewer position hypotheses were exhibited as practice continued among those groups that eventually achieved criterion (Tables 5.2–5.4). Among the children in Group 7, neither the win–stay object component nor the lose–shift position component strengthened with practice. Consequently, they continued to exhibit position hypotheses in more than 60% of their probes.

The conditional probabilities for the second graders of each criterion group were also computed. The only entry in the fourfold matrix in which there were enough observations to provide meaningful estimates was when object hypotheses were followed by positive feedback. These probabilities, for maintaining the same object hypothesis and switching to a new object hypothesis, are presented in Table 5.16. Win–stay object was relatively weak in Groups 2A and 2B during the first two blocks of five problems. This was probably the reason they failed to achieve criterion on the first day. The probabilities that the children shifted from object to position hypotheses following positive feedback are not presented, but they may be derived by simply summing the probabilities in the cells of interest in the bottom and top of Table 5.16, and subtracting from 1.0. In general, they shifted to position hypotheses relatively infrequently. The one exception was Group 2A in the second block of five problems in the first session.

Data from the three other entries in the fourfold matrix are not presented, because at least five of the 10 cells in each table were empty when the 10-observation criterion was applied. In general, the second graders showed win–stay object, lose–shift object, win–stay position, and lose–shift position from the outset of acquisition. Each component unit was well established in their repertoires, and all that was required was that they consolidate them appropriately to meet the demands of the task. The one exception, as was already indicated, was Group 2A in their second block of five problems. There were 25 instances in which the children showed object hypotheses followed by positive feedback, and they shifted to a position hypothesis nine times. One child alone accounted for five of the nine instances.

BOWMAN'S ESTIMATES

Bowman's (1963) model was applied to the data of each criterion group in each session (preschoolers) or block of five problems (second graders). For a detailed description of this model and how it is applied,

TABLE 5.16
The Conditional Probabilities That Second-Grade Children Exhibited a Given Object Hypothesis in Two Consecutive Probes When Intervening Feedback Was Positive (Top), and Switched from One Object Hypothesis to a Different One When Intervening Feedback Was Positive (Bottom)

	Problems			
Criterion group	1–5	6–10	11–15	16–20
	Object Hypothesis + Same Object Hypothesis			
1A	.964			
1B	.815	.940		
2A	.731	.400	.833	
2B	.667	.692	.840	.964
	Object Hypothesis + Different Object Hypothesis			
1A	.015			
1B	.075	.036		
2A	.231	.240	.071	
2B	.148	.154	.100	.036

the interested reader is directed to Levinson and Reese (1963, 1967). In earlier applications (Bowman, 1963; Levinson & Reese, 1967) the model was applied only to the first two trials of each problem. In the present experiment the model was applied to each feedback trial and the (blank) trial that immediately followed it. It was also applied to the first two trials of each problem separately, but because the two procedures yielded essentially identical findings, only the results of the former are reported.

The model yields interval estimates of the proportions of responses controlled by each of the eight components described earlier in this chapter. The proportion of responses by which one component exceeds its complement (e.g., win–stay object versus win–shift object) may be calculated exactly; it is equal to the difference between the upper limits of the two components.

The data to which the model was applied in the present case were the following: (*a*) the object chosen on each of the two trials in question, same or different; (*b*) the position chosen on each of the two trials, same or different; and (*c*) the feedback on the first of the two trials, positive or negative. It is important to note that the model assumes responses on the two consecutive trials are either both to an object cue or both to a position cue; that is, the response determinant cannot shift from a position referent on one trial to an object referent on the next or vice versa. This assumption is strongly questioned by the hypothesis data presented in Tables 5.12 and 5.15. These data indicate that preschool children may shift from one referent to another following feedback more than 50% of the time during some phases of the acquisition process.

The interval estimates that result from the analyses range from 0.0 to 1.0. The upper and lower boundaries of each interval may be thought of as representing two children in the given group, the one who showed the most and the one who showed the fewest responses, respectively, that were controlled by the given component relative to its complement. The other children represented in the interval fell somewhere between the two. Alternatively, the range of the interval may be taken to indicate the amount by which the strength of the particular component increased or decreased, relative to its complement, during the block of trials over which it was computed. In fact, the upper and lower boundaries and the interval between them probably represent some combination of the two. If estimates of both components of a complementary pair are zero, or near zero, it implies that neither component occurred or they occurred very infrequently. If the upper and lower boundaries of an interval are identical, it implies that all children showed essentially identical performance during the block of problems in question, and the relative strength of the component did not change during the block.

Estimates of each of the four win components among the five groups of preschool children in two-dimensional problems during each daily session are presented in Figure 5.3. It should be explicitly stated that Bowman's estimates lump all object hypotheses together and all position hypotheses together and, consequently, these estimates cannot always be directly compared to the hypothesis data presented above. Win–shift object, for example, implies that the child shifted from one object cue to another. Bowman's model does not directly estimate shifts from object cues to position cues or vice versa. The groups of children who met criterion showed mostly win–stay object on the criterion day. The amount of win–shift object decreased across precriterion days and approached zero on the criterion day. These data correspond to the hypothesis data presented in Table 5.10. Bowman's procedures suggest, however, that win–stay object was stronger in precriterion sessions in Groups 3 and 4 and in Groups 7 than was obtained in the conditional probability data. Both win–stay position and win–shift position approached zero on the criterion day for each group. This, of course, indicates that position referents rarely controlled responses on criterion days. The preschoolers in Group 7 showed no discernable pattern in any of their win components across daily sessions.

The lose components of the preschool children in two-dimensional problems are presented in Figure 5.4. These estimates indicate that lose–shift object was relatively weak in Groups 2, 3, and 4 prior to the criterion day, not much stronger than lose–stay object. This is inconsistent with the hypothesis data presented in Table 5.13. Data in this table indicate that only Group 3, in their first and second sessions, maintained disconfirmed hypotheses with frequencies much above 10%. The children exhibited lose–stay position and lose–shift position with about equal frequencies in precriterion sessions, a finding that was reasonably close to that obtained in the hypothesis data (Table 5.14).

The win and lose components of the second graders in their two-dimensional problems in each block of five problems are presented in Figure 5.5. The estimates of win–stay object in Groups 2A and 2B suggest it was weaker than was indicated by the hypothesis data (Table 5.16). Also, the depressed win–stay object performance of Group 2A in their second block of five problems is not reflected in the data of Figure 5.5. In general, the patterns of win and lose components across problem blocks are similar to those obtained among the preschool children who met criterion.

Estimates derived from the four-dimensional problems for all groups of both age levels are presented in Figure 5.6. These data are essentially identical to those obtained in the hypothesis data. All groups showed

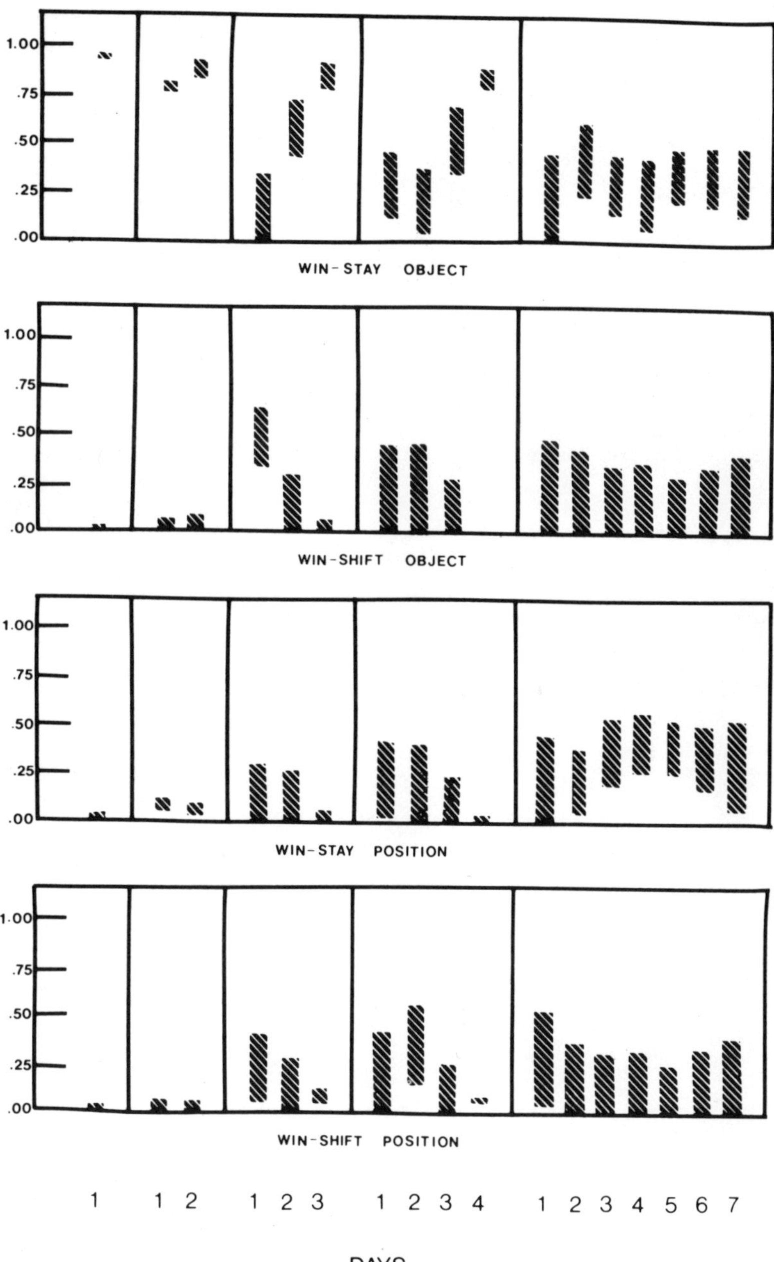

Figure 5.3. Estimates of each of the four win components for the five preschool groups in each daily session in two-dimensional problems.

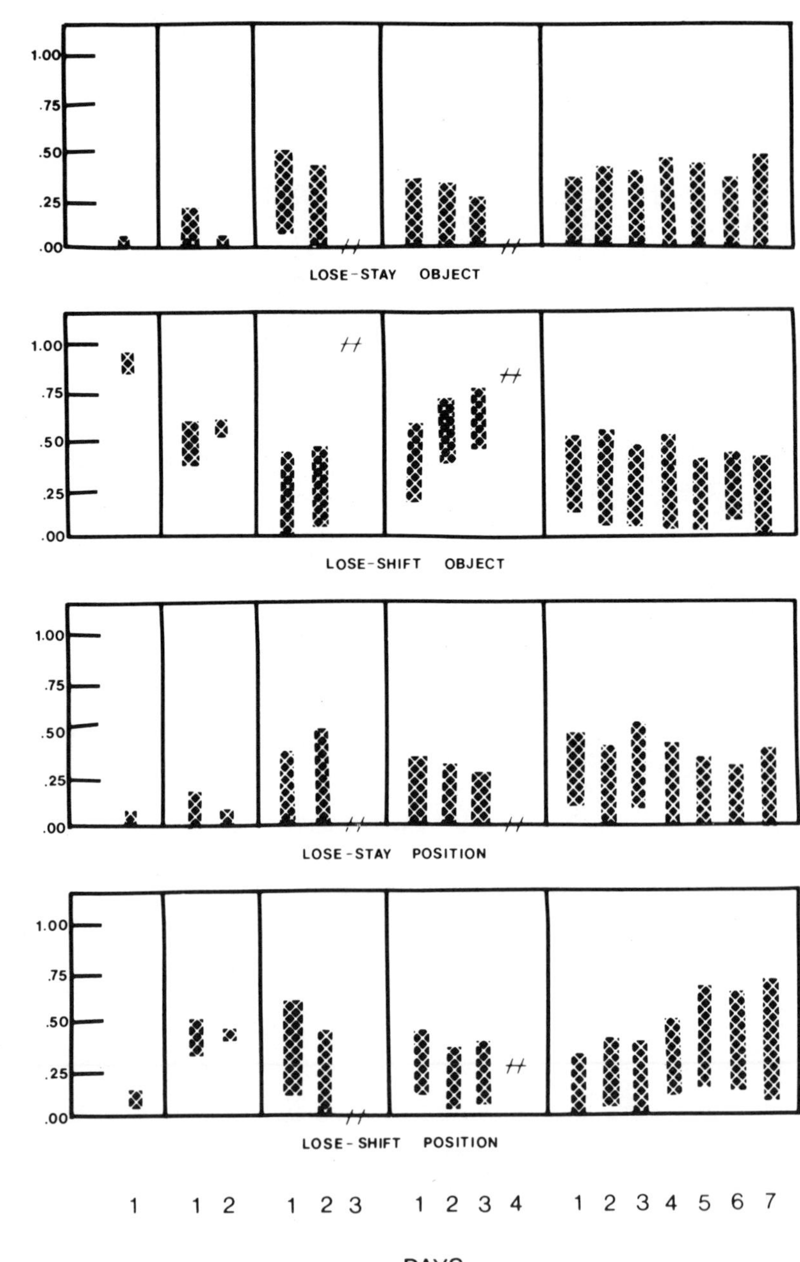

Figure 5.4. Estimates of each of the four lose components for the five preschool groups in each daily session in two-dimensional problems.

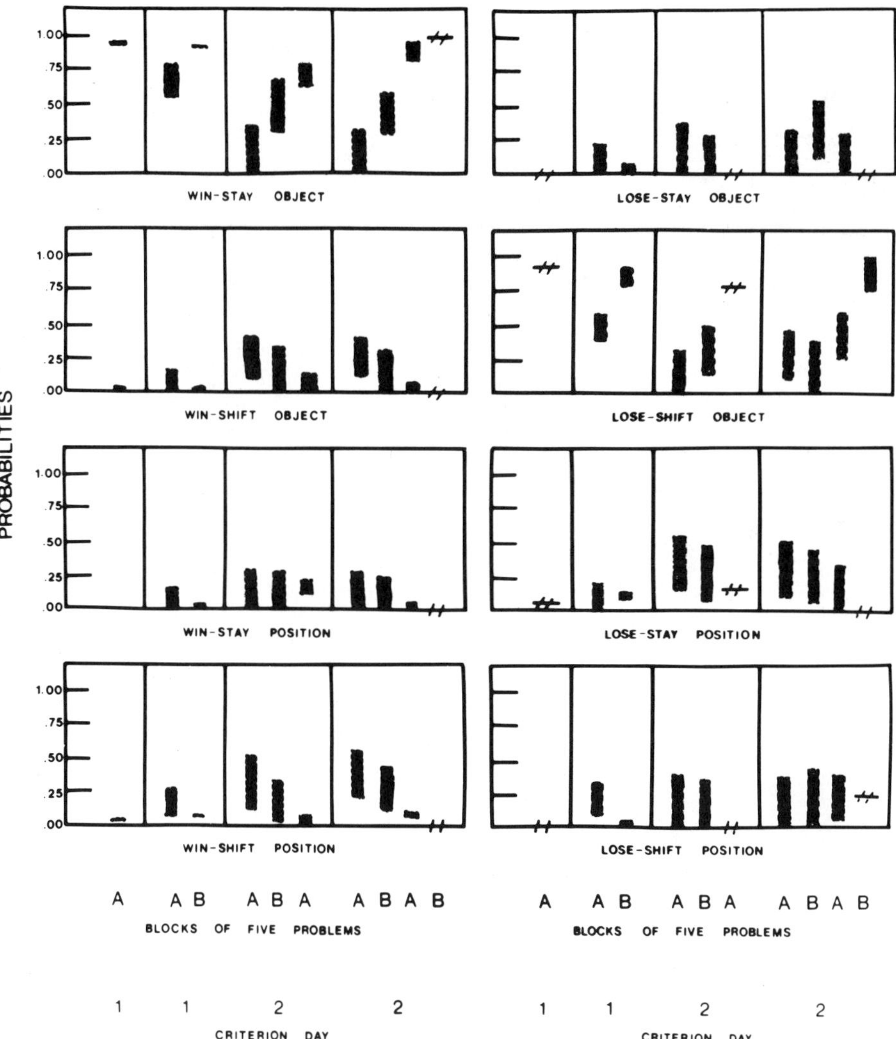

Figure 5.5. Estimates of each win and lose component for the four second-grade groups in blocks of five problems in their two-dimensional problems.

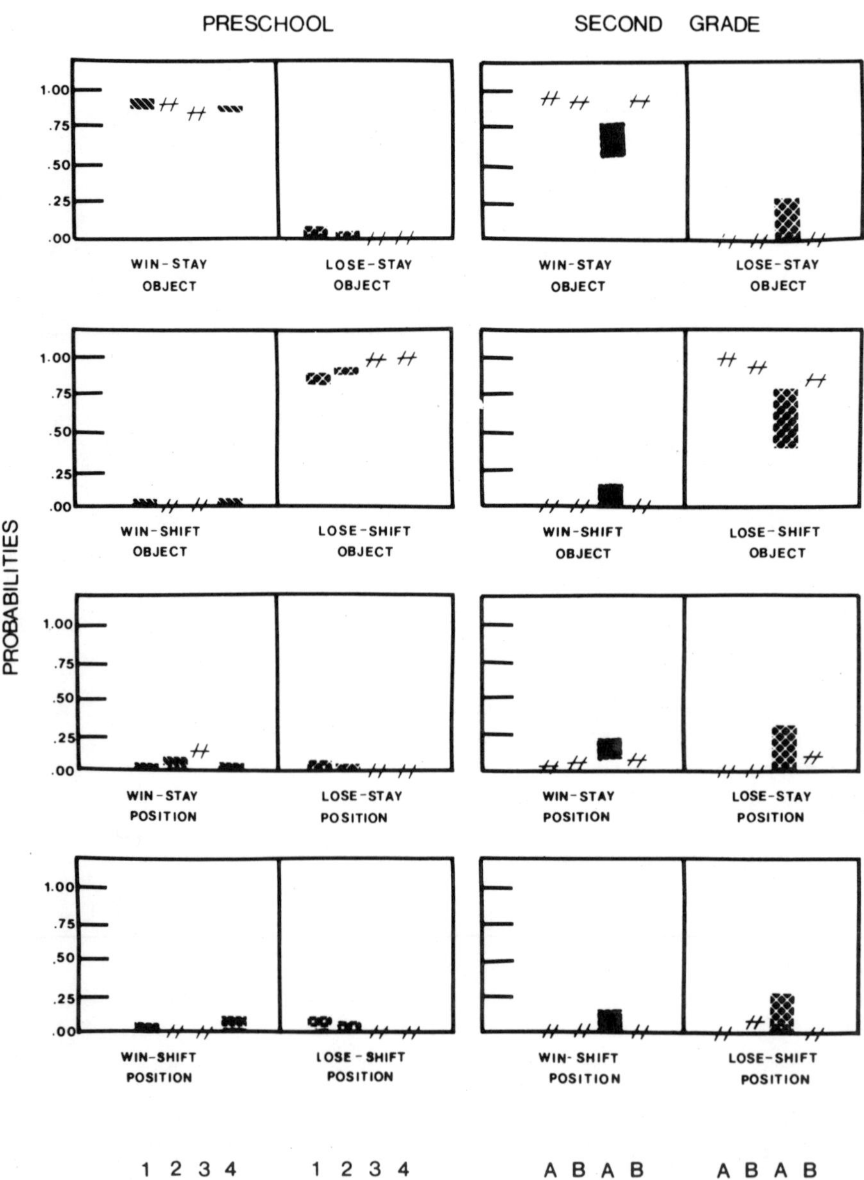

Figure 5.6. Estimates of each win and lose component for preschool children and second graders in their four-dimensional problems.

mostly win–stay object and lose–shift object. Position components hardly ever occurred. The one exception was Group 2A. They showed depressed performance on both win–stay object and lose–shift object, and they also showed more position components than any other group of second graders or preschoolers. This depression was reflected in the four-dimensional hypothesis data presented in Table 5.8. These children showed simple object hypotheses only 63% of the time, and showed no-hypothesis patterns in 15% of their probes.

Discussion

Results revealed by the hypothesis data and by the application of Bowman's procedures revealed several discrepancies. This was probably because Bowman's model assumes that responses on the two trials to which it is applied are both determined either by object cues or position cues, but the basic referent does not change. The data of Tables 5.10, 5.11, 5.13, and 5.14, however, revealed that this assumption is not viable. The children maintained a given hypothesis during a series of probe trials, but the preschool children switched from an object to a position hypothesis or vice versa very frequently following feedback during some phases of acquisition. The effect of these switches on Bowman's estimates of individual components cannot be directly determined, but if confirmed object hypotheses were replaced with position hypotheses the expected effect would have been an artificial inflation in the estimated amount of win–stay object. This is because the response to the position cue on the second trial would be misinterpreted as a response to an object cue. Similarly, when disconfirmed object hypotheses were replaced by position hypotheses, it inflated the estimated amount of lose–stay object. In both cases the predicted inflation of scores was borne out by the findings: Bowman's procedures estimated both more win–stay object and more lose–stay object than was obtained in the conditional probability data.

In addition, Bowman's procedures lump all object hypotheses together and all position hypotheses together, while the hypothesis-probe procedures permit the unique detection of the hypotheses that correspond to each object cue, each object-alternation cue, each position cue, and each position-alternation cue. One can only make inferences about specific hypotheses based upon the relative strengths of various components, however, when Bowman's procedures are applied (e.g., Levinson & Reese, 1967); and these inferences are not always easy either. One would be hard-pressed to determine, based upon the interval estimates of the preschool children in Group 7 (Figures 5.3 and 5.4), for example, that the frequencies of object hypotheses actually decreased during the first four sessions while position hypotheses increased. Thus it seems reasonable to suggest that hypothesis procedures should be used to monitor individual components whenever possible.

Except as indicated, the remaining discussion is confined to the hypothesis data generated by groups of children who met criterion. The findings of the various analyses are clear in their implications. The children showed response patterns that corresponded to hypotheses most of the time and well above chance levels. Children in each criterion group exhibited at least a few instances of each type of hypothesis the probes could detect. The striking finding was the relative weakness of some of the components at the outset of acquisition among the preschool children.

Win–stay object, for example, was weak among Groups 2, 3, and 4, but increased in strength systematically across daily sessions. When a response dictated by an object hypothesis was followed by positive feedback, the children of Groups 3 and 4 were about as likely to shift to a position hypothesis as they were to maintain the confirmed object hypothesis. This, of course, did not hold in the criterion session: The strength of win-stay object increased in the session preceding criterion and was very high on the criterion day.

The lose–shift object component was strong from the outset, but the children were about as likely to replace a disconfirmed object hypothesis with a position hypothesis as they were to replace it with a second object hypothesis early in acquisition. The frequency with which they shifted from a disconfirmed object hypothesis to another object hypothesis increased across the sessions preceding criterion.

The relative strengths of the position components were exactly the opposite of the object components. Win–stay position was strong from the outset of acquisition and it remained strong throughout. The children, of course, exhibited fewer position hypotheses as they approached the criterion run. In general, lose–shift position was much weaker than lose–shift object at the outset of acquisition, and it did not increase much across sessions. What did happen as the children approached the criterion session, though, was *(a)* they showed fewer position hypothesis, and *(b)* they were much more likely to replace a disconfirmed position hypothesis with an object hypothesis than a second position hypothesis.

The preschool children who failed to achieve criterion (Group 7) failed for several reasons. First, the strength of the win–stay object component remained weak throughout all seven sessions. Second, they very frequently replaced both confirmed and disconfirmed object hypotheses with position hypotheses. Finally, these children showed position hypotheses in more than 60% of their probes, and the frequency actually increased after the first session.

Among the second graders the win–stay object and lose–shift object components were generally strong from the outset. The children who required more than five problems to achieve solution mostly tested object-alternation and position-alternation hypotheses until they discovered that these were not the hypotheses demanded for solution. They then shifted to win–stay, lose-shift object. The one exception was Group 2A, whose performance included win–shift object in their second block of five problems and also in their four-dimensional problems. One child, however, appeared to be responsible for most of this discrepancy.

The findings of this preliminary experiment were consistent, then, with the analysis offered in Chapters 3 and 4 (cf. Gholson & Schuepfer, 1979). Prediction hypotheses do not emerge full-blown in the repertoire of the young (preschool) child. The components out of which they are consolidated are acquired independently and at different rates. Once the win–stay object and lose–shift object components are consolidated they appear to be durable, because the preschool children showed nearly perfect transfer from the two-dimensional to the four-dimensional problems. What remains to be done is to study the acquisition of other learning sets: win–shift, lose–stay object; win–stay, lose–shift position; and win–shift, lose–stay position. This research should provide us with a description of the time course of each component and of each consolidation process. An important issue that remains to be addressed concerns the relative dominance of position versus object hypotheses during different phases of the acquisition process, and what mechanism is responsible for the changes that occur.

Experiment 2: Coaching Preschool Children To Generate Prediction Hypotheses

JOHN E. KELLEY, BARRY GHOLSON, TED L. ROSENTHAL, AND ARTHUR S. PATTERSON

In Chapters 3 and 4 it was shown that Piaget's theory implies preoperational children should be capable of generating prediction hypotheses, that is, hypotheses that are maintained when they are confirmed and rejected when they are disconfirmed. Previous reports failed to confirm this prediction (Gholson *et al.*, 1972, 1976; Rieber, 1969; Schuepfer & Gholson, 1978; Weisz, 1977), but results of the learning-set research reported earlier in this chapter are consistent with it. Of the 71 preschool (preoperational) children who were studied, 65 met the acquisition criterion in two-dimensional problems and showed excellent transfer to four-dimensional problems. Because the learning set involved win–stay object combined with lose–shift object, it was necessary for the children to generate prediction hypotheses in order to attain criterion.

As was indicated earlier in this chapter, Piaget's description of the capabilities of young children indicates that the logical operations embodied in the preoperational processor are so restricted that they should be incapable of generating strategies (i.e., focusing, dimension checking, hypothesis checking) during problem solving. Preoperational children should exhibit prediction hypotheses *only* in unsystematic sequences. This is because they lack operative reversibility, sophisticated classification skills, and the ability to formulate a systematic plan and carry it through (see Chapter 4, pp. 67–69). Although the preschool children in the learning-set experiment reported above exhibited prediction hypotheses, the stimulus object designated correct in each problem contained the same cues on all feedback trials. The data that were obtained, therefore, did not lend themselves to a systems analysis, and the prediction from Piaget's theory concerning characteristics of the processor could not be evaluated. Thus, in the present experiment, procedures were devised to teach preschool children to generate prediction hypotheses. It was then possible to explore the sequences of hypotheses they exhibited in standard four-dimensional problems that contained blank-trial probes.

Because modeling procedures have been used successfully to teach children numerous types of conceptual materials—including information-processing strategies (e.g., D. R. Denney, N. W. Denney, & Ziobrowsky, 1973; Kelley, 1974; Richman & Gholson, 1978; Rosenthal, Kelley, & White, 1974; Rosenthal, Zimmerman, & Durning, 1970; Schadler, 1973; Tumblin *et al.*, 1979), conservation of the quantitative properties of materials that undergo perceptual transformations (e.g., Beilin, 1965, 1976; Rosenthal & Zimmerman, 1972, 1973, 1978; Siegler & Liebert, 1972; Zimmerman & Rosenthal, 1972a,b), and various aspects of language (e.g., Bandura, 1971; Liebert, Odom, Hill, & Huff, 1969; Rosenthal & Carroll, 1972; Whitehurst, 1972, 1976; Whitehurst, Ironsmith, & Goldfein, 1974)—a vicarious-learning format that included rule instruction was adopted in the present experiment. Procedures were devised which elicited response patterns that corresponded to nonpositional stimulus cues in more than 80% of the preschool children's blank-trial probes. They also rejected disconfirmed hypotheses and maintained confirmed hypotheses at high levels. The training procedures were the result of extensive pilot work and are complex, so they are described in detail in the appropriate section.

Method

SUBJECTS

The subjects were 40 preschool children (mean CA = 4:7 years) who were drawn from a private preschool system (Educare) in Memphis, Tennessee. The children were mostly from middle SES families. Eleven other children were excluded from the sample, nine because they consistently failed to identify stimulus attributes accurately as measured through penny placements, or they failed to cooperate during pretraining. The other two children refused to return to the experiment after a rest break. A male graduate student served as model and a female undergraduate served as experimenter.

STIMULUS MATERIALS

Each child was individually presented with a series of problems composed of bivalued four-dimensional stimulus materials. The four dimensions were sex of a child (boy versus girl), expression (smile versus frown), height (short versus tall), and color of clothing (e.g., pink versus gray). These dimensions were selected because earlier research (Kelley, 1974) had indicated that preschool children comprehend them more easily than they do the abstract dimensions that are typically used in research involving older children and adults. All stimulus materials were appended to 12- × 12-inch posterboard cards that were white in color. The two stimulus objects were clearly separated by a black line drawn down the vertical midline. The children were drawn with their hands depicted as behind their backs to indicate they were hiding something. Their faces were composed of two dots depicting eyes and a tight radius arc for the mouth (proportional in size). In the "happy" face the arc was concave up and in the "sad" face it was concave down. The tall figure was 8 inches in height and the short one was 4 inches. The girl figures were depicted with hair on their heads and in dresses. The boy figures were bald and in pants. Each figure was a solid color below the neck. The colors varied from one problem to the next, but values on all other dimensions were constant across problems.

Stimulus pairs presented on feedback trials were sequenced according to Levine's (1966) orthogonality criterion so that any three trials logically specified the solution. In blank-trial probes the response patterns that corresponded to simple cues always involved three responses to one side of the card and one response to the other side. A total of 11 problems were constructed: four were 5 trials in length, one was 16 trials, one was 26 trials, and five were 31 trials in length. Boundaries between problems were readily apparent due to alterations in color combinations and verbalizations of the model and experimenter.

PROCEDURE

The pretraining procedure consisted of four steps, the first three of which were identical for all 40 children. Half the children were assigned to an experimental condition and were coached in the use of prediction hypotheses. The remaining children were assigned to a control condition in which no coaching was given.

Step 1. The experimenter took the first card from a five-card problem and explained to the subject that the object of the game they were going to play was to find out what kind of child always had a penny. The experimenter then enumerated the values of each dimension. She then spread the remaining four cards on the table and gave the subject five pennies, saying "Put a penny on the same kind of child in all these pictures." The model then suggested that the subject place a penny on all the big children, then all the happy children, all the green children, and all the girl children. He helped the subject perform each of the four tasks.

Step 2. The experimenter spread out a new five-card problem, placed a penny on each boy figure, and instructed the subject to determine what kind of child always had the penny. The model pointed to the stimulus object on the first card and prompted the subject to describe the four stimulus cues relevant to solution. The model then said to the subject, "Why don't we always try *boy*, because this child is a boy and has the penny?" He helped the subject examine each card in order, prompting affirmations that each boy figure had a penny. The model then asserted that since the boy figure always had the penny, *boy* was the correct answer.

The experimenter then produced a new five-card problem, spread them out, placed a penny on each *sad* figure, and instructed the subject to "find what kind of child always had the penny." The model reminded the subject that children with any of the eight relevant attributes (concretely specified) might always have the penny. Pointing to the first card, the model induced the subject to describe the characteristics of the child with the penny and reasoned, "Since this *little* child has the penny, maybe all the little children have the penny. If *little* is the answer to this puzzle, a little child will always have the penny. Let's point to all the little children." The subject and model jointly pointed to the little children in succession until they reached a little child without a penny. The model protested, "Uh oh. This child (pointing to the big child) has the penny. The little child doesn't have the penny, so *little* isn't the correct answer. Since this child has the penny and is a boy, let's try all the boys. If *boy* is the answer to this puzzle, a boy will always have the penny." The model then returned to the first card in the problem and helped the subject (*a*) discover that boy was not the solution, (*b*) hypothesize sad, (*c*) ascertain that the sad children always had the penny, and (*d*) conclude that sad was the answer to the puzzle.

Step 3. The experimenter produced a new five-card problem, but this time kept them in a stack. She explained to the subject, "I've already given pennies to these children and they are hiding the pennies behind their backs. You can't see them, but I know who has the penny. You don't know, Art doesn't know, the chair doesn't know, and the wall doesn't know, but I know who has the penny. See if you can find out which kind of child always has the penny. Just point to the children you think have the penny." The model then reasoned aloud, "Since we can't see the penny, we'll have to guess the first time. What kind of child do you think always has the penny? Let's try *pink*. O.K., point to the pink child." The model then asked the experimenter if that was the child that had the penny and the experimenter replied that the kind of child that always had the penny was in the picture and pointed to it.

The experimenter then produced the next card and the model said, "O.K., let's see if pink children always have the penny." He then pointed to the pink picture and ask the experimenter if that was the kind of child who always had the penny. The experimenter pointed to the other stimulus object and said, "No, the kind of child that always has the penny is in *this* picture." The model then pondered that pink could not be the answer, and that it had to be something about the child in the picture to which the experimenter was pointing. The model then helped the child pick and disconfirm *big*, and then select and confirm *girl* as the solution to the problem. The model attempted to increase the subjects' feelings of personal control during the first three steps by soliciting their opinions and performing jointly, but he nevertheless steered choices in order to make sure all children had access to the same conceptual material during this part of the training. The format was designed to underscore the fact that the correct cue would perfectly correspond with pennies and that a single counterinstance amounted to disconfirmation.

Step 4. The procedure described in Step 3 was repeated with a 16-trial problem, but the experimenter explained at the outset that she would not always give feedback and that the model and subject were to "keep pointing at the same kind of child even if I don't tell you." Feedback was delivered on the first trial and every fifth trial thereafter.

Experimental Condition. The model induced subjects in the *coaching* condition to choose an attribute verbally, ensured that they pointed to the stimulus object containing that attribute on consecutive trials until negative feedback was given, and prompted them to choose their own alternative hypotheses from different dimensions in Step 4. Hence, the model forced the subjects in the experimental condition to choose hypotheses in a manner that corresponded to a sequence determined by a dimension-checking strategy, while emphasizing the importance of pointing to the stimulus object dictated by their stated hypothesis on each trial during the given blank-trial probe.

The children in this condition then received a series of eight problems. Odd-numbered problems were training problems in which the model encouraged the subjects to respond as independently as possible, but offered sufficient guidance to ensure that they selected hypotheses as dictated by a dimension-checking format until they achieved solution. The model induced subjects to state their hypotheses verbally in order to assess and correct their choice responses. He also stated his reasoning processes throughout each training problem in the manner illustrated in Steps 1, 2, and 3. Even-numbered problems were test problems in which the model allowed subjects to respond without any guidance whatsoever. Subjects were given a 30-minute rest break before starting the first test problem. All test problems were 31 trials in length and contained blank-trial probes between feedback trials.

Control Condition. During Step 4 these subjects were not forced to select hypotheses according to a dimension-checking format. They were encouraged to "choose the same kind of child" throughout a given blank-trial probe, but were not provided with any other suggestions. These subjects did not receive any exposure to the training problems, but otherwise received the test problems under exactly the same circumstances as the subjects in the experimental condition. The model did provide social feedback when necessary. Social interest and warmth on the part of the model were important ingredients in obtaining cooperation from the children of both groups throughout all phases of the experiment.

In order to maximize the amount of data available to the systems analysis, feedback was programmed during the first three feedback trials of each problem, rather than specifying a solution to each problem that the child might select at the outset. One of the four different combinations of positive (+) and negative (−) feedback that are possible in a three-trial sequence, given that feedback is negative on the third, was assigned to each of the four test problems (i.e., + + −, + − −, − + −, and − − −). After the third feedback trial, feedback was determined by the logical solution in each problem.

Results

Because training problems were interpolated between test problems in the experimental condition, it was possible that performance improved across test problems. A previous experiment (Tumblin *et al.*, 1979) in which the alternation format was used with first-grade children, but without pretraining, revealed some improvements across the first few problems. Performance also improved with practice for most of the preschool children and second graders in the first experiment reported in this chapter. Thus, a preliminary 2 (condition) × 4 (test problems) analysis of variance was performed on the hypothesis data to ascertain whether the children's performance improved with practice in the present experiment. There were no significant effects involving problems and no apparent trends in the means. The data were, therefore, collapsed across test problems and analyzed using one-way analyses of variance.

Each test problem contained only seven feedback trials, so a weak solution criterion was adopted. A problem was considered solved if the child exhibited the solution hypothesis during the last blank-trial probe of the problem (Trials 27–30) and chose the correct stimulus object on Trial 31. By this criterion the children in the experimental condition solved seven of their problems and those in the control condition also solved seven.

Data from the blank-trial probes fall into two basic categories: the eight 3 : 1 patterns of response that correspond to simple hypotheses and the eight patterns that do not (2 : 2 and 4 : 0 patterns). Children in the experimental condition exhibited response patterns that corresponded to simple hypotheses in 84% of their probes. The corresponding score was 59% among the children in the control condition. Analysis of variance revealed that this difference was significant, $F(1, 38) = 15.45, p < .05$ (the criterion adopted for all analyses). A closely related measure concerns the frequencies with which the children in the two conditions exhibited choice responses on feedback trials that were consistent with the immediately preceding hypothesis. The scores were 85% and 58% for the experimental and control groups respectively. This difference was significant, $F(1, 38) = 32.40$.

If we consider only those probes in which response patterns that corresponded to legitimate hypotheses were not exhibited, half the patterns of left (L) and right (R) responses that the children could show correspond to position-oriented response sets (i.e., LLLL, RRRR, LRLR, RLRL) and half do not (LLRR, RRLL, LRRL, RLLR). Children in the experimental condition showed such response sets in 51% of these probes, and those in the control condition did so in 63%. This difference was not significant in an analysis of variance.

The percentages of the times children in the two conditions (*a*) maintained confirmed hypotheses, that is, two consecutive probes yielded the same hypothesis when intervening feedback was positive (given that consistent hypotheses were shown in each and the appropriate stimulus object was chosen on the intervening feedback trial), (*b*) maintained disconfirmed hypotheses, and (*c*) resampled according to a local consistency rule following negative feedback, are presented in Table 5.17. In each case the performance of children in the experimental condi-

TABLE 5.17
The Probabilities That Two Consecutive Hypotheses Were Identical When Intervening Feedback Was Positive ($F_i = +$) or Negative ($F_i = -$), and the Local Consistency Data (LC) for Each Group

	$F_i = +$	$F_i = -$	LC
Experimental	.797	.154	.782
Control	.540	.465	.590

tion was better than that of children in the control condition. The $F(1,38)$ values were 6.53, 8.15, and 10.65 for the measures in the order listed. These data, along with data derived from the blank-trial probes, clearly indicate that children in the experimental condition exhibited prediction hypotheses.

The final measure derived from the data concerned the hypothesis-sampling systems and unsystematic hypothesis sequences observed among the children of each group. In order to avoid misrepresenting the children's performance in problems involving two of the feedback sequences (i.e., + + − and − + −), some restrictions were added to those described in Chapters 3 and 4. To see why this was necessary, consider a problem involving the sequence + + −. Suppose the child exhibited the hypothesis sequence "large, large, small" following the three feedback trials in question. One might infer that the child's hypotheses were determined by the hypothesis-checking strategy based upon this sequence. If this were the case, then the child should exhibit an hypothesis from a second dimension if negative feedback was received on some subsequent trial.

It is well known, however, that children frequently exhibit dimension preferences in problems of the kind used here (e.g., Cantor & Spiker, 1978; Suchman & Trabasso, 1966a,b). That is, they try one value on a dimension until it is disconfirmed, then the other value on the dimension, and if it is disconfirmed switch back to the first value, etc. Problems involving hypothesis sequences of this kind are classified as involving unsystematic hypothesis sequences when systems are analyzed (cf. Gholson & Beilin, 1979; Gholson *et al.*, 1972; Levine, 1975; Phillips & Levine, 1975). Because this performance could not be detected in the first three blank-trial probes when the + + − or − + − feedback sequences were used, it was required that the child exhibit an hypothesis from a second dimension if feedback were negative on a subsequent trial in order for the problem to be classified as involving hypothesis checking. It was not required, however, that this hypothesis from a second dimension occur in the probe immediately following the negative feedback. If, for example, the child received negative feedback on the fourth feedback trial (Trial 16) and failed to exhibit a consistent hypothesis in the probe that followed (Trials 17–20), this probe was ignored, and how the problem was classified depended upon the hypothesis shown in the next interpretable probe (i.e., Trials 22–25 or 27–30).

The systems analysis revealed that children in the experimental condition exhibited strategies in 12 problems, stereotypes in 7 problems, and unsystematic hypothesis sequences in 42 problems. Of the latter 42 problems, 39 involved dimension preferences; the children replaced a disconfirmed hypothesis with its complement on the same dimension each time negative feedback was received throughout each problem. Nineteen of these children's problems could not be classified, mostly because they showed nonhypothesis patterns during one or more of the blank-trial probes submitted to analysis. In their classifiable problems, then, these children exhibited unsystematic hypothesis sequences more than three times as frequently (68%) as strategies (19%). The children in the control condition exhibited classifiable protocols in only 18 of their problems (22%). They exhibited strategies in 2 problems, stereotypes in 5, and unsystematic hypothesis sequences in 11 problems. Ten of the latter involved dimension preferences.

Discussion

It seems clear, then, that preschool (preoperational) children can be induced to exhibit prediction hypotheses. The children in the experimental condition showed simple hypotheses in 85% of their blank-trial probes, maintained confirmed hypotheses 80% of the time, rejected disconfirmed hypotheses 85% of the time, and sampled according to a local-consistency criterion following negative feedback 78% of the time. Their performance was reasonably comparable to that exhibited by elementary-school children on each of these measures (e.g., Eimas, 1969; Gholson *et al.*, 1972, 1973; Ingalls & Dickerson, 1969; Nuessle, 1972; Phillips & Levine, 1975).

The similarities end, however, when the systems data are considered. In four-dimensional problems containing blank-trial probes to detect hypotheses, elementary-school children typically exhibit strategies in 70–75% of their problems and unsystematic hypothesis sequences in only about 10% (e.g., Gholson & Beilin, 1979; Gholson *et al.*, 1972, 1973; Levine, 1975; Phillips & Levine, 1975). The preschool children exhibited 68% unsystematic hypothesis sequences and only 19% strategies, even following the laborious training procedures that were used.

Thus, when preschool children are induced to exhibit prediction hypotheses, they fail to test them strategically (they solved only 7 of 80 problems, even with a very weak solution criterion). This finding was clearly in line with predictions derived from Piaget's theory. It should be explicitly stated, however, that the main emphasis of the training was upon eliciting prediction hypotheses from the children. The procedures were designed to accomplish this goal, but the children were largely left to their own devices in determining *how* the prediction hypotheses would be tested. Whether preschool children can be induced to exhibit sequences of hypotheses that correspond to the strategy categories remains to be investigated. The protocols of one child in the experimental condition suggested that more laborious training procedures might produce such sequences. She exhibited sequences of hypotheses that corresponded to strategy categories in all four of her problems. It was also possible, of course, that this child was precocious and was already concrete operational (no relevant assessment was made), in which case her behavior would be consistent with the model presented in Chapter 3. No other child exhibited a strategic sequence in more than one problem.

6

The Effects of Cognitive Level upon Hypothesis Testing across the Life Span

Two experiments are reported in this chapter. Both explore the effects of cognitive level upon problem solving. The aim of the first was to investigate further the transition from preoperational to concrete operational thought. A brief observational learning procedure was used to examine the acquisition of systematic problem-solving skills by preoperational, transitional, and concrete operational kindergarten children. In an earlier, related experiment (Gholson *et al*., 1976), much more laborious training procedures that required two sessions with each child were used. Also, in the earlier research, the behavior of transitional children was not studied systematically.

A second, exploratory experiment involved young, middle-aged, and older adults. Each subject was assessed according to Piaget's criteria prior to participation in the experiment proper. Previously, older adults have received little attention from those using hypothesis-testing methodologies (cf. Offenbach, 1974). In addition, a literature search located no research in which hypothesis-testing procedures were applied to the middle-aged. The model presented in Chapters 3 and 4 predicts, of course, that cognitive level will interact with task variables.

Experiment 3: Strategic Problem Solving among Kindergarten Children of Three Cognitive Levels

BARRY GHOLSON, DALE E. THEOBALD, AND SYDNEY T. YARBROUGH

The purpose of this experiment was to explore two implications of the model presented in Chapters 3 and 4: (*a*) that stage changes, as assessed by Piaget's criteria, produce qualitative changes in the processor that are reflected in main effects of developmental level; (*b*) experimental manipulations that produce changes in the functioning of various cognitive subprocesses lead to interactions between developmental level and task variables. A subsidiary purpose was to provide some systematic data concerning the transition from preoperational to concrete operational thought. Because it is well known that the shift from preoperational to concrete operational thought frequently occurs in the age range 5 to 7 years, and because it is desirable for the chronological ages of children assigned to various cognitive-level groups to be as comparable as possible (Schleser, A. W. Meyers, & R. Cohen, 1979), kindergarten children were selected as a subject population.

Children of each cognitive level observed a model solving a series of short problems containing blank-trial probes for hypotheses. The model either provided explicit rules for using a specific strategy to solve the problems, or just illustrated the basic skills underlying the use of any strategy. It was deemed unnecessary to include a nonmodeling control condition, because previous research has repeatedly demonstrated that under standard conditions, that is, several pretraining problems followed by a series of experimental problems, kindergarten children manifest only stereotype systems (e.g., Gholson *et al.*, 1972, 1976; Rieber, 1969; Schuepfer & Gholson, 1978; Weisz, 1977).

Method

SUBJECTS

The subjects were 246 kindergarten children drawn from the Memphis City Schools. It was necessary to pretest this number of children to obtain 54 who were preoperational (mean CA = 5:9), 54 who were transitional (mean CA = 6:0), and 54 who were concrete operational (mean CA = 6:1) according to the criteria used. The remaining 84 children were lost either because they were unavailable when the experiment proper was conducted or because their assigned group was already filled (preoperational groups filled first, followed by transitional groups). The main effect of chronological age reached significance in analysis of variance, even though all children were tested during their kindergarten year.

CONSERVATION PRETEST

Each child was individually administered two conservation tasks, number and liquid quantity, that were used to assess cognitive status 1972). Two sets of six checkers each were used in the number task. One set was presented in a straight line throughout, with individual checkers spaced about 1 inch apart. The other set was placed in six relative configurations: 1 : 1 correspondence; spread out; 1 : 1 correspondence; contracted; 1 : 1 correspondence; a circle. The child was asked, upon presentation of each configuration, to judge whether the two sets of checkers contained the same number and then explain the answer that was given.

Similarly, the quantity conservation task involved two equal portions of colored water. One portion was presented in a standard-size beaker throughout. The other portion was first presented in a second standard-size beaker so the child agreed each "had the same amount to drink." The contents of one beaker were then transformed as follows: taller, narrower beaker; standard-size beaker; shorter, wider beaker; standard-size beaker; three small, equal-size beakers. The child judged the relative quantities following each transformation and then provided an explanation for the judgment.

Only those children who gave correct answers followed by reasonable (logical) justifications (Beilin, 1971, 1976; Piaget, 1952, 1968) to all questions in both conservation tasks were included in the concrete operational groups. Children who answered correctly and justified at least one, but not all questions, were included in the transitional groups (Piaget, 1968, pp. 154–157). Children who gave no correct answers in either task were classified as preoperational. The conservation pretest required about 10 minutes per child.

PROBLEM SOLVING

Within a week following the conservation assessment, each child participated individually in a session approximately 50 minutes in length. The children first received pretraining, then viewed a 10-minute modeling tape, and were then presented with six problems that constituted the main experiment. The stimuli used in all three phases of this session were bivalued, four-dimensional problems of the kind described earlier. The same four dimensions (alphabetic letter, size, color, line position) were used in all problems, but each involved a different combination of 20 alphabetic letters and 10 colors. The heights of the small and large letters were 1.25 and 3.0 inches. The line positions were "line over" and "line under" the letter. The lines, measuring 2.5 × .5 inches and always black in color, were located .25 inch above or below the letter. All stimuli were appended to white 5- × 8-inch cards with center lines clearly separating the stimulus objects.

Pretraining. The pretraining procedure was standard (e.g., Eimas, 1969; Gholson *et al.*, 1972; Weisz, 1977). The first two problems each contained 12 consecutive feedback trials. The third and fourth problems contained blank trials, introduced in sets of two and then four, that were used to infer the children's hypotheses. Following each pretraining problem the children were asked to state the solution. If they were correct they were told "very good" and went on to the next problem (or the modeling tape). If the child was wrong, a hint of the following type was given: "Why not try the colors, red or green, to see if one of them is the answer?" The latter procedure was followed during pretraining only. At the outset of each problem during both pretraining and the main experiment, the possible solutions were described by dimension to the children.

Modeling. Immediately following the fourth pretraining problem the children were told that they were now going to see a TV show in which a child solved the problems very well and that they (the subjects) should watch and listen very carefully so they could do as well as the child on the TV. The experimenter and child then watched a 10-minute black-and-white videotape presented on a 19-inch screen. Four short problems, each illustrating a solution drawn from a different dimension, were presented by a female experimenter to a female subject. Only the stimulus materials and the hands of the experimenter and subject were visible on the tape. Each problem was 16 trials in length. Trials 1, 6, 11, and 16 were feedback trials. Intervening trials involved blank-trial probes. Half the children of each cognitive level were assigned to a dimension-checking condition in which the modeling subject both verbally described and visually illustrated the rules underlying the use of a dimension-checking strategy. The remaining children were assigned to a basic-skills condition in which the video portion of the tape and the modeling experimenter's verbalizations were identical to those described above, but no rules were verbalized by the modeling subject. At the beginning of each problem the modeling experimenter described the possible solution hypotheses dimensionally. The modeling experimenter also delivered feedback on appropriate trials by saying either "correct, the answer is in this picture" or "wrong, the answer is in *this* picture." In either case, the modeling experimenter simultaneously pointed to the correct stimulus object.

In the videotape viewed by children assigned to one condition, the modeling subject verbalized rules underlying the dimension-checking strategy on feedback trials. After receiving feedback on the first trial of each problem, for example, the modeling subject verbalized a variant of the following: "Let's see, the answer could be any one of the four things in this picture. It could be white or T or big or line on the top. I'll try the sizes first, and since big is in the correct picture, I'll try big." The modeling subject then chose the large stimulus on every trial until negative feedback was received and then verbalized some variant of the following: "Now I'm sure the answer isn't either of the sizes, big or little, so it must be something else. I'll try the letters next. If it's one of the letters, it has to be T, because that's in the correct picture. Yes, I'll try the T." The latter kind of statement always followed negative feedback on Trials 6 and 11. The modeling subject always selected the correct hypothesis following Trial 11 and received positive feedback on Trial 16.

At the beginning of the third problem, the modeling subject made the following statement:

> *I think I know how to do these puzzles. I only have to try one of each pair of things, like big or little, and I always choose the one of each pair that's in the picture you just told me was correct. Then if that's wrong, I've eliminated both the sizes, big and little, and I just pick something else, like the letter that's in the correct picture, and try that. I just check one of each pair of things—the one that's in the picture you just told me was correct—until I find the answer. I know I only have to check one of each pair because once you've told me, for example, that the picture with the big letter is correct, the small letter has to be in the wrong picture, so I never need to check that. And I can do that for each pair of things—just check the one that's in the correct picture. That way I can always find the answer.*

The children assigned to the basic-skills condition observed a tape in which both the video portion and the verbalizations by the modeling experimenter were identical to those presented in the dimension-checking condition. The modeling subject, however, provided no explicit strategy. The modeling subject's verbalizations were restricted to simply stating the hypothesis she was going to try at the outset of each problem and following negative feedback on any subsequent trial, for example, "I'll try *big*."

Experimental Problems. Immediately after viewing the modeling tape each child was told: "I'll bet you can do those puzzles as well as the child on TV did. Now it's your turn to do some more puzzles." The child then received a series of six 31-trial problems in which a blank-trial probe was inserted between consecutive feedback trials. Thus, each problem consisted of seven feedback trials and six blank-trial probes. On feedback trials the experimenter said either "Yes, the answer is in this picture," or "No, the answer is in *this* picture," and pointed to the correct stimulus complex for about three seconds before turning the card to expose the stimuli for the next trial. On blank trials the card was turned immediately following response.

The stimuli for each problem met the special restrictions specified by Levine's (1966) orthogonality criterion: Any three consecutive feedback trials logically specified the solution, and each of the eight stimulus cues corresponded to a unique 3 : 1 pattern of left and right responses during each four-trial probe. Within these restrictions the stimulus pairs were ordered randomly. After completing the sixth problem the child was lavishly praised and escorted back to the classroom.

Results

Because this research addressed hypothesis sampling and not learning, each problem involved only seven feedback trials and six blank-trial probes. Consequently, a weak criterion of solution performance was adopted. This criterion was a correct response on each of the last two feedback trials (Trials 26 and 31) and manifestation of the correct hypothesis during the intervening blank-trial probe (Trials 27–30). Not surprisingly, few problems were solved: The concrete operational children solved a total of 50 of their 324 problems (15.4%); the transitional children solved a total of 22 problems (6.7%); and the preoperational a total of 15 problems (4.6%). A test of independence indicated that these differences were not statistically significant.

Data from the blank-trial probes for hypotheses fall into two basic categories: the eight 3:1 patterns of response that correspond to simple cues and the eight remaining response patterns that do not (i.e., 2 : 2 and 4 : 0 patterns). Among the concrete operational children the percentages of probes that led to the inference children held hypotheses were 68.3 (664 of 972) and 72.2 (702 of 972) for the dimension-checking and basic-skills conditions, respectively. Corresponding scores were 56.4 (548 of 972) and 53.8 (523 of 972) for the transitional children and 51.2 (498 of 972) and 45.4 (441 of 972) for the preoperational. The two concrete groups exhibited more consistent hypothesis patterns than would be expected by chance (50%), but the other groups did not. A two-way analysis of variance (modeling condition, cognitive level) performed on scores revealed that only the effect of cognitive level was significant, $F(1, 156) = 18.15, p < .05$ (the criterion adopted for all analyses).

The blank-trial probes in which the children failed to exhibit hypotheses were separated into two categories of left (L) and right (R) responses: response sets (LLLL, RRRR, LRLR, RLRL) and residual (LRRL, RLLR,

LLRR, RRLL). The concrete operational, transitional, and preoperational children showed response sets in 23, 31, and 35% of their probes, respectively. Analysis of variance performed on scores revealed, as expected, that the effect of cognitive level was significant. Taken together, hypothesis patterns (3 : 1) and response-set patterns accounted for 83–93% of the probe data.

If we consider *only* those blank-trial probes in which no hypothesis was exhibited, half the possible patterns correspond to the response-set category and half do not. Thus, if no systematic processes were operating during probes in which no hypothesis was exhibited, 50% of the observed response sequences would be expected to correspond to each category. Response-set percentages ranged from 65.5 to 74.5 (mean = 69.4); each of the six groups differed significantly from chance expectation. Analysis of variance performed on these percentages, normalized by arcsin transformations (Guilford, 1954), revealed no significant differences among groups. Thus children of the three cognitive levels differed in the frequency with which they exhibited hypotheses dictated by relevant stimulus cues, but when we consider only those probes in which hypotheses were not exhibited, the three groups showed position-oriented response sets with about equal relative frequencies.

Four other conventional measures of performance were derived from the data and submitted to two-way analyses of variance: The probabilities children of the six groups retained confirmed hypotheses; rejected disconfirmed hypotheses; manifested locally consistent hypotheses following negative feedback; and on feedback trials chose the stimulus object that contained the cue corresponding to the hypothesis inferred from the immediately preceding blank-trial probe.

Two of these measures yielded no significant effects: The mean percentage of the time the same hypothesis was manifested during two consecutive blank-trial probes when intervening feedback was negative was 29.8 (range 24.7–37.7), and the mean percentage of the time locally consistent hypotheses were manifested immediately following negative feedback was 65.7 (range 60.8–70.5). In each case, though, the data were ordered in favor of the concrete operational groups. Analysis of the percentage of the time children of the various groups manifested the same hypothesis in two consecutive blank-trial probes when intervening feedback was positive yielded a significant effect of cognitive level, $F(2, 156) = 3.69$. The percentages were 79.5 for concrete operational, 70.5 for transitional, and 62.3 for preoperational children. Similarly, the percentage of the time that choice responses on feedback trials were consistent with the immediately preceding hypothesis yielded only an effect of cognitive level, $F(2, 156) = 7.68$. The percentages here were 85.4, 77.5, and 71.7 for concrete operational, transitional, and preoperational children.

The final measure of performance concerned the hypothesis-sampling systems observed during each problem. Due to restrictions dictated by the criteria for categorization of problems as involving systems (see Chapter 3), only about 27% of the problems (267 of 972) could be used in this analysis. This was comparable to the 15–30% obtained in previous research in which blank-trial probes were used with children and adults.

Results of the systems analysis for each cognitive level and modeling condition are presented in Table 6.1. A multiple-contingency chi square (Winer, 1971, p. 858) was performed on the data collapsed into three categories: strategies, stereotypes, and unsystematic. The interaction between cognitive level and response category was significant, $\chi^2(4) = 23.43$. This interaction reflects a main effect of cognitive level in that it indicates there were different frequencies of observation in the dependent-measure categories as a function of cognitive level. This finding is in line with the predicted main effect of developmental level. The three-way interaction (Modeling condition × Cognitive level × Response category) was also significant, $\chi^2(4) = 11.89$, indicating that the modeling conditions had differential effects as a function of cognitive level. The theory, of course, predicts interactions between developmental level and task variables.

The concrete operational children performed nearly identically under the two conditions, $\chi^2(2) = .82$, manifesting strategies in about half their problems, stereotypes in 35%, and unsystematic hypothesis sequences in about 15%. The transitional children exposed to the dimension-checking condition performed similarly to the two concrete groups, $\chi^2(2) < 3.81, p > .10$ in each case. They did, hoewever, manifest fewer strategies (34%) and more stereotypes (50%) than the concrete operational children. The transitional children assigned to the condition involving only basic skills, however, differed significantly from both the first transitional and the two concrete operational groups, $\chi^2(2) > 6.47$, in each case. They manifested few strategies (11%), but many unsystematic hypothesis sequences (32%). This latter performance was strikingly similar to the performance of preoperational children in the dimension-checking condition, $\chi^2(2) = .59$, who manifested 15% strategies and 37% unsystematic sequences. Preoperational children provided with only a visual demonstration, while exhibiting strategies with about the same frequency (16%), manifested unsystematic hypothesis sequences in only 14% of their problems. The difference between the two preoperational groups approached, but did not reach significance, $\chi^2(2) = 5.67$, $.10 > p > .05$.

Because the systems analysis dictates that problems meet stringent criteria in order to be categorized, individual subjects contributed differ-

TABLE 6.1
The Relative Frequency of Each Hypothesis-Sampling System for Each Modeling Condition and Cognitive Level (in Percentages)

	System[a]						
Modeling condition	Fo	D–ch	H–ch	S–P	P–A	P–P	Uns
Dimension checking							
Preoperational	0	5.0	10.0	12.5	30.0	5.0	37.5
Transitional	0	12.0	22.2	24.2	13.2	13.2	15.5
Concrete	0	28.5	21.4	19.6	7.1	8.9	14.2
Basic skills							
Preoperational	0	8.3	8.3	11.1	44.1	13.8	13.8
Transitional	0	9.2	2.3	27.9	23.2	4.6	32.5
Concrete	0	35.4	14.5	27.0	4.1	2.0	16.6

[a] The systems are: focusing (Fo), dimension checking (D–ch), hypothesis checking (H–ch), stimulus preference (S–P), position alternation (P–A), position preference (P–P), and the nonsystem category labeled unsystematic hypothesis sequences (Uns).

TABLE 6.2
The Number (and Percentage) of Children, Identified by Cognitive Level and Modeling Procedure, Yielding Problems in Each System Category

Condition	Strategy	Stereotype	Unsystematic	Total
Dimension checking				
Preoperational	82.0 (10.5)	9.0 (47.4)	8.0 (42.1)	19/27
Transitional	6.0 (31.6)	10.0 (52.6)	3.0 (15.8)	19/27
Concrete operational	11.0 (47.8)	10.0 (43.5)	2.0 (08.6)	23/27
Basic skills				
Preoperational	3.7 (18.3)	14.0 (70.0)	2.3 (11.7)	20/27
Transitional	2.2 (09.1)	11.4 (51.8)	8.4 (38.3)	22/27
Concrete operational	9.0 (47.4)	6.7 (35.0)	3.3 (17.6)	19/27

ent numbers of problems (from zero to five) to the analyses. Thus it was considered possible (Cantor & Spiker, 1978) that the data of Table 6.1 might not truly characterize the behavior of individual children assigned to the various groups. In an attempt to explore this possibility the systems data were reevaluated using a procedure in which the data of each child were weighted equally. These data, representing about 75% of the children (122 of 162; 40 children yielded no categorizable problems) are presented in Table 6.2. The findings are essentially identical to those of the preceding table, indicating that the data presented in Table 6.1 accurately characterize the behavior of the individual children in each group.

The proportion of each child's score placed in each category was assigned so that the sum equaled unity. A child who manifested two categorizable problems that both reflected strategies, for example, was assigned 1.0 in the strategy category. Another child, whose data yielded three categorizable problems, two stereotypes and one unsystematic sequence, was assigned .66 in the stereotype and .33 in the unsystematic category. Protocols of 74 of the 122 children represented in the table yielded two or more categorizable problems. Thirty-four of these protocols were split among the various categories as follows: 19 children exhibited both strategies and unsystematic sequences; 10 children manifested both stereotypes and unsystematic sequences; 3 children showed both strategies and stereotypes; and 2 children exhibited problems in all three categories. Previous research (Gholson & McConville, 1974; Gholson *et al*., 1976) had indicated that a given child of this age range *never* exhibited both strategies and stereotypes.

Discussion

The purpose of this experiment was to examine further the implications of the model presented in Chapter 3. The change from preoperational to concrete operational thought produced several main effects of developmental level, as predicted by the model. In addition, the task manipulation interacted with developmental level in the systems analysis. It should be explicitly stated, though, that it is impossible to specify which cognitive subprocesses were differentially affected by the two modeling conditions (cf. Beilin, 1976). A second purpose was to obtain data from children classified as transitional according to Piaget's criteria. A modeling procedure was chosen because there is considerable evidence from several domains that rule learning may be accomplished rapidly and effectively through observational procedures (Bandura & Harris, 1966; D. R. Denney, 1972, 1975; Odom, Liebert, & Hill, 1968; Richman & Gholson, 1978; Rosenthal & Zimmerman, 1978; Zimmerman & Rosenthal, 1972, 1974). In an earlier study (Gholson *et al.*, 1976) in which preoperational and concrete operational kindergarten children received extensive stimulus-differentiation training, concrete operational children manifested strategies in 45% to 75% of their problems, while preoperationals manifested mostly stereotypes with few strategies or unsystematic hypothesis sequences. Thus the data obtained from corresponding groups in the present investigation following brief observational procedures (10 minutes) compare favorably with those obtained previously following more laborious training (about 40 minutes).

Present results revealed significant effects of cognitive level upon four dependent measures. In each case performance of the concrete operational children was best, transitional children intermediate, and preoperational children poorest. In addition, performance was similarly ordered on three of the measures that revealed no significant effects. Additional research should probably involve a longitudinal tracking of the transition from preoperational to concrete thought.

While the high degree of variability among the children of each group indicates that the procedures that were used need further refinement, the data clearly support the view that information-processing efficiency is contingent upon developmental level. If one is willing to grant that the assessment procedures that were used may not have been perfect and/or that the short videotape presentations may not have been adequate to elicit the characteristic mode of processing of some children of each cognitive level, these results, in conjunction with the earlier experiments, warrant several conclusions. First, concrete operational kindergarten children have available to them the underlying cognitive capabilities necessary to impose a systematic information-processing strategy upon the problem-solving situation. These children appear to require no more than a brief demonstration of the basic skills involved in such a strategy or stimulus-differentiation training in order to organize their capabilities accordingly. Transitional kindergarten children also have available the cognitive capabilities requisite to systematic problem solving, but seem to require complete verbal rule instruction (cf. Beilin, 1976; Siegler &

Liebert, 1972) in conjunction with a demonstration in order to organize their cognitive capabilities appropriately and exhibit a strategic approach to the problems (Tumblin *et al*., 1979). When such children simply observe a (largely) silent model, they tend to exhibit hypotheses in unsystematic sequences. Preoperational children have not yet acquired at least some of the underlying cognitive skills necessary to impose *any* logical structure on a complex problem-solving task. These children, following observation of a modeling procedure involving complete rule instruction, appear to consolidate prediction hypotheses (see Chapter 5), but these are not tested systematically. Instead, these children show unsystematic hypothesis sequences at least twice as frequently as strategies. Without rule instruction, however, preoperational children exhibit mostly stereotypes, with few unsystematic hypothesis sequences or strategies.

Experiment 4: Systematic Problem Solving among Young, Middle-Aged and Older Adults of Two Cognitive Levels

DIANA M. BYRD, THERESE SCHUEPFER, AND BARRY GHOLSON

This experiment was related to the model described in Chapter 3, but strictly speaking, it was exploratory. The behavior of young adults (college students) has been intensively studied in the context of hypothesis theory (see Chapter 2), and children have recently received increasing attention. The middle-aged and elderly, however, have been largely neglected. Two experiments were located, though, that bear directly on the present study. One was reported by Offenback (1974).

He used an hypothesis-testing task to investigate the behavior of children of various grade levels (first, third, fifth), college students, and older adults (mean CA =74:8 years, range 65:10–87:1). The older subjects all lived in their own homes and none was known to suffer from neurological impairment. Cognitive level was not assessed. Offenbach used conventional bivalued four-dimensional problems, but did not use blank trials as probes for hypotheses. Instead, he required the subjects to make two responses on each trial. First, the subject chose one of the two four-dimensional stimulus objects. The second response was to a display in which the eight cues were decomposed and presented separately. The second response was used to infer which specific cue, or hypothesis, determined the prior choice response. Feedback was provided *only* following the second response on each trial, but feedback was determined by the first-choice response, that is, by whether the chosen stimulus object contained the cue that was designated the solution to the given problem.

In general, where comparisons were possible, Offenbach's results among his children and college students were reasonably consistent with those obtained when blank-trial probes are used to detect hypotheses. The elderly subjects exhibited much poorer performance than even the youngest children. The first graders, for example, maintained confirmed hypotheses 69% of the time, but the elderly did so only 49% of the time. Similarly, the young children maintained disconfirmed hypotheses with probability .125, but among the older subjects the score was .20. Offenbach (1974, p. 489) concluded that the elderly did not recognize when they selected the correct cue and, consequently, their behavior was less systematic than that of the college students, or even the youngest children.

Parallel decrements in performance among the elderly have been reported by numerous other researchers (e.g., Cicirelli, 1976; Papalia, 1972; Rubin, Attwell, Tierney, & Tumulo, 1973). Some have attributed these decrements to a decline in fluid intellectual abilities that may be unavoidable due to neurological changes (Birren, 1964; Hooper, Fitzgerald, & Papalia, 1971; Horn & Cattell, 1966). Others, however, deny that intellectual decrements are inevitable in old age. Instead, they posit that the *apparent* cognitive deficits are situationally or experientially determined (Flavell, 1970; LaBouvie-Vief, Hoyer, M.M. Baltes, & P.B. Baltes, 1974).

Hornblum and Overton (1976) have argued that poor performance among the elderly can be explained in terms of a distinction between competence and performance factors (Flavell & Wohlwill, 1969). They define competence in terms of the formal logical knowledge possessed by the individual. In the present conception, then, competence would be embodied in the processor. Performance factors refer to the psychological processes by which information is used in daily life. In the model presented in Chapters 3 and 4, performance factors correspond to the functioning of various cognitive subprocesses involved in the flow of information to and from the processor. The notion is that the individual's competence does not deteriorate in old age; but performance factors do deteriorate.

Some research based upon Piaget's theory tends to support the argument based on a competence-performance distinction (N.W. Denney, 1974; N.W. Denney & Lennon, 1972; Schultz & Hoyer, 1976; Tomlinson-Keasey, 1972). Hornblum and Overton (1976) demonstrated, for example, that elderly subjects (mean CA =70:2 years) who failed to conserve surface area in a pretest quickly acquired the skill during feedback training. The skill generalized to other conservation tasks, and it was maintained in a delayed posttest. They concluded that their subjects had the appropriate knowledge available to them, but it was necessary to activate that knowledge through a brief training procedure before it was used.

Richman (personal communication, January 3, 1979) has recently completed an hypothesis-testing experiment in which cognitive level was assessed among college students. Subjects of three cognitive levels were obtained: concrete operational, transitional from concrete to formal operations, and formal operational. The transitional subjects were easiest to locate; concrete operational were very difficult. (The criteria used to assess cognitive level are described directly below, *Method* section.) Following the assessment each subject first received standard pretraining (four problems), was then exposed to an observational learning procedure via a videotape, and finally was presented with a series of bivalued four-dimensional problems that contained blank-trial probes.

Three 10-minute observational learning procedures were used: (*a*) a focusing condition in which this strategy was explicitly illustrated in four short problems and detailed rule instruction was provided; (*b*) a basic-skills condition in which the model stated the hypothesis that was to be exhibited at the outset of each blank-trial probe and the experimenter gave feedback on appropriate trials, but no specific strategy was described; (*c*) a time-control condition in which a randomly chosen stimulus card was presented for 10 minutes and the subjects were told to think about ways the problems might be solved.

In general, the formal operational and transitional subjects showed very similar performance on all measures except the strategies they exhibited (solution data, however, were not made available to me). They rejected disconfirmed hypotheses, maintained confirmed hypotheses, and sampled according to a local-consistency rule following errors with very high probabilities. The concrete operational subjects showed good, but slightly depressed performance on each measure. The formal operational subjects exhibited more focusing after exposure to this observational procedure (about 65%) than after exposure to the basic-skills or time-control conditions. The latter did not differ from each other (about 50% focusing). The formal operational subjects showed more focusing than the transitionals after exposure to the focusing tape, but the two cognitive levels did not differ after exposure to the basic-skills or time-control tapes. The concrete operational subjects in the focusing condition showed focusing in about 25% of their problems, and even fewer under the other two conditions.

In the present study subjects who were transitional to formal operations were compared with those who were formal operational at three points on the adult life span. Thus characteristics of the processor (competence) were held constant in order to detect any changes in performance that were associated with age level. According to the present model, then, any changes in performance that are correlated with age are due to changes in the functioning of one or more of the cognitive subprocesses. This assumes, of course, that cohort effects and differences in the educational experiences of each generation are not reflected, per se, in the subjects' performance in the learning task (P.B. Baltes, 1968, 1978; Botwinick, 1967; Nesselroade, Schaie, & P.B. Baltes, 1972; Schaie, LaBouvie, & Buech, 1973).

Method

SUBJECTS

The subjects were 40 college students, 17–25 years of age (mean CA = 20:4 years), 40 middle-aged adults, 40–49 years of age (mean CA = 43:8), and 40 elderly adults, 60–80 years of age (mean CA = 70:1). The college students were all volunteers from introductory psychology sections at Memphis State University. The middle-aged were employees of Colt Industries in Beloit, Wisconsin, or were parents of the college students. The elderly were volunteers from Senior Citizens' Centers, Senior Citizens' apartment complexes in Memphis, or were grandparents of the college students. They were all living in their own private dwellings, and none was known to be suffering from any neurological impairment. There was no relationship between where the subjects were obtained and cognitive level. Subjects of each age level were pretested using Piaget's tasks until 20 who were transitional from concrete to formal operations and 20 who were formal operational were located. College students of the two cognitive levels were located with about the same frequencies, but among the middle-aged and elderly the transitional groups filled first. Initially, the experiment was to include concrete operational individuals of each level, but they could not be located. Only two concrete operational subjects were located during extensive pilot work: one middle-aged and one elderly person. No college student who was tested was concrete operational. The differences between the present population of college students and Richman's cannot be determined. The only difference that can be specified is that her subjects were drawn largely from rural backgrounds, while Memphis State University students are mostly from urban areas.

PIAGETIAN ASSESSMENT

The subjects were tested individually throughout all phases of the experiment. The assessment consisted of three conventional conservation tasks: number, continuous-quantity, and volume (Beilin, 1976; Piaget, 1952) and the oscillating pendulum problem (Inhelder & Piaget, 1958; Neimark, 1975b). The number and continuous-quantity tasks were the same as those described in Experiment 3. The volume task involved two balls of clay which were placed in two identical beakers that were filled with equal quantities of liquid. The subject first agreed that the two balls of clay displaced equal volumes of liquid, or that the liquid went up an equal distance in both beakers. One ball of clay was then removed from a beaker and was transformed into the shape of a sausage. The experimenter, pointing to the ball of clay that remained in its beaker, then asked the subject, "When I put this piece of clay [referring to the sausage] back into the water, will the water go up the same amount as this one or a different amount?" The subject was then required to justify the answer that was offered.

In the oscillating pendulum problem, the subject was presented with a pendulum in the form of an object suspended from a string. The subject was given three lengths of string, and three different weights. Thus it was possible to vary the length of the string, the weight of the object that was suspended, the height of the point from which the object was set in motion, and the force of the push with which the object was set in motion. The task was to find the factor or factors that determined the frequency of oscillation, or, "what would make the pendulum swing faster or slower?" In order to be considered formal operational, the subject was required to demonstrate that three factors should be held constant while one was varied, and to systematically isolate the length of the string as the only factor that determined the frequency of oscillation.

EXPERIMENTAL PROBLEMS

Immediately following the assessment tasks, each subject was presented with a series of standard bivalued four-dimensional problems. Following pretraining a series of ten 26-trial problems was presented. Stimulus sequences were constructed according to an orthogonality criterion, and feedback was delivered every fifth trial beginning with the first. Feedback was always negative on the third feedback trial. Thus the response-feedback sequence on the first three feedback trials determined the solution to each problem. The logical solution then determined feedback on Trials 16, 21, and 26. On feedback trials the experimenter said either "Yes, the answer is in this picture," or "No, the answer is in *this* picture" while pointing to the correct stimulus complex for approximately three seconds following response.

Results

Seven conventional measures of performance were derived from the data. Six of these were submitted to 3 × 2 (Age level × Cognitive level) analysis of variance. The seventh measure was analyzed by partitioning a chi square (Winer, 1971). Only the effect of age was significant in five of the analyses of variance: (*a*) the probabilities that consistent hypothesis patterns were exhibited during blank-trial probes, $F(2, 119) = 4.34, p <$ .05 (the criterion adopted for all analyses); (*b*) the probabilities that confirmed hypotheses were maintained, $F(2, 119) = 5.63$; (*c*) the probabilities that disconfirmed hypotheses were replaced, $F(2, 119) = 10.49$; (*d*) the probabilities that hypotheses were sampled according to a local-consistency criterion following negative feedback, $F(2, 119) = 25.75$; and (*e*) the probabilities that responses on feedback trials were consistent with the hypothesis exhibited during the immediately preceding blank-trial probe, $F(2, 119) = 5.36$. In each case the college students and the middle-aged showed statistically equivalent performance, but both differed significantly from the elderly subjects. Data from the five measures are presented in Table 6.3.

Because the problems were short—only six feedback trials and five blank-trial probes—a weak solution criterion was adopted. This criterion was a correct response on each of the last two feedback trials (Trials 21 and 26) and manifestation of the correct hypothesis in the intervening blank-trial probe (Trials 22–25). Two significant effects were obtained in analysis of variance: the age effect, $F(2,119) = 55.15$; and the Age level × Cognitive level interaction, $F(2,119) = 5.81$. The college students solved more problems than the middle-aged, who solved more than the elderly. Each difference was significant. The data for each age group and cognitive level are presented in Table 6.4. The significant interaction indicated that among the transitional groups there were significant differences between each age group: college>middle-aged>elderly. Among the formal operational subjects the college students and middle-aged did not

TABLE 6.3

The Probabilities That the Adults of Each Age Level and Cognitive Level Exhibited Consistent Hypotheses during Probes, P(H), Maintained Confirmed Hypotheses, P(H = H | +), Replaced Disconfirmed Hypotheses, P(H = H | −), Resampled According to a Local Consistency Criterion, (LC), and Chose the Stimulus Complex on Feedback Trials That Was Consistent with the Immediately Preceding Hypothesis, P(F | H)

		Age		
Measure	Cognitive level	College	Middle-aged	Elderly
P(H)	Transitional	.927	.892	.851
	Formal	.927	.931	.839
P(H = H | +)	Transitional	.980	.945	.889
	Formal	.979	.970	.847
P(H ≠ H | −)	Transitional	.976	.941	.881
	Formal	.982	.983	.925
P(LC)	Transitional	.979	.930	.821
	Formal	.974	.931	.838
P(F | H)	Transitional	.981	.981	.946
	Formal	.984	.988	.934

TABLE 6.4
The Probabilities That the Adults of Each Age Level and Cognitive Level Solved Their Problems According to the Criterion Adopted

	Age level		
Cognitive level	College students	Middle-aged	Elderly
Transitional	.925	.640	.310
Formal	.840	.765	.400

differ, but both showed significantly better performance than did the older adults: college = middle-aged>elderly.

The systems data are presented in Table 6.5. In order to best articulate with related research, the data are (first) presented in terms of the relative frequencies of the total number of categorizable problems for each group. The number of categorizable problems, which ranged from 84 to 129 (out of 200), is also given in the table. These data were submitted to a 3 (age level) × 2 (cognitive level) × 5 (category: focusing, dimension checking, hypothesis checking, stimulus preference, unsystematic sequence χ^2 for analysis (Winer, 1971). The main effect of age level, $\chi^2(8) = 135.76$, and cognitive level, $\chi^2(4) = 24.16$, were significant, as was their interaction, $\chi^2(8) = 17.87$.

College students of the two cognitive levels showed performance that was roughly comparable to that obtained in previous research in which cognitive level was not assessed (Gholson *et al.*, 1972, 1973). They exhibited focusing in 43–55% of their problems and dimension checking in most of the remainder. The two groups of college students did not differ significantly from each other, $\chi^2(4) = 6.31$, $p>.10$. Among the two middle-aged groups, however, the formal operational subjects showed better performance that the transitional, $\chi^2(4) = 22.44$. The middle-aged formal operational subjects performed comparably to the two groups of college students, $\chi^2(4) <7.27$, $p>.10$, in each case, but the middle-aged transitional subjects differed significantly from both, $\chi^2(4)>23.79$, in both cases. The middle-aged transitional adults *did*, however, exhibit better performance than either group of elderly adults, $\chi^2(4)>15.48$, in each case. Finally, the effect of cognitive level approached, but did not reach significance among the older adults, $\chi^2(4) = 9.38$, $p>.05$.

Because the data presented in Table 6.5 included only those problems that could be classified according to one of the five categories, a second set of analyses was performed that included all 1200 problems. For this analysis the protocols were placed into three basic categories: strategies, processing errors, and nonhypothesis. The data are presented in Table 6.6.

Because strategies are inferred from the first three feedback trials and the hypothesis that follows each, only these trials were considered in

TABLE 6.5

The Relative Frequency of Each Hypothesis Sampling System and Unsystematic Hypothesis Sequences for Each Age Level and Cognitive Level [a]

Age	Fo	D–ch	H–ch	Uns	S–P	(Number of problems)	Total percentage
Transitional	43.3	50.4	3.1	3.1	0	(127)	63.5
College							
Formal	55.0	38.0	0.7	5.4	0	(129)	64.5
Transitional	16.0	64.0	4.0	10.0	6.0	(100)	50.0
Middle-aged							
Formal	43.4	45.0	2.3	9.3	0	(129)	64.5
Transitional	2.4	61.9	13.1	14.3	8.3	(084)	43.0
Elderly							
Formal	8.0	43.2	14.8	25.0	9.1	(088)	44.0

[a] The systems are: focusing (Fo), dimension checking (D–ch), hypothesis checking (H–ch), the nonsystem category labeled unsystematic hypothesis sequences (Uns), and stimulus preference (S–P).

TABLE 6.6
The Probabilities That the Adults of Each Age Level and Cognitive Level Exhibited Strategies, Processing Errors, and Nonhypothesis Patterns

	Category		
Age	Strategy	Processing errors	Nonhypothesis
Transitional	.61	.06	.32
College			
Formal	.60	.08	.31
Transitional	.42	.10	.47
Middle-aged			
Formal	.58	.12	.29
Transitional	.32	.21	.46
Elderly			
Formal	.29	.26	.44

classifying problems. The strategy category includes, of course, focusing, dimension checking, and hypothesis checking. Four kinds of processing errors that prevent a problem from being placed in a strategy category have been identified (Mims & Gholson, 1977): (*a*) unsystematic hypothesis sequences (see Chapter 3); (*b*) failure to sample according to a local consistency criterion following errors; (*c*) stimulus preference, which is a subclass of the failure to exhibit local consistency; and (*d*) the subject's failure to maintain a confirmed hypothesis. The category labeled "nonhypothesis" includes those problems in which the subjects failed to exhibit consistent hypotheses in at least one of the first three blank-trial probes. In those cases in which more than one kind of error occurred, the problem was placed in the nonhypothesis category if any nonhypothesis pattern occurred, otherwise the first processing error dictated how the problem was categorized.

These data were analyzed by partitioning a 3 (age level) × 2 (cognitive level) × 3 (category: strategy, processing error, nonhypothesis) χ^2 (Winer, 1971). The findings were similar in every respect to those based upon the data of Table 6.5. Age level, $\chi^2(4) = 91.89$, cognitive level, $\chi^2(2) = 10.28$, and their interaction were significant, $\chi^2(4) = 10.18$. Comparisons of individual groups also yielded a similar pattern of findings. Thus the data of Tables 6.5 and 6.6 lead to essentially identical conclusions regarding the relationship between age level and cognitive level.

Discussion

To summarize, then, the main effect of age level was significant on each of seven measures of performance. The young and middle-aged adults showed comparable performance on five of these measures; performance of the elderly was depressed in each case. The systems data and the solution data revealed age-level by cognitive-level interactions. In each case the formal operational middle-aged subjects performed at about the same high level as the two groups of college students. The middle-aged who were transitional showed intermediate performance: worse than the college students and formal operational middle-aged, but significantly better than either group of older subjects. The latter did not differ from each other.

The experiment was, of course, exploratory, and any interpretation of the findings is qualified by cohort effects, the different educational processes of each generation, and so forth (P.B. Baltes, 1978; P.B. Baltes & Schaie, 1973; N.W. Denney & Wright, 1975; Overton, 1975; Riegel, 1973). Firm conclusions, then, will have to await further research in which these factors are controlled and evaluated. In addition, various training regimens may elicit more sophisticated strategies and generally better performance than was obtained here (Hornblum & Overton, 1976).

It does seem fair to say, though, that age level, whether due to cohort effects, educational experiences, a general decline in information-processing skills, or some other factor (Reese, 1976, 1977), produced some of the same effects on performance as does the manipulation of various task variables. That is, in two analyses, age level interacted with cognitive level, producing effects similar to those produced by the manipulation of coding demands, memory demands, and various training regimens (cf. Chapter 4, Chapter 7, and Expt. 3). It is possible to speculate that some specific cognitive subprocess, such as memory organization (Reese, 1976) was responsible for the general decline in performance associated with old age.

Comparison of the two middle-aged groups, however, casts some doubt on this interpretation. They showed equivalent performance on five measures of information-processing efficiency that presumably reflect how efficiently some cognitive subprocesses function. It should be explicitly stated, though, that none of the five measures directly reflect the subject's memory organization (cf. Eimas, 1970; Gholson & Danziger, 1975; Neimark *et al.*, 1971; Nuessle, 1972). Thus it is possbile that memory organization differs among middle-aged people who are transitional versus formal operational. The problem with this interpretation was that memory organization did not, at least as reflected in the strategies they exhibited, differ among transitional and formal operational college students. Such an interpretation would require the assumption of differential rates of memory decline among the formal operational and transitional during the years that intervene age 20 and middle age. This does not appear plausible.

Conclusions

In general, the results of Experiment 3 were very congenial to the model presented in Chapters 3 and 4. Training condition interacted with cognitive level, as predicted. The preoperational children failed to exhibit strategies under either training condition. The concrete operational showed equally good performance under both. The transitional children exhibited strategies almost as frequently as those who were concrete operational following rule instruction; they showed mostly unsystematic hypothesis sequences (and stereotypes) in the absence of specific rule instruction.

The model did not fare so well in Experiment 4. Age level interacted with cognitive level, a result that cannot be predicted by the model as it is presently stated. Other research indicates that specific cognitive deficits which would be reflected in the efficiency with which the cognitive subprocesses function may be associated with age level (cf. Horn, 1978; Reese, 1976). Only if these deficits can be identified and related to specific cognitive subprocesses that regulate the flow of information to and from the processor will the model remain viable. In our present state of understanding this does not seem to be an unreasonable possibility. Minimally, the empirical implications of the question are clear and researchable.

7

The Effects of Cognitive Subprocess Manipulations upon Problem Solving

Four experiments are reported in this chapter. Each was designed to explore how task variables that are identified with specific cognitive subprocesses affect problem solving. The attentional processes of elementary-school children were investigated in the first two experiments. The third involved manipulations of memory and coding processes in children and adults. In the fourth, attention and memory processes in normal and underachieving readers were explored. Blank-trial probes for hypotheses were not used to obtain hypothesis data in any of this research. Instead, the subjects were trained to give verbal statements of their hypotheses in three experiments (Phillips & Levine, 1975); a technique proposed by Kornreich (1968), in which the stimulus cues are decomposed, was used in one experiment.

Experiment 5: Training Attention Control: Effects of Rule Provision and Instructional Feedback upon the Voluntary Control of Attention among Elementary-School Children[1]

ANITA L. TUMBLIN AND BARRY GHOLSON

Mims and Gholson (1977) reported an experiment in which they used three different *kinds* and three different amounts of feedback. The children (CA range 7–9 years) were trained to state their hypotheses verbally

1. This report is based upon a thesis submitted to the faculty at Memphis State University by the first author as part of the requirements for the M.S. degree. The second author directed the work.

on each trial (this procedure is described in detail in the *Method* section). They received either (*a*) verbal–directional feedback, in which the correct stimulus complex was indicated by the experimenter pointing to it, (*b*) verbal-only feedback, in which the experimenter said whether the response was correct or wrong, but the correct stimulus object was not overtly indicated, or (*c*) material feedback in which a marble was moved by the experimenter following responses to indicate whether choices were correct or wrong. In each case the stimulus object remained in the child's view for about four seconds following response. The three kinds of feedback were factorially combined with three amounts: (*a*) correct–wrong, in which feedback followed both correct and incorrect choice responses; (*b*) wrong–blank, in which feedback followed incorrect responses, but nothing (no feedback) followed correct responses; and (*c*) correct–blank in which feedback followed correct responses, but did not follow incorrect responses.

Children in the verbal–directional correct–wrong and wrong–blank conditions showed strikingly better performance than those in any other group. They solved more problems (70% versus 50–57%), resampled according to a local-consistency criterion more frequently (about 90% versus 60–70%), and exhibited strategies in more of their problems (about 75% versus 30–48%) than the children of any of the remaining seven conditions. The crucial factor responsible for the differences appeared to be the overt attentional guidance provided by the directional component of the feedback. Because the verbal–directional correct–wrong and wrong–blank conditions showed equally good performance while the corresponding correct–blank group showed poor performance, it appeared that the attentional guidance was important only following errors.

In one form or another, the directional component has been part of the feedback procedure in much of the hypothesis-testing research that involved children (Eimas, 1970; Gholson & Danziger, 1975; Gholson *et al.*, 1972, 1973, 1976; Goldfield, 1974; Moss, 1976; Phillips & Levine, 1975). The overt guidance does not appear to provide the child with additional information concerning the correctness of the response per se. Instead, it serves strictly as an attentional aid.

To date, the issue of attentional guidance has not been addressed by those working within the framework of hypothesis theory. Although the importance of this type of directional feedback has been demonstrated in a few experiments involving three- and four-choice problems (e.g., Bourne & Pendleton, 1958; Comstock & Chumbley, 1973; Gholson & O'Connor, 1975; Gumer & Levine, 1971), the logical requirements of these tasks following errors are different from those following errors in two-choice tasks. That is, pointing to the correct stimulus object following an error in a two-choice task provides no new logical information; but in a three- or four-choice task, pointing reduces the number of logically viable stimulus objects from two or three to one.

Thus it was deemed important to examine aspects of children's attention systematically during two-choice problem solving. The present experiment explores the possibility of teaching children to control their own voluntary attentional processes more efficiently. Extensive pilot work involving numerous techniques indicated that the most effective training combined rule provision with instructional feedback in a training procedure administered over the course of several pretraining problems. After pretraining, all attentional training was discontinued. Rule provision consisted of instructing the child that being told "wrong" meant the solution was not in the stimulus object that was chosen and, therefore, "wrong means look in the other picture." The instructional feedback involved telling the child "correct, the answer is in that picture," or "wrong, the answer is in the other picture" after choice responses, but the correct stimulus object was never overtly indicated by the experimenter's pointing to it. Because pilot work indicated that the most effective procedure involved a combination of the manipulations, it was of interest to evaluate each independently.

The basic experiment consisted of four groups that were formed by combining two levels of rule provision (present versus absent) with two levels of instructional feedback (present versus absent) to yield a 2 × 2 factorial design. In each case the attentional training was administered only during pretraining, and the children were then given a 10-problem series of experimental problems in which all training procedures were omitted. In the experimental problems, feedback consisted of having the experimenter simply say "correct" or "wrong" following choice responses (i.e., verbal-only feedback).

In order to directly articulate with previous research, two additional groups were included. These conditions were identical to two used by Mims and Gholson (1977)—those called verbal–directional correct–wrong, and verbal-only correct–wrong. The first of these, hereafter referred to as verbal–directional/verbal–directional, involved complete feedback which included a directional component (pointing by the experimenter) throughout all trials of both pretraining and experimental problems. In the second, called verbal–directional/verbal-only, the children received directional feedback during pretraining, but were transferred to non-directional feedback for the experimental problems (i.e., the experimenter said only "correct" or "wrong"). Previous research (e.g., Gholson *et al.*, 1973; Mims & Gholson, 1977) and pilot data suggested these groups would yield, respectively, the upper and lower boundaries of performance.

Method

SUBJECTS

The subjects were 150 children from third- and fourth-grade classes in the Memphis City Schools, equally divided into six groups (mean CA = 9:5–10:0 years). The children were drawn from schools that serve families of lower SES levels. An attempt was made to assign approximately equal numbers of third- and fourth-grade boys and girls to each cell. Otherwise the assignment was haphazard.

GENERAL PROCEDURE

Children of all six groups were exposed to preliminary instructions and pretraining that consisted of five problems, and then received 10 experimental problems that were used to assess the training effects. Each child was seen individually for one session of about 50 minutes. The same stimulus materials, feedback sequences, and 10 different problem-order sequences were used in each group. Standard bivalued four-dimensional stimulus sequences were used in each problem. Each problem involved the same four dimensions (shape or alphabetic letter, color, size, line position), but employed a different combination of 18 letters and eight colors. The heights of the small and large letters were 1.25 and 2.5 inches. Line positions were "over" and "under" the letters. The lines measured 2.5 × .5 inches, were black in color, and were positioned .5 inch above or below the letters. Stimulus materials were appended to white 5- × 8-inch index cards with distinct black center lines separating the two stimulus objects.

The stimulus sequences of each problem were arranged to conform to Levine's (1966) orthogonality criterion. The stimulus pairs were ordered so that any three consecutive trials within a problem logically specified the solution, and no one cue alternated or perseverated for more than three consecutive trials. Beyond these restrictions, the stimuli were ordered randomly.

PRETRAINING PROBLEMS AND INTROTACTS

The general pretraining procedure was adapted from a method developed by Phillips (1974, 1976; Phillips & Levine, 1975) for teaching children to voluntarily generate verbal statements of their hypotheses on each trial. Using Phillips' procedure, introtacts, or verbal probes for hypotheses, are introduced gradually during pretraining. The child is asked to state a "best bet" as to the solution on various trials beginning with the third pretraining problem and increasing thereafter until, on the fifth and final pretraining problem, a "best bet" is voluntarily given (or requested) on every trial. Requests for "best bets" are discontinued after pretraining. Care was taken to emphasize to the child that hypotheses were to be stated *before* choice responses were made on each trial. The choice response involved pointing to the stimulus object thought to contain the solution.

Feedback was always delivered immediately after the child's choice response, and stimuli remained in view for about four seconds following feedback. The pretraining problems were 24, 24, 24, 10, and 10 trials in length in the order presented. The solutions were a color, a letter, a size, a line position, and a color, respectively.

Following the twelfth and/or twenty-fourth trial of the first three, and the tenth trial of the last two pretraining problems, the children were asked if they had "figured out what is always correct," and to state the solution. If they were unable to do so, a hint about the solution dimension was given, for example, "try one of the colors, see if red is always correct or green is always correct," and the problem was either continued or presented again. A solution was requested again on the appropriate trail and, if the child was still unable to state the solution, the answer was given, for example, "the answer to this puzzle is red, see if you can choose all the pictures that are red," and the problem was presented yet again. No further hints were given. If multiple or conjunctive hypotheses were stated, the child was reminded that the answer could be only one thing. For continuation beyond pretraining, a criterion of 10 consecutive correct responses was required in the first three problems, and five consecutive correct responses in problems four and five. No child failed to meet this criterion. Thus all children received comparable pretraining on the mechanics of the task itself, the nature of solution, and the use of verbal probes for hypotheses.

PRETRAINING FEEDBACK PROCEDURES

Although a common body of information and task experience was communicated in the pretraining of all six groups, there were important differences in the attentional training administered during pretraining. These differences were due to deliberate variations in the feedback-delivery procedures and were designed to produce changes in performance in the subsequent experimental problems.

Verbal-Only Condition. Throughout all trials of all pretraining problems, the children (mean CA = 9:6 years) in this condition were simply told "correct" or "wrong" after each choice response.

Instructional-Feedback Condition. Pretraining feedback for children (mean CA = 9:6) in this condition consisted of the following: On Problems 1 and 2, choices on every trial were responded to with the statement "correct, the answer is in that picture" or "wrong, the answer is in the other picture." No directional component was combined with the instructional statement. On Problem 3, instructional feedback was given on Trials 5, 6, 11–13, 17–19, and on Trial 23. On all other trials of this problem, feedback was of the verbal-only form described above, that is, "correct" or "wrong." In the fourth pretraining problem, instructional feedback was delivered on Trials 4, 8, and 9 with verbal-only feedback on the remaining trials. In the final pretraining problem verbal-only feedback was given on all trials.

Rule-Provision Condition. Children (mean CA = 9:9) in this condition received verbal-only feedback on all trials of the first two pretraining problems. Following the second problem, but before presentation of the third, they were told, "There is something I would like you to remember about how to play these puzzles. Whenever you pick and I tell you 'wrong,' I want you to think to yourself that 'wrong means the answer is not in the picture I chose, so wrong means I have to look at the *other* picture.' OK? So remember, whenever you hear 'wrong,' just think 'wrong means look in the other picture.' " Problem three was then presented and on Trials 1–4, 7–10, 14–16, 20–22, and 24 the children were again told that "wrong means look in the other picture," or "after awhile I am not going to remind you any more, so I want you to try really hard now and remember that 'wrong means look in the other picture.' " For the remaining trials of the problem the children received just verbal-only feedback. On pretraining Problem 4, rule provision was provided on Trials 1–3, 5–7, and 10. The fifth problem involved verbal-only feedback on all 10 trials. Following this final pretraining problem, the children were reminded once more that "wrong means look in the other picture." The children frequently parroted this statement, suggesting that this training constituted, at least in part, a self-instruction procedure (Meichenbaum, 1977).

Instruction-Plus-Rule Condition. Children (mean CA = 9:5) in this condition received instructional feedback on trials corresponding to that condition, and rule provision on trials corresponding to the rule-provision condition. Thus the two training procedures were simply combined for children in this group.

Verbal-Directional/Verbal-Directional Condition. For children (mean CA = 9:5) in this condition, the feedback procedure involved the experimenter saying "correct, the answer is in this picture," or "wrong, the answer is in *this* picture" as dictated by the solution. At the same time that the verbal statement was being made, the experimenter also pointed directly to the stimulus object containing the solution for about four seconds. This procedure was followed for every trial of the five pretraining problems and the 10 experimental problems.

Verbal-Directional/Verbal-Only Condition. During pretraining these children (mean CA = 10:0) received directional feedback identical to the verbal–directional/verbal–directional condition. They received verbal-only feedback during the 10 experimental problems.

EXPERIMENTAL PROBLEMS

Upon completion of the pretraining problems, all children received a randomized series of 10-trial problems. In these problems feedback was predetermined on the first three trials: Half the problems involved three negative feedbacks; in the remainder the child was told "correct" on the first trial and "wrong" on the second and third. Specific solutions to each problem were determined by the child's choice responses and the feedback sequence during the three trials. After the third trial, the logically specified solution determined feedback. Children in five of the conditions received verbal-only feedback during experimental problems. Those in the verbal–directional/verbal–directional condition, of course, received verbal–directional feedback on each trial.

Results

All analyses were based on data derived from the 10 experimental problems administered to each child. All children were instructed in the basic mechanics of the task, and all met the same solution criterion in each pretraining problem. Thus the data of interest concerned the transfer effects of the various training procedures. No analyses were performed on the data of the five pretraining problems.

The basic design of the experiment involved the factorial combination of two levels of instructional feedback and two levels of rule provision. Thus these data were analyzed as a 2 × 2 factorial design. The two other groups were included only for purposes of comparison and to articulate with previous research. Thus they were treated separately. The verbal–directional/verbal–directional condition was included to provide a ceiling against which the training conditions could be compared to assess their effects. The verbal–directional/verbal-only condition was included to compare against the verbal-only condition. These planned comparisons were performed with *t-tests*.

Seven dependent measures were derived from the data. Two of these, response consistency and choice description (Phillips & Levine, 1975), were used to evaluate the use of verbally stated hypotheses. The third—the percentage of problems solved—was a measure of learning. Three measures were used to evaluate feedback effects: the probabilities that confirmed hypotheses were maintained, that disconfirmed hypotheses were rejected, and that locally consistent hypotheses followed negative feedback. The final measure involved the strategies that were exhibited and the processing errors which prevented problems from fitting one of the strategy categories. The feedback-effects data were normalized by arcsin transformations (Guilford, 1954) prior to analyses.

RESPONSE CONSISTENCY AND CHOICE DESCRIPTION

Response consistency concerns the degree to which the children's stated hypotheses conformed to their actual choice responses. In all six groups, the stimulus complex that contained the child's stated hypothesis was chosen 100% of the time. This was in line with previous research in which Phillips' procedures were used. Phillips and Levine (1975), for example, obtained 99% response consistency in their work with second graders; similarly, Moss (1976) and Mims and Gholson (1977) each reported 100% response consistency among second- and third-grade children.

Choice description involves problems in which the child meets a solution criterion in terms of the choice responses exhibited, but never *states* the solution hypothesis. Rather, in cases of this sort, hypotheses from another, irrelevant dimension are verbalized despite the fact that the child makes the correct choice response on each trial. A child might, for example, give the sequence of hypotheses "big, little, little, big, little," during a five-trial series in which the stimulus complex containing the solution (e.g., red) is always chosen. Phillips and Levine (1975) showed that such protocols result when children misunderstand the instruction to give a "best bet" as a request to predict which of two stimulus objects is correct on a particular trial, rather than as a request to predict which *attribute* is correct on *all* trials. Despite this confusion, the nature of the task itself is understood; otherwise the child would not solve problems. Actually, Phillips and Levine reported that problems involving choice description were solved at a rate comparable to other problems (about 70%).

In the present experiment, problems were classified as involving choice description if the child's last four choice responses were correct (Trials 7–10), and the appropriate value of one irrelevant dimension was given as an hypothesis on each. A total of 24 problems of this type occurred, ranging from 0 to 7 per cell (of 250). This amounts to about 1.6% of the data. Thus problems involving choice description were of no special concern.

SOLUTION DATA

The solution criterion was a correct choice response on each of the last four trials in the problem. Analysis of variance performed on the factorial data revealed effects of rule provision, $F(1, 96) = 17.78, p<.05$ (the significance criterion for all analyses) and instructional feedback, $F(1, 96) = 16.33$. The data for all six groups are presented in Table 7.1. Scheffé tests revealed that the verbal-only group solved fewer problems than did any other group in the factorial, but the three remaining groups did not differ among themselves. The verbal–directional/verbal–directional group solved more problems than the children in the instruction-plus-rule condition, $t(48) = 3.82$, and those in the verbal–directional/verbal-only condition solved more than those in the verbal-only group, $t(48) = 2.10$.

EFFECTS OF FEEDBACK

The probabilities that confirmed and disconfirmed hypotheses were maintained, and the probabilities that hypotheses were sampled according to a local-consistency criterion following errors are presented in Table 7.2. The local-consistency measure is particularly important because it indicates whether the child switched attention from the chosen stimulus object to the correct one (and coded a cue) during the four seconds the stimulus card was present following negative feedback. Analysis of the local-consistency data derived from the factorial design revealed significant effects of rule provision, $F(1, 96) = 99.34$, instructional feedback, $F(1, 96) = 42.46$, and their interaction, $F(1, 96) = 7.21$. Scheffé tests revealed that the instruction-plus-rule group was superior to all other groups; the rule-provision group was comparable to the instructional-feedback group, but differed significantly from the verbal-only group. The instructional-feedback and verbal-only groups did not differ significantly from each other. The verbal–directional/verbal–directional group showed better performance than children in the instruction-plus-rule

TABLE 7.1
The Average Probabilities That Problems Were Solved by the Children of Each Group

Group	Percentage
Verbal-only	.364
Instructional-feedback	.460
Rule-provision	.464
Instruction-plus-rule	.548
Verbal–directional/verbal-only	.436
Verbal–directional/verbal–directional	.600

TABLE 7.2
The Probabilities That Confirmed (+) and Disconfirmed (−) Hypotheses Were Maintained, and the Probabilities That Hypotheses Were Sampled According to a Local-Consistency Criterion (LC) following Negative Feedback

	Measure		
Group	(+)	(−)	(LC)
Verbal-only	.879	.026	.615
Instructional-feedback	.919	.015	.683
Rule-provision	.909	.012	.734
Instruction-plus-rule	.954	.004	.875
Verbal–directional/verbal-only	.876	.031	.591
Verbal–directional/verbal–directional	.961	.004	.919

condition, $t(48) = 3.21$, but the verbal-only and verbal–directional/verbal-only groups did not differ from each other, $t(48) = 1.01$.

Analyses of the percentages of confirmed hypotheses that were maintained among the four groups of the factorial revealed only a main effect of instructional feedback, $F(1, 96) = 9.38$. Scheffé tests revealed that the instruction-plus-rule group differed from the verbal-only group, but no other differences were significant. The verbal–directional/verbal–directional condition did not differ from the instruction-plus-rule condition, and the verbal–directional/verbal-only condition did not differ from the verbal-only condition, $t(48) = 1.28$ and .06, respectively.

Analysis of variance performed on the probabilities that disconfirmed hypotheses were maintained, that is, the probabilities that two consecutive hypotheses were identical when intervening feedback was negative, revealed significant effects of instructional feedback, $F(1, 96) = 6.98$, and rule provision, $F(1, 96) = 6.61$. The instruction-plus-rule condition differed from the verbal-only condition; no other differences were significant by Scheffé tests. The verbal–directional/verbal–directional condition did not differ from the instruction-plus-rule condition, and verbal-only did not differ from verbal–directional/verbal-only, $t(48) =$ .19 and .06, respectively.

SYSTEMS ANALYSES

Each problem was classified as involving one of the three strategies (focusing, dimension checking, hypothesis checking), a stereotype (stimulus preference), or one of the three processing errors (unsystematic hypothesis sequence, local-consistency error, shift) that were described in Experiment 4 (Chapter 6). These data for all six groups are presented in Table 7.3. The four groups of the factorial design were analyzed by partitioning a multiple contingency (Instructional feedback × Rule pro-

TABLE 7.3

The Number of Problems in Each Strategy, Stereotype, and Processing-Error Category for Each Group

	Category [a]						
	Strategy			Stereotype	Processing error		
Group	Fo	D–ch	H–ch	S–P	Uns	LCE	Shift
Verbal-only	3	10	30	1	51	155	0
Instructional-feedback	0	26	38	0	39	147	0
Rule-provision	1	40	34	0	58	117	0
Instruction-plus-rule	0	76	51	0	56	67	0
Verbal–directional/verbal-only	1	11	33	1	43	161	0
Verbal–directional/verbal–directional	15	77	48	0	66	44	0

[a] The categories are: Focusing (Fo), dimension checking (D–ch), hypothesis checking (H–ch), stimulus preference (S–P), Unsystematic hypothesis sequence (Uns), local-consistency error (LCE), and confirmed hypothesis rejected (shift).

vision × Response class: strategies, stereotypes, processing errors) chi square (Winer, 1971). This analysis revealed significant effects of instructional feedback, $\chi^2(2) = 25.76$, and rule provision, $\chi^2(2) = 43.01$. The interaction between instructional feedback and rule provision was not significant. Two additional chi square analyses, each involving two groups and three categories, revealed no differences between the verbal–directional/verbal–directional condition and the instruction-plus-rule condition, or between the verbal–directional/verbal-only condition and the verbal-only condition. The data of Table 7.3 are reasonably orderly, with the verbal–directional/verbal-only and the verbal-only groups showing strategies in 17% and 18% of their problems, the instructional-feedback and rule provision groups showing strategies in 25% to 30%, and the instruction-plus-rule and verbal–directional/verbal–directional groups showing strategies in 50% to 56%.

Discussion

The results may be summarized as follows:

1. The children who received the most extensive attentional training (instruction-plus-rule) performed at levels superior to the three other training groups, and comparably on several measures to the verbal–directional/verbal–directional group that was included to provide an upper boundary for comparison,

2. Children who received no attentional training at all (verbal-only) performed at low levels that were generally comparable to those exhibited by the verbal–directional/verbal-only condition,

3. Children in the partial-training conditions (instructional-feedback, rule-provision) generally performed at intermediate levels on each dependent measure. That is, they did not perform as well as children in the instruction-plus-rule condition, but did not perform as poorly as those in the verbal-only condition.

It seems reasonable to conclude, then, that it is possible to teach children appropriate control of their voluntary attentional processes. The children who were given instruction-plus-rule training over a series of five preliminary problems, when transferred to problems in which the training conditions were omitted, showed performance at levels almost equal to that of a group given external guidance in the form of attention-directing feedback throughout. The verbal-rule instruction mobilized previously unintegrated attentional operations. (Beilin, 1976, p. 101) that were then brought to bear on the problem. The successful performance of children in this condition contrasts sharply with the inferior performance exhibited by children who received no specific attentional training (verbal-only) and those who received attention-directing feedback during pretraining but were transferred to experimental problems involving the verbal-only procedure (verbal–directional/verbal-only).

In comparing results of the present verbal–directional/verbal–directional group and the instruction-plus-rule condition with results obtained from comparable verbal–directional/verbal–directional groups in previous research that involved children of the same age range and similar procedures (cf. Mims & Gholson, 1977; Moss, 1976; Phillips & Levine, 1975), two curious inconsistencies appeared. First, the percentage of unsystematic hypothesis sequences obtained in the present study was considerably higher than levels obtained previously. In the earlier research these sequences occurred in roughly 10–15% of the problems, but present findings revealed them in about 22–26%. Second, the two groups of children in the present study exhibited strategies in only about 50–56% of their problems, but children in the previous research exhibited them in 65–80%.

Thus, despite the success of the instruction-plus-rule training in bringing performance to a level almost comparable to that of the verbal–directional/verbal–directional condition, the failure to replicate previous systems data obtained under the verbal–directiona/verbal–directional condition indicated that something was amiss. The only differences that could be specified between the present experiment and previous research concerned the populations from which children were drawn. Each of the earlier experiments involved middle- and upper-middle-SES children, but those in the present study were from lower-SES families.

It was deemed necessary to provide a preliminary evaluation of these differences in SES level. Therefore, a second experiment, involving children drawn from Memphis State University School, was conducted. These children are drawn mostly from middle-SES familiies, employees of Memphis State University. The children, 15 third graders per group, were trained under three of the conditions described above: verbal–directional/verbal–directional, instruction-plus-rule, and verbal-only.

The children exhibited only three problems involving choice description and their choice responses were dictated by the hypotheses that were stated 100% of the time. Children in the verbal–directional/verbal–directional and the instruction-plus-rule conditions showed comparable performance that was superior to that of the verbal-only condition on each dependent measure. They solved more problems (84–86% versus 48%), sampled more frequently according to a local-consistency criterion following errors (95–97% versus 64%), maintained more confirmed hypotheses (97% and 97% versus 93%), and were less likely to maintain a disconfirmed hypothesis (2–3% versus 11%). The systems data are presented in Table 7.4.

TABLE 7.4
The Number of Problems in Each Strategy, Stereotype, and Processing-Error Category for Each Group

	Category						
	Strategy			Stereotype	Processing error		
Group	Fo	D–ch	H–ch	S–P	Uns	LCE	Shift
Verbal–directional/verbal–directional	29	77	11	0	24	9	0
Instruction-plus-rule	38	62	18	0	19	13	0
Verbal-only	5	11	19	0	21	21	0

Children in the verbal–directional/verbal–directional and instruction-plus-rule conditions showed very comparable performance: about 78% strategies and 12–16% unsystematic hypothesis sequences. These proportions are very similar to the ones obtained previously among middle-SES children of this age range using verbal–directional feedback procedures, verbal statements of hypotheses, and four-dimensional problems (Mims & Gholson, 1977; Moss, 1976; Phillips & Levine, 1975). Children in the verbal-only condition exhibited 23% strategies and 14% unsystematic sequences. The comparable group in the main experiment showed 17 and 20%, respectively.

Comparing the verbal–directional/verbal–directional and instruction-plus-rule groups in Table 7.3 and 7.4 reveals that the middle-SES children exhibited strategies in about 23% more of their problems than the lower-SES children. Thus the lower-SES children committed processing errors in about twice as many of their problems as the middle-SES children (about 46 versus 22%). It was not surprising, then, that the lower-SES children also solved fewer of their problems (about 55 and 60% versus 84 and 86%).

Unfortunately, the mechanism responsible for the SES differences cannot be specified at present. Anecdotal observations suggested that the lower-SES children were less planful, in a long-term sense, than those of middle-SES levels. The middle-SES children appeared to view each problem comprehensively and then try to formulate a plan that led to solution within the 10 trials. Lower-SES children were more concerned with being correct on each trial, that is, they seemed more concerned with responding correctly than formulating a long-term objective that led to problem solution. Previous research indicates that lower-SES children are frequently more impulsive (Kagan & Kogan, 1970) and field dependent (Langer, 1970) than middle-class children. The relationship between these cognitive styles and SES level has not been investigated using hypothesis-testing procedures (cf. Nuessle, 1972).

Conclusions

It seems clear, then, that children of elementary-school age can be induced to integrate their attentional processes and achieve voluntary control over them. Children in the verbal–directional/verbal-only and verbal-only conditions attended to inappropriate stimulus information; thus this was the information that was coded and reached the processor. The result was that these children exhibited very poor information-processing performance. Conversely, children in the instruction-plus-rule condition performed at a level nearly comparable to those who received external attentional guidance through having the experimenter explicitly point to the stimulus array that contained the solution on each trial. These children switched attention as demanded by the task and, consequently, appropriate stimulus information was coded and reached the processor.

As predicted by the model presented in Chapter 3, the task manipulation strongly influenced how efficiently the children's attentional processes functioned. Because other age groups were not included, the predicted interaction between developmental level and the attentional manipulation cannot be directly determined. There is clear evidence, however, that high-school and college students would show comparable performance in all six conditions (cf. Gholson *et al.*, 1973; Schonebaum, 1973).

Experiment 6: The Effects of Material Feedback upon Children's Attentional Processes

CYNTHIA DANIEL, ANITA L. TUMBLIN, AND BARRY GHOLSON

In a series of research reports, J.T. Spence (1964, 1966a, b, 1970a, b, 1971; Spence & Dunton, 1967; Spence & Segner, 1967) contrasted the effects of verbal, symbolic (e.g., a light flash), and material feedback (e.g., tokens, trinkets, candy) upon children's conceptual learning. In each case, the verbal and symbolic feedback procedures produced equivalent performance that was highly superior to that produced by material feedback conditions. She concluded that material feedback interferes with the child's attentional processes, that is, it distracts the child's attention away from relevant stimulus information. This *distraction* hypothesis has received some attention (e.g., Leeming, Blackwood, & Robinson, 1978; Ratliff & Root, 1974; Ratliff & Tindall, 1970; Spence, 1970a, b; Spence & Dunton, 1967; Tindall & Ratliff, 1974), but the antecedents of distraction have not been systematically assessed (Barringer & Gholson, 1979, reviewed these issues).

In an experiment described in the introduction to Experiment 5, Mims and Gholson (1977) attempted to explore the effects of material feedback by using hypothesis-testing procedures. In one of their conditions, the experimenter moved marbles to and from the child's marble board to signal correct and incorrect responses. This group was contrasted with conditions in which children received verbal–directional feedback and verbal-only feedback. As expected, the verbal–directional condition produced the best performance, but the verbal-only and material-feedback groups did not differ on any dependent measure. This was surprising, because in the material condition it was necessary for the child to glance away from the stimulus materials and observe the experimenter's movements in order to determine whether feedback was positive or negative (the stimulus array persisted for about four seconds following response); whereas in the verbal-only condition, feedback was auditory, so it was not necessary for the children to switch their visual attention away from the stimulus array.

The performance of children in both the verbal-only and material-feedback conditions was, however, very poor relative to the verbal–directional condition. This suggested that the similarities in performance might have been artifactual, that is, the similarities may have resulted from floor effects. The present experiment was designed to explore this possibility. Material and verbal feedback were contrasted, using directional and nondirectional procedures.

In order to equate, as nearly as possible, the material and verbal feedback conditions, the children were instructed during pretraining that "green" meant their response was correct and "red" meant it was incorrect. Thus, following a correct response, the experimenter either said "green" (verbal conditions) or handed the child a green token (material conditions). Similarly, following incorrect responses, the experimenter said "red" or handed the child a red token. In the verbal–directional condition, the experimenter pointed to the top of the correct stimulus array while saying "red" or "green," and in the material–directional condition she held a red or green token at the top of the array. In the nondirectional conditions the children were simply told "red" or "green," or were handed a token of the appropriate color. These four conditions yield a 2 × 2 factorial design. The children were taught during pretraining to verbalize their hypotheses on each trial.

Method

SUBJECTS

The subjects were 56 second- and third-grade children (mean CA = 8:0) drawn from Memphis City Schools serving middle-SES-level families. Approximately equal proportions of second- and third-grade boys and girls were assigned to each cell. Otherwise, the assignment of 14 children to each of the four conditons was random.

GENERAL PROCEDURE

All the children were presented with preliminary instructions and pretraining during a sequence of five problems, and then received ten 10-trial problems that were used to assess effects of the various feedback-delivery procedures. The techniques used to train the children to state their hypotheses verbally were identical to those used in the experiment described earlier in this chapter (Expt. 5). Standard bivalued four-dimensional (shape, color, size, line position) stimulus materials, sequenced according to an orthogonality criterion, were used in each of the 15 problems. Different pairs of shapes and colors were used in each problem, but values on the size and line-position dimensions were constant. The colors red and green were, of course, excluded from the stimulus materials. The stimulus array was always left in the child's view for about four seconds following response.

At the outset of the session the experimenter asked the child how to play the game "red light, green light." Following the child's explanation she asked what red light and green light meant (red means stop, green means go). She then explained that these referents were similar to those that would be used in the experimental task. The experimenter then placed six tokens, three of each color, on the table and asked the child to hand them to her one at a time as she requested them by their color name (e.g., "hand me one red bead"). This screening procedure was used to identify any child who was red–green color-blind (no child was).

Verbal Conditions. At the outset of each pretraining problem, the experimenter told the child that when she said "green" it meant the choice response was correct, and when she said "red" it meant that the response was incorrect. Following each response in the first pretraining problem, the experimenter said either "green, green means you are correct, the answer is in the picture you picked," or "red, red means you are wrong, the answer is not in the picture you picked." The experimenter continued to give feedback of this kind through the first five trials of the second pretraining problem. The children were then told that they would no longer be reminded what red and green meant following each response, so they should try to remember. On the remaining trials of this problem, the experimenter just said "green" or "red" following choice responses. The full feedback statement was given following the child's first correct and first incorrect response in pretraining Problem 3, but the experimenter said only "red" or "green" on the remaining trials of this problem and all trials of pretraining Problems 4 and 5.

Children in the verbal-only condition received no other instructions regarding feedback. Children in the verbal–directional condition, however, were also told that when the experimenter said "green," that meant the choice response was correct and she (the experimenter) would point to the stimulus array the child chose, but that when she said "red" that meant the response was incorrect and she would point to the other stimulus object, that is, the one that was correct. This was explained at the outset of the first two pretraining problems. The experimenter pointed each time to the correct stimulus array during the 4 seconds the stimuli persisted following response.

Material Conditions. The meaning of the red and green tokens (.5-inch square plastic beads) was explained at the outset of each pretraining problem. During the first pretraining problem the children were told either "the green block means that you are correct, the answer is in the picture you picked," or "the red block means you are wrong, the answer is not in the picture you picked" and were handed a token of the appropriate color on each trial. This procedure was followed through the first five trials of the second pretraining problem, and following the first correct and first incorrect responses in the third. On all other trials during pretraining, the experimenter just handed the child a token of the appropriate color. In the token-only condition the child was simply handed the token. In the token–directional condition a token of the appropriate color was held at the top of the stimulus array (where the experimenter pointed in the verbal–directional condition) that contained the solution during the 4-second interval the stimulus array remained in view following response. It was handed to the child at the end of the interval. The children placed tokens of both colors in a single cup.

Experimental Problems. On each trial of all experimental problems the children received feedback appropriate to the condition to which they were assigned. In the verbal–directional condition the experimenter said "red" or "green" and pointed to the correct stimulus object for approximately 4 seconds. In the material–directional condition a token of the appropriate color was placed at the top of the correct array during the 4-second interval and then handed to the child. In the nondirectional conditions the child was simply told "red" or "green," or was handed a token of the appropriate color. The stimulus array remained in the child's view for about 4 seconds following response on all trials in all conditions.

Results

The seven dependent measures described in the preceding experiment (Expt. 5) were derived from the data. There was only one instance in which a child failed to choose the stimulus array that contained the hypothesis that was stated. The children exhibited choice descriptions in a total of 20 problems. Twelve of these occurred in the verbal-only condition, four in verbal–directional, three in material–directional, and one in material-only.

The solution data are presented in Table 7.5. These data were submitted to a 2 (attention direction: present, absent) × 2 (feedback type: verbal, material) analysis of variance. One problem was lost due to an experimenter error., so the data were converted to proportions and normalized by arcsin transformations (Guilford, 1954) prior to analysis. The analysis of variance revealed significant effects of attention direction, $F(1, 52) = 37.04, p < .05$ (this criterion was used in all analyses), feedback type, $F(1, 52) = 5.61$, and their interaction, $F(1, 52) = 4.56$. Further analyses revealed that children in the verbal–directional condition solved more problems than those in the material–directional condition, $F(1, 26) = 7.27$. The verbal-only and material-only conditions did not differ ($F < 1$). Verbal–directional exceeded verbal-only, $F(1, 26) = 36.51$, and material–directional exceeded material-only, $F(1, 26) = 7.29$.

Three measures of the effects of feedback on individual trials were derived from the data. These measures, the probabilities that children of each group exhibited locally consistent hypotheses following errors, rejected disconfirmed hypotheses, and maintained confirmed hypotheses are presented in Table 7.6. The data were normalized by arcsin transformations before analyses of variance were performed. Analysis of the local-consistency data revealed effects of attention direction, $F(1, 52) = 86.14$, and an attention–direction × feedback-type interaction, $F(1, 52) = 6.09$. The children in the verbal–directional condition performed better than those in verbal-only, $F(1, 26) = 58.75$, and material–directional outperformed material-only, $F(1, 26) = 28.26$. The difference between verbal–directional and material–directional approached, but did not reach, significance, $F(1, 26) = 2.98$, $.05 < p < .10$. The difference between verbal-only and material-only did not approach significance ($p > .10$).

Analysis of the probabilities that disconfirmed hypotheses were maintained revealed significant effects of attention direction, $F(1, 52) = 5.92$, and feedback type, $F(1, 52) = 5.35$. The interaction did not approach significance ($F < 1$). Surprisingly, the material conditions showed better performance on this measure than the verbal conditions. The directional

TABLE 7.5
The Probabilities That Children of Each Group Solved Their Problems

Condition	Probability
Verbal-only	.489
Verbal–directional	.850
Material-only	.478
Material–directional	.664

TABLE 7.6
The Probabilities That Confirmed (+) and Disconfirmed (−) Hypotheses Were Maintained, and That Hypotheses Were Sampled According to a Local-Consistency Criterion (LC) following Negative Feedback

	Measure		
Group	(+)	(−)	(LC)
Verbal-only	.832	.124	.562
Verbal–directional	.967	.047	.886
Material-only	.946	.047	.638
Material–directional	.948	.009	.823

TABLE 7.7
The Number of Problems in Each Strategy and Processing-Error Category for Each Group

	Category[a]					
	Strategy			Processing error		
Group	Fo	D–ch	H–ch	Uns	LCE	Shift
Verbal-only	3.5	1.5	12	46	68	8
Verbal–directional	31.8	46.2	20	29	15	4
Material-only	0.5	13.5	21	23	78	7
Material–directional	17.3	29.7	24	22	41	6

[a]The categories are: focusing (Fo), dimension checking (D-ch), hypothesis checking (Hch), unsystematic hypothesis sequence (Uns), local-consistency error (LCE), and confirmed hypothesis rejected (Shift).

conditions were again superior to the nondirectional. Analysis of the probabilities that confirmed hypotheses were maintained revealed effects of attention direction, $F(1, 52) = 8.77$, and the interaction between attention direction and feedback type, $F(1, 52) = 7.17$. Children in three of the conditions did not differ from each other: verbal–directional = material–directional = material-only, but all three showed better performance than children in the verbal-only condition, $F(1, 26) > 9.28$, in each case.

The systems data are presented in Table 7.7. The frequencies with which each processing error occurred are also presented in the table. Because no instances of stimulus preference were observed, this category was omitted from the table and the analyses. The data were analyzed by partitioning a multiple contingency (Attention direction × Feedback type × Strategies versus processing errors) χ^2 (Winer, 1971). The main effect of attention direction was significant, $\chi^2(1) = 107.19$, as was the interaction between attention direction and feedback type, $\chi^2(1) = 13.71$. Further analyses revealed significantly better performance among children in the verbal–directional than the material–directional condition, $\chi^2(1) = 10.86$, and in the material-only than the verbal-only condition, $\chi^2(1) = 4.08$ (after Yate's correction in the latter case).

Discussion

In the following discussion it will be useful to identify some specific cognitive subprocesses and how they are reflected in the present task. Coding processes, recoding, and attention are monitored through the trial-by-trial use of feedback information. Following an error, for example, children must (*a*) reject the hypothesis that determined their choice response, (*b*) switch attention from the stimulus complex that was just disconfirmed to the stimulus object that logically contains the solution, and (*c*) code a new cue. Following positive feedback, of course, the subject must only maintain (i.e., remember) the hypothesis that determined the choice response. Thus performance following negative feedback provides good measures of attentional and coding processes. Performance following positive feedback gives some indication of the child's memory, at least for the hypothesis that was just exhibited.

Children in the material–directional condition used feedback at least as effectively as did children in verbal–directional. The two groups showed statistically equivalent performance on two measures: exhibiting locally consistent hypotheses following errors (attention) and maintaining confirmed hypotheses. Children in the material–directional group were actually more likely to reject disconfirmed hypotheses (recode) than were those in the verbal–directional group. Thus the material–directional condition produced no detectable deficits in the children's attentional, coding, or memory processes. These children attended to, coded, and remembered information at the same high level as those in the verbal–directional condition. Presumably, then, comparable amounts of appropriate information made their way to the processor among children in both groups.

The material–directional condition, however, did not produce efficient processing. Children in the verbal–directional group manifested strategies, rather than processing errors, in significantly more problems (70 versus 50%) than did those in the material–directional group. Thus the findings seem to indicate that the necessity for the child to manipulate the tokens during the intertrial interval caused the processor to malfunction.

The data of Table 7.7 and the local-consistency data of Table 7.6, however, suggest another interpretation that may be equally viable. Notice that the children in the verbal–directional condition showed strategies in 27 more problems than did those in material–directional; conversely, children in material–directional showed local-consistency errors in 26 more problems than did children in verbal–directional. Similarly, the data of Table 7.6 show that the verbal–directional condition produced 88.6% locally consistent hypotheses, while material–directional produced 82.3%. This difference approached, but did not reach, significance ($p<.10$). Thus the two measures, taken together, suggest that the presence of a token at the top of the correct stimulus array and/or the necessity for the child to manipulate the token at the end of the feedback interval interfered with attentional processes rather than the functioning of the processor per se. In the absence of further research it is impossible to specify which explanation is more viable.

The verbal-only and material-only conditions both produced very poor performance. These findings, along with those reported earlier (Expt. 5, this chapter; Mims & Gholson, 1977) indicate that a directional component of some sort should be combined with feedback whenever elementary-school children are to be taught conceptual material (cf. Dalton, Rubino, & Hislop, 1973; O'Leary & Kent, 1973; Staats, Minke, & Butts, 1970). The material-only condition produced slightly but significantly better performance on three measures: the proportion of confirmed hypotheses that were maintained, the proportion of disconfirmed hypotheses rejected, and the proportion of problems involving strategies. The analysis offered above suggests that memory and recoding deficits accounted for the relatively inefficient processing shown by the verbal-only condition. The differences between the two conditions are, however, inconsistent with results obtained in closely related research (Mims & Gholson, 1977), and other research on conceptual learning (e.g., Penney, 1967; Spence, 1970a, 1971; Spence & Dunton, 1967; Spence & Segner, 1967). In previous research verbal-only conditions have produced performance that was at least comparable, and frequently superior to, that produced by material-only conditions.

Mims and Gholson, for example, obtained comparable performance among second- and third-grade children in their verbal-only and material-only conditions (e.g., about 35% strategies in both conditions). In contrast, the verbal-only condition produced about 13% strategies in the present study, and material-only produced only 23%. The one comparable experiment (Expt. 5, *Discussion)* that involved middle-SES children who were both pretrained (Mims & Gholson gave all groups directional pretraining) and tested under the verbal-only condition yielded better performance on several measures than was obtained in the present study: 10% more confirmed hypotheses were maintained, and strategies were exhibited in 10% more problems.

One possible explanation for the discrepancy is that the use of colors to identify correct and incorrect responses produced some unexpected effects that differentially affected performance in the directional and nondirectional conditions. To see how this might have occurred, consider the processing requirements in the nondirectional conditions. In the verbal-only condition it was necessary for the child (*a*) to immediately attend to and code the brief auditory signal ("red" or "green"), (*b*) translate the color name into its appropriate meaning, and (*c*) either maintain the hypothesis that dictated the choice response or reject it and switch attention to the other stimulus complex. In the material-only condition the immediacy of the first step was considerably reduced. The children were handed a token of the appropriate color and there followed a 4-second interval during which they could attend to the color, translate its meaning, etc.

It was possible, then, that children in the verbal-only condition sometimes failed to code the brief auditory signal and/or were less likely to translate the color name into its appropriate meaning than were the children who manipulated the token during the feedback interval. According to this explanation the distracting effects of material feedback were more than compensated for by the facilitation it provided during earlier phases of the processing sequence. The feedback data provide some support for this possibility: The verbal-only condition produced performance decrements relative to material-only on all three measures (Table 7.6).

Similar effects would not have been expected, however, in the directional conditions. It was not necessary for children in the verbal–directional condition to either code the brief auditory signal or translate it into its appropriate meaning. All they were required to do was attend to the stimulus complex to which the experimenter pointed and determine whether it contained the cue that corresponded to the current hypothesis. While this was also the case for children in the material–directional condition, the distraction produced by the presence of the token and the necessity to manipulate it placed these children at a relative disadvantage.

While this explanation is post hoc, it would also account for the discrepancy between present findings and those obtained by Mims and Gholson (1977) and in Experiment 5. Conclusions and clarifications will have to await an expanded replication and more systematic treatment of the variables.

Experiment 7: Effects of Explicit Memory Aids and Coding Demands upon Problem Solving

SHERIDAN PHILLIPS AND BARRY GHOLSON

There presently exists a growing body of research in which blank-trial probes or verbal statements were used to monitor children's hypotheses. Each of these procedures has certain advantages and disadvantages. The blank-trial probe detects both position-oriented response sets and those dictated by stimulus cues; but it also imposes extra memory demands because the child must attempt to remember stimulus information acquired on feedback trials during intervening blank trials (Foreit, 1974; Phillips & Levine, 1975). In addition, when children fail to show consistent hypothesis patterns or position patterns during consecutive probes, data are lost to other analyses that are performed on the data. Verbal statements of hypotheses reduce the memory demands imposed by blank trials and less data are lost for analysis, but they cannot detect position responses and they may influence the way in which the child approaches the task (Phillips & Levine, 1975). The two hypothesis probe procedures do, however, yield reasonably consistent findings (see Chapter 4).

The present experiment explored the use of a very different hypothesis-monitoring device that was described by Kornreich (1968). Kornreich used standard bivalued four-dimensional problems (Levine, 1966), but to monitor hypotheses he presented college-student subjects with a decomposed list of the eight different hypotheses and instructed them to indicate "which could still be correct" following each choice response and feedback. The apparatus that was used to monitor hypotheses consisted of a box upon which eight large buttons were mounted. Next to each button was a representation of one of the eight hypotheses from which the solution was drawn. Subjects pushed the appropriate button(s) to indicate which hypotheses they thought were still viable following each choice response. Schematically, on each trial the subject made a choice response, received feedback, and then pushed buttons that designated individual hypotheses.

After pretraining in the dynamics of the task and the use of the hypothesis-monitoring device, the subjects were presented with a series of four-dimensional problems in which the stimulus sequences were constructed according to an orthogonality criterion. A perfect processor would show four hypotheses following the first choice response, two following the second, and one hypothesis, the solution, following the third response. The four-dimensional stimulus array was extinguished immediately following the subjects' choice responses, so it was necessary for them to designate individual hypotheses in the absence of the visual stimulus materials.

In general, Kornreich's findings indicated that college students are nearly perfect processors in this task. Most of the time his subjects showed four hypotheses, two hypotheses, and one hypothesis following the first, second, and third feedback trials, respectively. There were occasional errors, but the pattern was perfect processing. Thus the procedure produced somewhat better performance than is usually obtained when blank trials or verbal statements of hypotheses are used with college-student subjects (cf. Gholson *et al.*, 1972, 1973; Karpf & Levine, 1971).

Kornreich's procedure included a specific memory aid in the form of the decomposed set of hypotheses, and this may have produced the improved performance. In addition, the instruction to indicate those hypotheses that were still viable following each choice response may have facilitated processing. Despite the pattern of findings obtained by Kornreich, no research was located in which his techniques were used in research with children. Because the procedure might be expected to illuminate aspects of children's problem solving that have not been explored previously, it was used in the present study. The performance of third- and sixth-grade children and college students was studied under two levels of coding demands. In one condition the visual stimulus objects terminated immediately following choice responses. Thus the subjects indicated which hypotheses were still viable in the absence of the four-dimensional stimulus objects. It was necessary for these subjects to remember aspects of the chosen stimulus, at least long enough to specify individual hypotheses and, when necessary (following errors), recode without benefit of the four-dimensional stimulus objects. In the second condition, the stimulus objects remained in view until subjects finished choosing from among the decomposed list of hypotheses. In both conditions a feedback lamp, mounted directly above the panel on which the correct stimulus object was projected, flashed on immediately following choice responses and remained illuminated until the subject finished choosing individual hypotheses.

Method

SUBJECTS

The subjects were 40 third graders (mean CA = 8:8 years), 40 sixth graders (mean CA = 11:9) and 40 college students (mean CA range 18–22 years). The children were drawn from schools serving middle- and upper-middle-SES families. Twenty subjects of each age level were randomly assigned to each condition.

MATERIALS AND GENERAL PROCEDURE

Each subject received a series of eight bivalued four-dimensional problems in which stimulus sequences were constructed according to an orthogonality criterion. Each problem was 10 trials in length. Four pretraining problems were followed by four experimental problems. The same four dimensions (shape, size, color, line position) were used in all problems, but each involved a different pair of shapes (e.g., circle versus square). The solution to each of the four pretraining problems was drawn from a different dimension. This was also true in the experimental problems.

The stimuli, 35-mm slides, were projected from behind a large interface that hid the apparatus from view, were presented on two 4- × 5.5-inch screens mounted 1.25 inches apart. The heights of the projected figures were 1 and 2 inches.

A red feedback lamp was mounted 1 inch above the vertical midline of each screen. After subjects indicated their choice responses by pushing one of the two screens upon which the stimuli were projected, the lamp above the screen containing the correct cue was illuminated, and it remained lit until the subjects finished choosing among the decomposed hypotheses.

These decomposed hypotheses were presented on the front of the interface, above the feedback lamps. Each of the eight individual hypotheses was appended to white 3- × 5-inch cards, and these cards were mounted on sheets of heavy black construction paper measuring 13.5 inches vertically and 22 inches horizontally. The printing on the 3 × 5 cards was black. Below the printing that designated the individual hypothesis was a circular "red button" that was .75 inch in diameter. The subject was instructed to push the buttons to indicate "which things could still be correct" following each choice response. An example of the

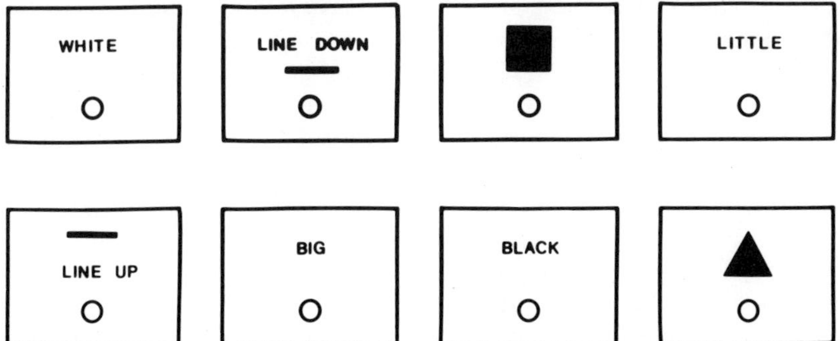

Figure 7.1. An example of the decomposed set of hypotheses presented to the subjects on each trial.

decomposed set of hypotheses is presented in Figure 7.1. The cards in the 2 × 4 array were mounted on the bottom half of the sheet of black construction paper, separated by .375 inch.

A different array of decomposed hypotheses was presented on each trial. This was done to prevent the subjects from using the positions, or locations, of individual hypotheses as mnemonics. No individual hypothesis occupied the same location in the 2 × 4 array on two consecutive trials; otherwise the locations were randomly determined.

On each trial the subject first pushed the screen that contained the chosen four-dimensional stimulus object. The feedback lamp was illuminated immediately when the screen was depressed. In one condition, called "stimulus absent," the stimuli projected on the screens terminated when choice responses were executed. In the other condition, "stimulus present," the four-dimensional stimuli remained in view while the subject selected individual hypotheses from among the decomposed array. In both conditions the feedback lamp remained illuminated until the subject finished selecting individual hypotheses. The experimenter then pressed a button that terminated the feedback lamp and advanced the slide projector to the next stimulus pair. There was then a 2-second intertrial interval. During this interval the experimenter lifted the exposed array of decomposed hypotheses, suspended from four large ringbinders, over the top of the interface to expose the next array.

Results

All analyses were based on data derived from the four experimental problems presented to each subject. The design of the experiment was a 3 (age level) × 2 (stimulus condition: present versus absent) factorial. Newman–Keuls tests were used to evaluate simple effects. Four kinds of processes were evaluated: learning, number of hypotheses sampled, coding, and memory.

The trial of last error (TLE) was taken as the measure of learning efficiency. The average TLE for each age level and stimulus condition, along with the average number of problems solved out of the 80 administered to each group, is presented in Table 7.8. The solution criterion was four consecutive correct feedback-trial responses. Analysis of variance performed on the TLE data revealed significant effects of age, $F(2, 114) = 40.35$, $p < .05$ (the criterion adopted in all analyses), and stimulus condition, $F(1, 114) = 8.11$. The interaction did not quite reach significance, $F(2, 114) = 3.01$. Newman–Keuls tests revealed that the college students showed better performance than the sixth graders, who showed better performance than the third graders.

Hypothesis sampling was measured by evaluating the average

TABLE 7.8
The Learning Data for Each Stimulus Condition and Age Level

	Measure			
	Trial of last error		Number of problems solved	
	Stimulus condition		Stimulus condition	
Age level	Present	Absent	Present	Absent
Third grade	4.64	5.70	54/80	39/80
Sixth grade	3.26	4.85	72/80	53/80
College students	2.05	1.91	80/80	80/80

TABLE 7.9
The Average Number of Hypotheses Exhibited on Each of the First Three Trials for Each Stimulus Condition and Age Level

	Stimulus condition					
	Present			Absent		
Age level	Trial 1	Trial 2	Trial 3	Trial 1	Trial 2	Trial 3
Third grade	2.81	2.15	1.90	2.98	2.73	2.38
Sixth grade	3.34	2.55	1.99	3.66	2.84	2.30
College students	3.94	2.03	1.03	3.99	2.04	1.14

number of hypotheses exhibited by the subjects of each group on each of the first three trials. These data are presented in Table 7.9. As may be seen in the table, all groups showed a steady reduction across the three trials, but only the college students showed essentially perfect processing. The college students narrowed the set from almost four hypotheses to slightly more than one hypothesis across the three trials. The overall analysis indicated that the Age × Stimulus condition × Trials interaction was significant, $F(4, 228) = 3.44$. Therefore, analyses were performed on each trial separately.

Analysis of variance performed on the first-trial data revealed only an effect of age, $F(2, 114) = 10.95$. The college students showed significantly more hypotheses than the sixth graders, who showed more than the third graders. On the second trial both age, $F(2, 114) = 5.52$, and stimulus condition were significant, $F(1, 114) = 3.14$. The third and sixth graders did not differ from each other, but both showed more hypotheses than the college students. On the third trial only the age effect was significant, $F(2, 114) = 17.84$. Again, there was no difference among the third and sixth graders, but both exhibited more hypotheses than the college students. Thus the college students began with a larger set of hypotheses on the first trial than either group of children, but narrowed the set more quickly so that it was smaller on the second and third trials than was the set considered by either the third-grade or sixth-grade children. The sixth graders began with a larger set than the third graders, but the two did not differ on trials two or three.

On each trial the subjects selected one or more hypotheses from among the decomposed set of eight. Thus the extent to which these hypotheses were consistent with the cues included in the four-dimensional stimulus object designated as correct on the given trial provided a measure of how efficiently the subjects coded the stimulus of choice when feedback was positive. When feedback was negative, these data provided a measure of recoding efficiency. The analyses were first performed only on the trials that preceded the TLE. The proportions of hypotheses that corresponded to those included in the stimulus object designated as correct on each of these trials following positive and following negative feedback are presented in Table 7.10.

Analysis of variance performed on the data following positive feedback revealed significant effects of age, $F(2, 114) = 12.33$, stimulus condition, $F(1, 114) = 27.49$, and their interaction, $F(2, 114) = 10.11$. Newman–Keuls tests indicated that the two groups of college students did not differ from each other or from the third and sixth graders in the stimulus-present condition, but all four groups exhibited better coding performance than the third and sixth graders in the stimulus-absent condition. The latter two groups did not differ from each other. Analysis of the data following negative feedback again revealed effects of age, $F(2, 114) = 18.76$, stimulus condition, $F(1, 114) = 46.12$, and their interaction, $F(2, 114) = 9.30$. Newman–Keuls tests revealed the same pattern of differences that was obtained following positive feedback. Thus the two adult groups and the children in the stimulus-present condition exhibited equally good coding and recoding processes, as measured by the proportions of hypotheses that were consistent with the four-dimensional stimulus object designated as correct on each trial. The children in the stimulus-absent condition, however, showed significantly worse performance on both the coding and recoding measures.

TABLE 7.10
The Average Proportions of Hypotheses Exhibited on Each Trial Prior to the Trial of Last Error That Were Consistent with the Stimulus Information Provided When Feedback Was Positive and When It Was Negative

	Feedback			
	Positive		Negative	
	Stimulus condition		Stimulus condition	
Age level	Present	Absent	Present	Absent
Third grade	1.00	.85	.99	.74
Sixth grade	.98	.90	.96	.75
College students	1.00	1.00	1.00	.97

The same analyses were performed on the post-TLE data, when by definition feedback was positive, and on the TLE data themselves when, of course, feedback was negative. Analyses of variance revealed the same significant effects obtained in the pre-TLE data, and Newman-Keuls tests revealed the same pattern of findings among the six groups. The two groups of college students and the children in the stimulus-present condition showed statistically equivalent performance that was superior to that exhibited by the children in the stimulus-absent condition.

Two measures of memory were derived from the data. The first concerned the proportions of hypotheses exhibited on a given trial, F_i, that were consistent with the stimulus information provided on Trial F_i and on the preceding feedback trial, $F_i - 1$. On Trial F_i, for example, the correct stimulus object might contain the cues "large, black, square, line up." Suppose that on Trial $F_i - 1$ the correct stimulus object contained "small, black, circle, line up." This measure was concerned with the proportion of individual hypotheses exhibited on Trial F_i that were globally consistent with stimulus information provided on Trials F_i and $F_i - 1$; that is, of all hypotheses exhibited on Trial F_i, what proportion was either "black" or "line up?" These were the only two cues that were contained in the stimulus object designated correct on both Trial F_i and Trial F_i. The measure was derived from only the pre-TLE data.

The proportions following positive and negative feedback on Trial F_i, for $F_i = +$ and for $F_i = -$ for each age level and stimulus condition are presented in Table 7.11. The data were collapsed over positive and negative feedback on Trial F_i in computing the proportions in the table. Analysis of variance performed on the data for $F_i = +$ revealed significant effects of age, $F(2, 98) = 15.19$, and stimulus condition, $F(1, 98) = 7.63$. The interaction approached significant, $F(2, 98) = 2.98$, $p < .10$. The number of degrees of freedom is reduced on these measures because a few

TABLE 7.11

The Proportions of Hypotheses Exhibited on a Given Trial (F_i) That Were Consistent with Stimulus Information Provided on Trial F_i and the Immediately Preceding Trial, F_i-1, When Feedback Was Positive ($F_i = +$) and Negative ($F_i = -$) on Trial F_i

	Feedback on Trial F_i			
	$F_i = +$		$F_i = -$	
	Stimulus condition		Stimulus condition	
Age level	Present	Absent	Present	Absent
Third grade	.62	.63	.57	.43
Sixth grade	.74	.64	.55	.49
College students	1.00	.91	.90	.77

subjects solved all of their problems by the second trial. The analyses were adjusted for unequal numbers of observations per cell. The college students showed better performance than either the third or sixth graders, who did not differ from each other. Following negative feedback at F_i, age, $F(2, 98) = 18.91$, and stimulus condition reached significance, $F(1, 98) = 5.90$. The third and sixth graders did not differ from each other, but both showed worse performance than the college students.

The second memory measure concerned the extent to which hypotheses exhibited on Trial $F_i - 1$ were remembered on trial F_i. This measure evaluated the extent to which the hypotheses exhibited on the preceding trial that are confirmed on the present trial are remembered and exhibited again. Assume, for example, that the subject exhibits the hypotheses "large, black, circle" on some $F_i - 1$ trial. Suppose on Trial F_i this subject chooses the four-dimensional stimulus object containing "small, black, circle, line down" and receives positive feedback. If the subject exhibited the hypotheses "black, circle," or "black, circle, line down," the score would be 1.00 (2 of 2). If, however, the exhibited hypotheses were "small, black," or "small, black, line down," the score would be .50. Unlike the preceding measure, which evaluated the subjects' memories for information included in the four-dimensional stimulus objects, this measure evaluated the extent to which they remembered the hypotheses they exhibited on Trial $F_i - 1$ when these hypotheses were included in the stimulus object that was chosen and was correct on Trial F_i. The measure was computed only over the first three feedback trials. The data are presented in Table 7.12. Analysis of variance revealed that only the effect of age was significant, $F(2, 114) = 23.51$. Newman–Keuls tests revealed that the college students remembered more than the children, but the third and sixth graders did not differ from each other.

TABLE 7.12
The Probabilities That Hypotheses Exhibited That Were Confirmed on Trial F_i-1 Were Exhibited on F_i [a]

	Stimulus condition	
Age level	Present	Absent
Third grade	.66	.58
Sixth grade	.67	.64
College students	.98	.94

[a] This measure was computed only over the first three trials.

Discussion

The model presented in Chapter 3 predicts interactions between age (or cognitive level) and task variables. These interactions were obtained on three of the seven dependent measures derived from the data: coding efficiency, recoding efficiency, and narrowing the set of hypotheses across the first three trials. In addition, two interactions approached significance ($p<.10$): the learning measure and memory for Trial $F_i - 1$ stimulus information on Trial F_i when $F_i = +$.

Only the results yielded by the college students in the present study can be directly compared with previous research. Kornreich (1968) reported that college students showed four hypotheses on the first trial, two on the second, and one (the solution) on the third trial in most of their problems. College students in the present experiment showed this pattern in 143 of their 160 problems (89%). Of the 40 subjects, 27 showed the pattern in all four of their problems, and all but two of the remainder did so in three of them.

Among the children, however, things were quite different. Only two children, both sixth graders, showed the perfect-processing pattern in all four of their problems. Three others showed the pattern in three problems (one was a third grader). Two sixth graders showed the pattern in two problems, and 10 children did so in one problem (three were third graders). None of the remaining 63 children ever showed the four, two, one pattern.

Schonebaum (1973, described in Chapter 4) reported an experiment in which he addressed some of the issues of concern in the present study. One datum he reported involved the number of hypotheses coded by third-, fifth-, and seventh-grade children and college students on the first trial of each of a series of four-dimensional problems. His estimate for third graders was about 3.3 hypotheses, and among fifth and seventh graders, about 3.5. Schonebaum's estimate for third graders is somewhat higher than the 2.9 hypotheses obtained in the present experiment (Table 7.9); his estimate for fifth and seventh graders was almost identical to the score for sixth graders presented in Table 7.9. Schonebaum's estimate for college students was nearly 4.0, as was the score (3.96) obtained in the present study.

Schonebaum gave his subjects a series of two-trial problems. A pair of multidimensional stimulus objects was presented on the first trial, and feedback followed the choice response. The second trial was a probe: All dimensions were neutralized except one that was tested in the given problem. In one condition, the first-trial stimulus object persisted for 4 seconds following response and feedback; then following a short interval the pair of stimulus objects that served as a probe was presented. In the second condition, the first-trial stimuli were extinguished immediately following feedback.

Schonebaum published the probabilities that his subjects made errors on probe trials following positive and negative feedback in the two conditions. These measures are similar to the measures of coding and recoding that were used in the present experiment. Although the methodologies were considerably different, the two experiments yielded roughly comparable results. His results, which were collapsed over two-, four-, and six-dimensional problems, are presented in Table 7.13 (Schonebaum, 1973, p. 420). For convenience, the comparable measures from the present experiment (see Table 7.10) are also presented (the scores in parentheses) in Table 7.13. Schonebaum's fifth and seventh graders exhibited very similar performance, and were averaged for comparison with the sixth graders in the present experiment.

In the stimulus-absent condition the findings of the two experiments were similar following both positive and negative feedback, despite the differences in the procedures that were used. In the stimulus-present condition Schonebaum's subjects did not perform as well as the ones in the present experiment. This was not surprising, though, because Schonebaum permitted the first-trial stimulus objects to persist for only 4 seconds following response (and feedback), and they were not present when the probe stimuli were presented. In the present experiment the four-dimensional stimulus objects persisted until the subject finished selecting among the

TABLE 7.13
The Proportions of Hypotheses Exhibited That Were Consistent with the Stimulus Information Provided on the Given Trial When Feedback Was Positive and When It Was Negative [a]

	Feedback			
	Positive		Negative	
	Stimulus condition		Stimulus condition	
Age level	Present	Absent	Present	Absent
Third grade	.90 (1.00)[b]	.83 (.85)	.86 (.99)	.77 (.74)
Sixth grade[c]	.91 (.98)	.89 (.90)	.89 (.96)	.80 (.75)
College	.98 (1.00)	.97 (1.00)	.95 (1.00)	.92 (.97)

[a] Adapted from Schonebaum, 1973, p. 420.

[b] Data from the present study are presented in parentheses.

[c] Schonebaum's data for fifth and seventh graders were averaged for comparison with sixth graders in the present study.

The memory data obtained in the present experiment indicated that on a given trial, F_i, the children had considerable difficulty remembering stimulus information contained in the four-dimensional stimulus object designated correct on the preceding trial, $F_i - 1$. When feedback was negative on Trial F_i, the probabilities that they showed hypotheses consistent with stimulus information from both F_i and $F_i - 1$ ranged from .43 to .57 (see Table 7.11). Chance level, given that no subject ever showed more than four hypotheses on a given trial, is .50. Following positive feedback on Trial F_i, the performance was somewhat better; the probabilities ranged from .62 to .74. A second memory measure was concerned with how well the children remembered the hypotheses they exhibited on the preceding trial. Hypotheses that were exhibited on Trial $F_i - 1$ and confirmed on Trial F_i ($F_i = +$) were exhibited on Trial F_i with probabilities ranging from .58 to .67 (Table 7.12). Thus the children apparently had some difficulty even remembering which hypotheses they just exhibited. Among the college students the probabilities ranged from .94 to .98.

The results of the present experiment were presented in terms of simple averages for each age level and stimulus condition. There were, however, considerable differences in the modes of approach taken by different subgroups of the children. A few children chose one hypothesis from the decomposed array on each trial. Others chose three or four hypotheses on each trial before TLE. The remaining children usually started the problem with three or four hypotheses, but then narrowed the set on subsequent trials.

Thus the children of each group were classified according to performance on the first three trials of each problem: *(a)* children who showed three or four hypotheses on most of these trials (31 of 80); *(b)* those who exhibited one hypothesis on each trial (16 of 80); and *(c)* the remaining children (33 of 80). Because the college students all showed the same perfect-processing approach, their protocols were not considered. The average number of hypotheses exhibited by each of the subgroups on the first, second, and third trial among the children of each grade level and stimulus condition is presented in Figure 7.2. The number of children in each subgroup is indicated in the figure. The average number of hypotheses exhibited by each of the subgroups from the fourth trial before TLE through the criterion of four consecutive correct feedback-trial responses is presented in Figure 7.3.

The general pattern was for the various subgroups of children who exhibited more than one hypothesis to narrow the set somewhat by the TLE and to continue to narrow the set during the criterion run. The subgroup of third graders in the stimulus-present condition who showed

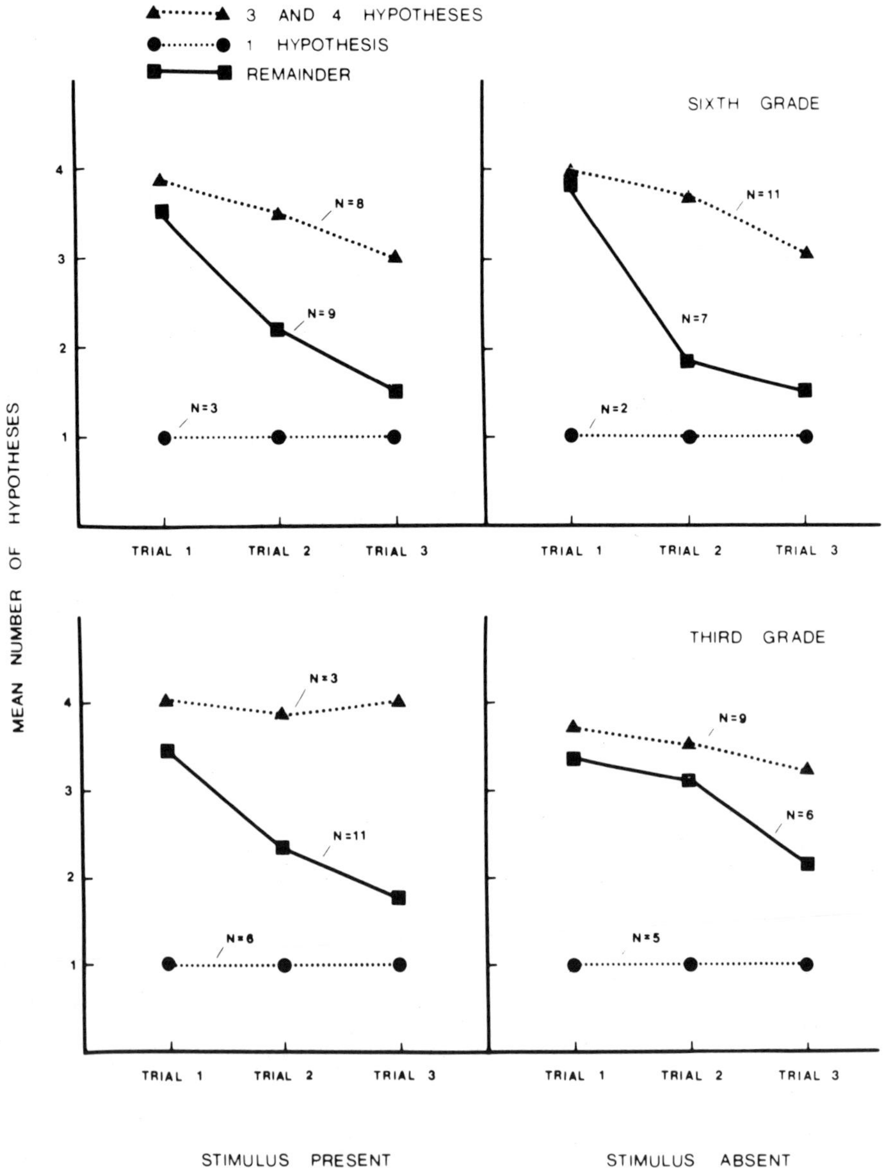

Figure 7.2. The average number of hypotheses exhibited by each of the three subgroups of children of each grade level (sixth grade top) and stimulus condition on the first three trials. The number of children in each subgroup is indicated in the figure.

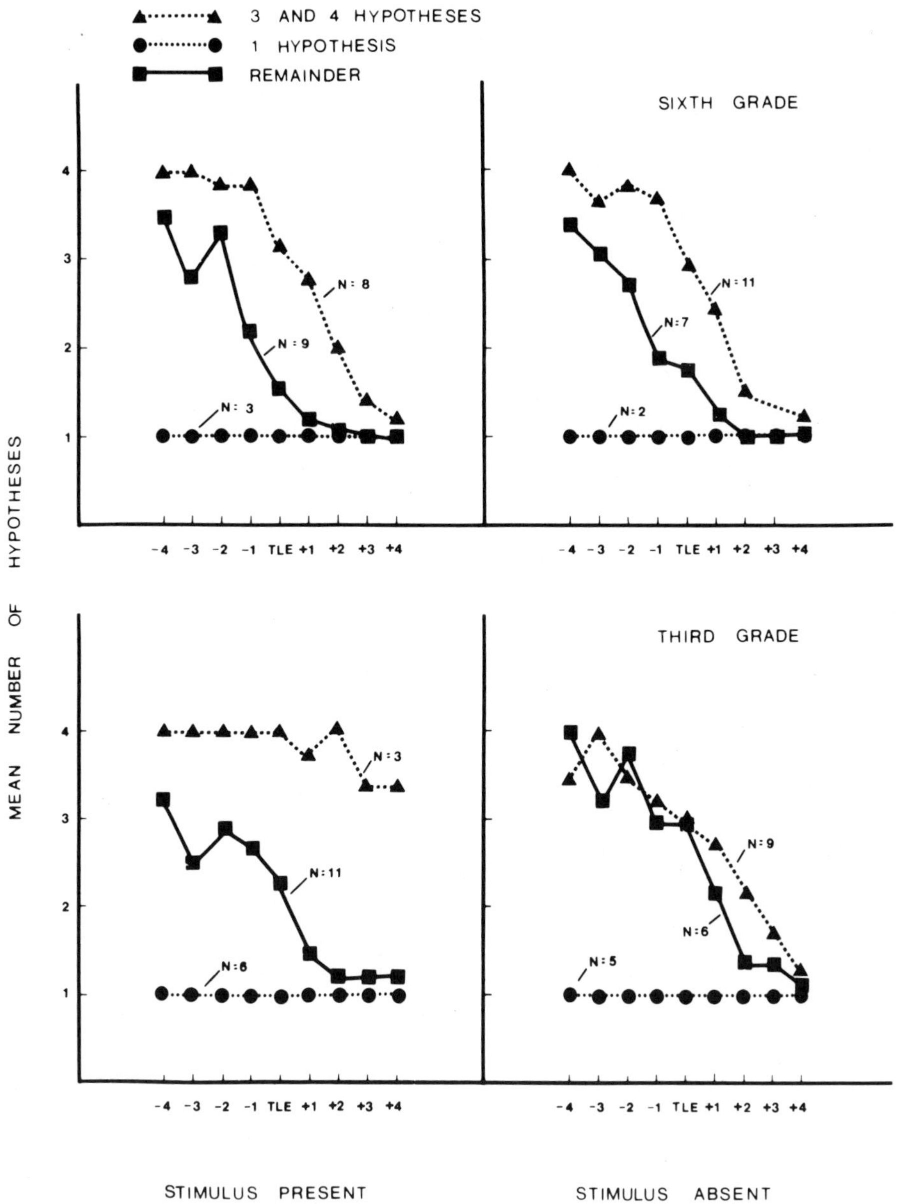

Figure 7.3. The average number of hypotheses exhibited by each of the three subgroups of children of each grade level (sixth grade top) and stimulus condition both before and after the last error (TLE). The number of children in each subgroup is indicated in the figure.

three or four hypotheses on each of the first three trials, however, showed 3.5 hypotheses even on the last criterion trial. These children solved their problems with about the same frequency (75%) as the remaining third graders in the stimulus-absent condition (Table 7.8). Their performance suggests they may have treated the decomposed stimulus array as a matching-to-sample task (Fellows, 1968).

Most of the children (64 of 80) began the problems by monitoring three or four hypotheses. They reduced the set somewhat during the trials that preceded the TLE and, with the exception of three children, continued to reduce the set that was monitored during the criterion run. By the fourth trial after the TLE the average number of hypotheses exhibited ranged from 1.0 to 1.3 (excluding the same three children). Levine (1970) has shown that college students routinely monitor several hypotheses both before the TLE and after it. After the TLE they continue to narrow the set until it contains only the solution hypothesis. To our knowledge, however, this is the first demonstration that children can be induced to behave similarly.

Previous research indicates that most children work with only one hypothesis at a time under standard conditions that do not include a decomposed array of the possible solutions (e.g., Cantor & Spiker, 1978; Eimas, 1969; Gholson *et al.*, 1972, 1973; Ingalls & Dickerson, 1969; Offenbach, 1974, 1979; Phillips & Levine, 1975; Reese, 1977; Rieber, 1969; Weisz, 1977). The children's poor memories for stimulus information from Trial $F_i - 1$, and even for the hypotheses they tried on that trial (Tables 7.11 and 7.12) prevent them from processing with the same efficiency as college students. At least in part, they appear to approach the decomposed array of hypotheses as a matching-to-sample task. The decomposed array serves as a constant remainder as to the possible solutions to the task, which may be a very important part of the procedure, because Ingalls and Dickerson (1969) have shown that most children completely omit one or two dimensions from consideration during standard four-dimensional problems that contain blank-trial probes.

Kornreich's (1968) procedure appears promising because it yields orderly results and provides measures of performance that are not obtained when other approaches are used to study children's problem solving. Unfortunately, the exact role of the decomposed array of hypotheses on the children's approaches to the task cannot be specified at present. Identifiable subgroups of children appear to use the array differently both before and after the TLE. The general procedure appears to enhance processing, but exactly what is responsible for the improved performance remains to be determined.

Experiment 8: Selective Attention and Information Processing in Normal and Underachieving Readers[2]

CRAIG BARRINGER AND BARRY GHOLSON

In recent years theorists have frequently cast the study of reading processes in an information-processing mold (e.g., Geyer, 1972; K. S. Goodman, 1970, 1972, 1973; Rayner & Kaiser, 1975; Samuels, Begy, & Chen, 1976). K. S. Goodman's model, a well-known example, assumes that reading is a predictive process: The reader samples textual information from several levels (e.g., graphic, morphemic, syntactic) and uses the sampled information to generate and test hypotheses about forthcoming material. Thus skilled reading—as opposed to unskilled—is said to result from more accurate first guesses based upon better sampling techniques, greater control over language structure, broadened experiences, and increased conceptual development (p. 266). This model of reading is similar to other theoretical positions (e.g., Allport, 1955; Bruner & Postman, 1948; Savin, 1963; Solomon & Postman, 1952), which have been referred to collectively as hypothesis/test models (cf. Samuels *et al.*, 1976). In general, the evidence is in line with these conceptualizations (cf. K. S. Goodman, 1970, 1972; Y. M. Goodman, 1972; LaBerge & Samuels, 1974; Rayner & Kaiser, 1975; Samuels *et al.*, 1976; Samuels, Dahl, & Archwamety, 1974).

Samuels *et al.* (1976), for example, compared the word recognition skills of normal and underachieving readers. As predicted by the hypothesis/test theory, normal readers exhibited relatively shorter word recognition latencies and used contextual cues more accurately to predict forthcoming words than did underachievers. These findings corroborated the results of an earlier training study (Samuels *et al.*, 1974), which was also based upon the hypothesis/test model. In general, findings of this kind are taken to support the contention that normal readers sample and use information more efficiently than underachievers.

The information-sampling mechanism, then, plays an important role according to these models of reading; what remains to be explained is the development of better information-sampling techniques (K. S. Goodman, 1970). Because appropriate attentional responses are requisite to efficient information sampling, LaBerge and Samuels (1974) have

2. This report is based upon a doctoral dissertation submitted to the faculty at Memphis State University by the first author as part of the requirements for the Ph.D degree. The second author directed the work.

formulated an information-processing model of reading that outlines the development of automatic attention responses. Schneider and Shiffrin (1977) have discussed a similar mechanism within a more general theory of cognition. Each of these theories postulates two different modes of attention. One is labeled *accuracy* (LaBerge & Samuels, 1974) or *controlled processing* (Schneider & Shiffrin, 1977). The other is referred to as *automaticity* (LaBerge & Samuels, 1974) or *automatic detection* (Shiffrin & Schneider, 1977). The distinction between the two modes has been confirmed by a respectable amount of empirical evidence.

Controlled processing (accuracy) is characteristic of the initial phase of solving any problem, including the problems that are inherent in reading. It involves the conscious deployment of attention at a micro-level of stimulus analysis; that is, an attempt is made to focus attention on the relevant stimulus components in the problem environment. Thus controlled processing involves decisions to attend to some aspects of a stimulus complex and to ignore, or screen out, others. The level at which controlled processing is implemented depends upon task demands. If the task involves, for example, matching colors, selectivity may occur at a relatively peripheral level. In a complex task like reading, however, attentional selectivity will occur at a more central, semantic level (Shiffrin & Schneider, 1977, p. 184). The level at which controlled processing is deployed, then, depends upon the novelty and complexity of the problem at hand. The efficiency of controlled processing at any level would depend upon the child's cognitive abilities (e.g., Gholson & Beilin, 1979; Piaget, 1970; Stauffer, 1970).

When a high degree of accuracy is achieved by the child, an alternative information-sampling mode may be employed. This mode, automaticity, does not involve the conscious, purposeful deployment of attention. Instead, as the label implies, "automatic detection refers to the case when a stimulus gives rise to an automatic attention response that bypasses the need for serial search through either memory or the display [Shiffrin & Schneider, 1977, p. 143]." The achievement of automaticity depends upon practice, degree of attention control, and the constancy of stimuli relevant to solution (LaBerge & Samuels, 1974; Shiffrin & Schneider, 1977).

In line with the general conception discussed in the preceding paragraphs, a number of investigators have demonstrated that children who differ on tests of reading achievement show corresponding differences on various measures of attention (e.g., Hallahan, 1975; Ross, 1976; Tarver & Hallahan, 1974). This covariation has been taken to support the contention that attentional deficits are, at least in part, responsible for reading underachievement (cf. Dykman, Ackerman, Clements, & Peters, 1971; E.

J. Gibson, 1970; Ross, 1976). The usual approach has been to measure some facet of attention and then relate performance on the attention measure to scores obtained on reading-achievement tests (e.g., Anderson, Halcomb, & Doyle, 1973; Noland & Shuldt, 1971).

Dyckman and his colleagues (Dykman *et al.*, 1971; Dykman, Walls, Suzuki, Ackerman, & Peters, 1970), for example, used a vigilance task, which tested the child's ability to detect and respond to periodic light signals. Their general finding was that children who did poorly on tests of reading (and other academic skills) also made significantly more detection-response errors than normal readers. Based on these findings, Dykman *et al.* (1971) proposed a neuropsychological theory of learning disabilities. Specifically, they suggested that underachievers of normal IQ cannot inhibit reticulo-cortical arousal; hence, they are overresponsive to irrelevant stimuli. Other researchers have obtained corresponding differences between normal and underachieving readers in vigilance tasks (Anderson *et al.*, 1973; Douglas, 1972; Grassi, 1970; Noland & Shuldt, 1971); but theoretical interpretations vary.

Normal and underachieving readers have also been compared on various matching tasks (Elkind, Larson, & Van Doorninck, 1965; Guyer & Friedman, 1976; Kagan, Rosman, Day & Phillips, 1964). Kagan (1965) used the matching familiar figures task to assess children as either reflective or impulsive (see Chapter 4). He reported that, compared to their reflective peers, impulsive children exhibited more errors on tests of word recognition. Others have obtained similar results (e.g., Hallahan, Kauffman, & Ball, 1973). Hagen and Kail (1975) concluded that impulsive responders are relatively less planful than their reflective peers when they search a stimulus configuration for relevant information. Thus they show deficits in tasks such as reading that require controlled processing (Day, 1975; Wright & Vlietstra, 1975).

Hidden- and embedded-figures tasks also reveal differences between normal and underachieving readers. Elkind *et al.* (1965), for example, reported that children who were two years behind their peers on tests of reading achievement showed more errors on a hidden-figures task. Others have obtained similar findings using Witkin's (e.g., Witkin, Dyk, Paterson, Goodenough, & Karpf, 1962) disembedding problems as measures of field independence (Guyer & Friedman, 1975; Sabatino & Ysseldyke, 1975). This research has shown that there is a developmental increase in the child's perceptual independence from background stimuli and, compared to normal readers, underachievers progress toward field independence at a slower pace.

Another procedure that is commonly used to study children's attention involves a central-incidental recall task (Gottfried, 1976; Hagen,

1967, 1972; Hagen & Hale, 1973; Hale & Green, 1976; Hale & Morgan, 1973). The child is presented with paired pictures on successive trials, with prior instructions to selectively remember one member of the pair. No instructions are usually given regarding the second member of each pair. The central (relevant) stimulus objects are drawn from one class (or dimension) and the others (incidental) are drawn from a second. Subsequently, serial-recall trials are administered, first on the central and then on the incidental materials.

Among normal readers the general finding is that recall of central (relevant) information increases during the elementary-school years, while incidental recall remains unchanged or falls slightly (Hagan, 1967, 1972; Hagen & Hale, 1973). Hallahan (e.g., Hallahan *et al.*, 1973) and others (e.g., Ross, 1976) have hypothesized that the underachieving reader lags behind the normal reader in this developmental progression. In line with this suggestion, numerous investigators have reported that underachieving readers show deficits in selective attention relative to normal readers (e.g., Baker & Maddell, 1965; Hallahan *et al.*, 1973; Mercer, Cullinan, Hallahan, & LaFleur, 1975; Mondani & Tutko, 1969; Silverman, Davids, & Andrews, 1963; Tarver, Hallahan, S. Cohen, & Kauffman, 1977; Tarver, Hallahan, Kauffman, & Ball, 1976).

These experiments on vigilance, figure matching, disembedding, and selective attention represent a growing body of research concerned with attentional deficits that accompany low reading-achievement scores. This convergence of findings, along with reports that children's scores on various measures of attention are highly correlated (e.g., Hallahan *et al.*, 1973; Keogh & Donlon, 1972), has led to the conclusion that a single cognitive deficit underlies the performance of underachieving readers in all the tasks described above (e.g., Ross, 1976). Hagen and Kail (1975) have summarized this growing theoretical concensus: "There appears to be an emerging tendency (developmentally) to employ task-appropriate strategies . . . which certainly involve perception, but also involve a central, cognitive component [p. 188]." If the attentional performance exhibited by underachieving readers is, in fact, due to a central-processing deficit, then the processes involved must be both conceptualized *and* studied within a broad cognitive framework (K. S. Goodman, 1972; LaBerge & Samuels, 1974; Rosenthal & Zimmerman, 1978; Shiffrin & Schneider, 1977; Wright & Vlietstra, 1975). Tasks in which attention is studied in relative isolation from other cognitive processes may reveal the deficits, but they will not yield much information about the cognitive mechanisms responsible for them.

The present experiment, then, involved an attempt to explore the cognitive mechanisms responsible for attention deficits that are obtained when normal readers are compared with underachievers. Experiments 5 and 6, reported earlier in this chapter, were concerned with one facet of children's attention during problem solving. This involved the efficiency with which they switched their attention from a multidimensional stimulus object that was disconfirmed on a given trial to the one that contained the solution. This attentional process is fundamental, because the stimulus object that contains the solution must be attended to before the correct cue can be coded for further processing.

There is, however, a second facet of attention that must also be considered. This involves selecting out, from among all the cues available, those which are to be coded into the system for further processing (Adams & Shepp, 1975; T. S. Kendler, 1979; Neisser, 1966; Sperling, 1960; Zeaman & House, 1963). Because this second, *selective* aspect of attention involves controlled processing (LaBerge & Samuels, 1974; Shiffrin & Schneider, 1977), it was chosen for study in the present experiment. Normal and underachieving readers were presented with problem-solving tasks in which stimulus cues specified as relevant to solution were embedded in multidimensional stimulus objects that contained both relevant and incidental (irrelevant to solution) information. The children's performance was studied in a series of problems in which the relevant stimulus information either varied from problem to problem or was constant.

Method

SUBJECTS

The subjects were 160 children drawn from fourth- and fifth-grade classes in a public school that serves families of middle SES levels. Half the children were at least 1.5 years below grade level on a test of reading achievement (Durost, Bixler, Hildreth, Lund, & Wrightstone, 1971). The remaining children, normal readers, scored at or above grade level. The age, IQ, and reading-level data for the normal and underachieving readers are presented in Table 7.14. Analyses of variance ($2 \times 2 \times 2$, see p. 205) performed on the age and IQ data revealed no differences among the groups. Except for restrictions specified below, the assignment of children to groups was random.

DESIGN

Half the children at each reading level were presented with bivalued four-dimensional problems. This was called the 4-dimension condition. The remaining children at each reading level were presented with eight-

TABLE 7.14

The Age, IQ, and Reading Level Data for the Normal and Underachieving Readers [a]

Reading level		Measure		
		Age	IQ	Reading score
Normals	(Mean)	10:6 years	97.4	5.2
	(Range)	8:9–12:1	91–110	4.0–8.7
Underachievers	(Mean)	10:5 years	98.7	2.69
	(Range)	9:4–11:1	92–112	1.5–3.5

[a]Both the mean and age range are included in the table.

dimensional problems: four dimensions were relevant to the solution and four were irrelevant. This was called the 8-dimension condition. The final factor involved division of the 4-dimension and 8-dimension conditions. Half the children in each of these conditions received problems in which the dimensions relevant to solution remained constant throughout 10 experimental problems. These conditions are labeled "constant" (4-dimension constant, 8-dimension constant). For the remaining children the dimensions relevant to solution varied from one experimental problem to the next. These conditions are called "variable" (4-dimension variable, 8-dimension variable). To summarize, then, the experiment compared the performance of children at two reading levels (normal, underachieving) in the presence or absence of irrelevant stimulus information (4-dimension, 8-dimension), with the dimensions relevant to solution either constant or variable from problem to problem (constant, variable). Thus the basic design was a 2 × 2 × 2 factorial.

MATERIALS

Each child was presented with a series of 15 bivalued problems. Each problem consisted of either four or all eight of the following dimensions: letter, color, size, border shape, border texture, box position, box volume (full versus empty), and number of borders (Gholson & Danziger, 1975; Levine, 1969, 1975). An example of an 8-dimension stimulus pair is presented in Figure 7.4. The stimulus sequence for each problem was constructed according to Levine's (1966) orthogonality criterion: Any series of three consecutive feedback trials logically specified the solution in all problems.

Additional unidimensional stimulus materials were used during pretraining. Each stimulus depicted only the two values of a given dimension. These were used to insure that the children had appropriate verbal labels for each dimension and could differentiate among the various dimensions. All stimulus materials were secured on 5- × 8-inch cards.

PRETRAINING

All subjects, tested individually, were pretrained with the procedures used to train children to give verbal statements of hypotheses on each trial. This procedure was described earlier in this chapter (Expt. 5). Modifications necessary to the present procedure are described below. All children were pretrained using stimulus sequences that corresponded to those presented in experimental problems in the 8-dimension variable condition.

At the outset of the first pretraining problem, the experimenter placed the eight unidimensional stimulus cards in front of the child. These surrounded the eight-dimensional stimulus pair. The experimenter labeled each value on each unidimensional stimulus card while pointing to it, and then to the corresponding cue in the bivalued eight-dimensional stimulus pair. These unidimensional stimuli were left in place during the entire problem (20 trials in lengths) and then removed.

At the outset of the second pretraining problem another set of unidimensional cards was produced (the sets were changed because values on the color and letter dimensions varied during pretraining). One card at a time was presented to the child. The child labeled each cue as the experimenter pointed to it; then the child was asked to point to the eight-dimensional stimulus object that contained the given cue. All errors were immediately corrected and the request was repeated. The four unidimensional cards containing cues relevant to solution were left in view while the child solved the problem. This procedure was repeated on pretraining Problems 3 and 4. The unidimensional stimulus cards were not used during the last (fifth) pretraining problem. The children met a criterion of 10 consecutive correct responses in the first three pretraining problems and five correct in the other two (see Expt. 5).

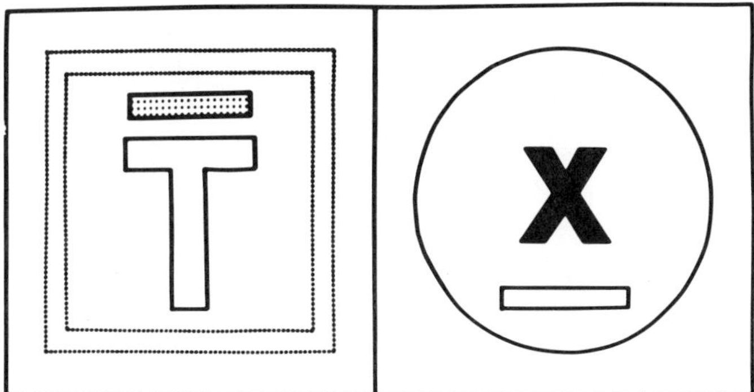

Figure 7.4. An example of an eight-dimensional stimulus pair.

EXPERIMENTAL PROBLEMS

The experiment proper consisted of ten 10-trial problems. The four types of problems were yoked to avoid any possible effects of differential dimension saliency (Odom, 1972, 1978). Consider, for example, the 4-dimension variable condition, in which the dimensions that were presented changed from problem to problem. In one problem size, color, border number, and box position were the cues that were presented. One or more of these dimensions was, of course, replaced in each of the remaining problems for children in this condition. Thus each problem was somewhat unique. Each of the 10 problems in this condition was yoked to a problem in the 4-dimension constant condition. Because one problem in the 4-dimension variable condition contained the dimensions size, color, border number, and box position, one set of 10 problems for the 4-dimension constant condition was composed entirely of these four dimensions. Thus 10 sets of 10 problems were used in the 4-dimension constant condition. Each set was assigned to two of the 20 children in each reading-level group in the 4-dimension constant condition.

The 8-dimension conditions were also yoked to one another in the manner described above. That is, the relevant dimensions in each of 10 sets of problems used in the 8-dimension constant condition were yoked to the relevant dimensions used in one of the 10 problems presented in the variable condition. In addition, each 8-dimension condition was yoked to its corresponding 4-dimension condition. The four relevant dimensions in the 8-dimension conditions corresponded to those in the comparable 4-dimension condition. Problem order was randomized independently for all children in each group.

One of the following feedback sequences was used in the first three trials of each problem: (*a*) positive feedback on the first two choice responses and negative on the third; (*b*) positive feedback on the first choice response and negative on the second and third; (*c*) negative feedback following the first choice response, positive following the second, and negative following the third. Feedback on trials after the third was determined by the logical solution to the problem. Feedback was verbal–directional: The experimenter said "yes, the answer is in this picture," or "no, the answer is in *this* picture." In either case he simultaneously pointed to the correct stimulus object for about 3 seconds before turning the card to expose the stimuli for the next trial.

Results

The children of both reading levels showed 100% response consistency and very few problems involving choice descriptions (about 1%), so these data will not be considered further (see Expts. 5 and 6 above). Six other dependent measures were derived from the protocols: solution data (correct choice responses on the last four trials), probabilities of maintaining confirmed hypotheses, maintaining disconfirmed hypotheses, sampling according to a local-consistency rule following negative feedback, and systems data. The first four measures were treated using $2 \times 2 \times 2 \times 10$ analyses of variance. The factors were reading level, presence versus absence of irrelevant information, constant versus variable relevant dimensions, and problems (practice). All the protocols, including both relevant and irrelevant hypotheses, were included in these analyses. The proportions were normalized by arcsin transformations (Guilford, 1954).

The solution data yielded significant effects of reading level, $F(1, 152) = 3.95, p < .05$ (the criterion adopted in all analyses), problems, $F(9, 1350) = 2.80$, and their interaction, $F(9, 1350) = 2.04$. The data for each reading level, in blocks of two problems, are presented in Table 7.15. The normal readers showed a significant increase in performance with practice but the underachievers did not.

The solution data also revealed significant effects of number of dimensions (4-dimension versus 8-dimension), $F(1, 152) = 14.19$, problem type (constant versus variable), $F(1, 152) = 7.48$, and their interaction, $F(1, 152) = 11.36$. These data are presented in Table 7.16. Children in three of the conditions showed statistically equivalent performance: 4-dimension constant, 4-dimension variable, and 8-dimension constant.

TABLE 7.15
The Probabilities That Children of Each Reading Level Solved Their Problems According to the Criterion Adopted, Presented in Blocks of Two Problems

	Problem blocks				
Reading level	1	2	3	4	5
Normal readers	.494	.612	.621	.684	.650
Underachievers	.543	.509	.578	.548	.513

TABLE 7.16
The Probabilities That Children in Each Condition Solved Their Problems

	Number of dimensions	
Problem type	Four	Eight
Constant	.630	.656
Variable	.619	.397

TABLE 7.17
The Probabilities That Children of the Two Reading Levels Maintained Confirmed Hypotheses, Presented in Blocks of Two Problems

	Problem blocks				
Reading level	1	2	3	4	5
Normal readers	.861	.912	.906	.897	.919
Underachievers	.861	.830	.881	.886	.851

Children in the 8-dimension variable condition exhibited significantly depressed performance.

Analysis of variance performed upon the probabilities that confirmed hypotheses were maintained revealed a main effect of problems, $F(9, 1350) = 2.52$, and a reading-level by problems interaction, $F(9, 1350) = 2.03$. The main effect of reading level approached significance ($p = .055$). The data for each reading level in blocks of two problems are presented in Table 7.17. Further analyses revealed that the performance of normal readers improved with practice, but that of the underachievers did not.

Analysis of the probabilities that disconfirmed hypotheses were maintained revealed only an effect of reading level, $F(1, 152) = 6.14$. The underachievers maintained disconfirmed hypotheses about twice as frequently (.081) as the normal readers (.044).

Analysis of the probabilities that hypotheses were sampled according to a local-consistency criterion revealed effects of reading level, $F(1, 152) = 5.45$, trials, $F(9, 1350) = 2.58$, and problem type, $F(1, 152) = 4.13$. The proportions were .865 and .824 among the normal and underachieving readers respectively. The scores were higher when relevant dimensions were constant (.862) across problems than when they varied (.828). The trials effect reflected a consistent increase in performance from the first problem (.803) to the seventh (.881). After the seventh problem, performance was constant in the range .86–.87.

The analyses presented above included all the data from the 8-dimension conditions; that is, no account was taken of whether stated hypotheses were those specified as relevant to solution. In order to evaluate the effects of the presence of irrelevant information upon the children's performance, the number of irrelevant hypotheses exhibited by the children of each group was analyzed separately. No child in the 4-dimension conditions ever stated an irrelevant hypothesis, that is, they confined their hypotheses to cues available in the stimulus objects that were presented. Thus only the 8-dimension conditions were included in this analysis.

The data were analyzed using a 2 (reading level) × 2 (constant versus variable relevant dimensions) × 10 (problems) analysis of variance. The

TABLE 7.18
The Probabilities That Children of Each Group Exhibited Hypotheses That Were Irrelevant to Solution in the Eight-Dimension Problems

	Reading level	
Problem type	Normals	Underachievers
Constant	.042	.159
Variable	.177	.239

effects of reading level, $F(1, 76) = 10.07$, problem type, $F(1, 76) = 18.38$, and problems were significant, $F(9, 680) = 3.14$. The children showed a slight improvement in performance over problems (about 6%). The data for each group, problems effects excluded, are presented in Table 7.18. The normal readers exhibited irrelevant hypotheses about half as frequently as the underachievers (11% versus 20%). When the relevant dimensions were constant from problem to problem, the percentage of irrelevant hypotheses was about 10%, but when they were variable the percentage doubled: 21%.

The final analysis involved the systems data for each group. The data from the 4-dimension conditions are presented in Table 7.19. Results from the 8-dimension conditions, including those problems in which the children exhibited irrelevant hypotheses, are presented in Table 7.20. The categories included in the tables are the three strategies and four processing errors (see Expts. 5 and 6): stimulus preference, unsystematic hypothesis sequences, local-consistency errors, and failure to maintain confirmed hypotheses. The rows in the tables do not sum to 200 problems per group because a few problems were excluded due to experimenter errors. No distinction was made between relevant and irrelevant hypotheses on this measure. This was done in order to avoid prejudicing the analysis in favor of the normal readers. Because systems are detected from the first three feedback trials and the hypothesis that follows each, only those data were considered in classifying the children's protocols.

The combined data of Tables 7.19 and 7.20 were submitted to a $2 \times 2 \times 2 \times 2$ (partitioned) χ^2 analysis. The factors were reading level, number of dimensions, problem type, and strategies versus processing errors. Only the effect of reading level was significant in this analysis, $\chi^2(1) = 7.39$. The normal readers showed significantly more strategies than the underachievers.

Discussion

Reading level produced significant effects on each dependent measure that was evaluated: four main effects and two interactions with practice. The normal readers either showed better performance through-

TABLE 7.19
The Number of Problems in Each Strategy and Processing-Error Category for the Normal and Underachieving Readers in the Four-Dimension Conditions (No Irrelevant Information)

	Category[a]						
	Strategy				Processing error		
Condition	Fo	D–ch	H–ch	S–P	Uns	LCE	Shift
Normal Readers							
Constant	25	76	28	5	28	19	11
Variable	25	84	23	2	17	37	11
Underachieving Readers							
Constant	19	58	26	11	31	35	15
Variable	22	62	20	14	41	33	7

[a]The categories are: focusing (Fo), dimension checking (D-ch), hypothesis checking (H-ch), stimulus preference (S-P), unsystematic hypothesis sequence (Uns), local-consistency error (LCE), and confirmed hypothesis rejected (Shift).

TABLE 7.20

The Number of Problems in Each Strategy and Processing-Error Category for the Normal and Underachieving Readers in the Eight-Dimension Conditions (Four Irrelevant Dimensions)

	Category[a]						
	Strategy				Processing error		
Condition	Fo	D–ch	H–ch	S–P	Uns	LCE	Shift
Normal readers							
Constant	10	90	17	8	20	35	8
Variable	0	100	24	4	26	32	9
Underachieving readers							
Constant	9	93	19	8	21	36	12
Variable	19	65	17	5	16	63	11

[a]The categories are: focusing (Fo), dimension checking (D-ch), hypothesis checking (H-ch), stimulus preference (S-P), unsystematic hypothesis sequence (Uns), local-consistency error (LCE), and confirmed hypothesis rejected (Shift).

out or improved with practice, while the underachievers did not. Problem type (constant versus variable relevant dimensions) and number of dimensions (4-dimension versus 8-dimension) also produced a few significant effects, but because neither variable interacted with reading level these effects will not be emphasized in this discussion.

The underachieving readers showed deficits in both facets of attention that were considered in designing this experiment. The local-consistency data indicated that they were less likely to switch their attention from a just-disconfirmed stimulus object to one that contained the solution. In addition, the underachievers exhibited irrelevant hypotheses about twice as often as normal readers (11 versus 20%). The underachievers, then, showed a controlled processing deficit relative to normal readers (LaBerge & Samuels, 1974; Schneider & Shiffrin, 1977).

It was suggested earlier, following Hagen and Kail (1975), that a central cognitive component was involved in the controlled processing deficits observed among underachieving readers. In terms of the present model, this central component would be embodied in the processor and would be reflected in the strategies that were exhibited. As expected, the underachievers showed significantly fewer strategies than the normal readers in both the 4-dimension and 8-dimension conditions. The differences obtained in the 8-dimension conditions could, of course, be accounted for in terms of the total amount of information the children attempted to process. The underachievers processed more irrelevant hypotheses and, consequently, there was a heavier load on the processor. The 4-dimension data revealed, however, that when no irrelevant information was contained in the stimulus materials, the underachievers showed strategies in about 15% fewer problems (52%) than the normal readers (67%).

It seems reasonable to conclude, therefore, that the inferior performance exhibited by underachieving readers was due to a central, logical deficit embodied in the processor (Hagen & Kail, 1975). Due to this deficiency the children sometimes failed to switch their attention from a disconfirmed stimulus object to one that contained the solution, were less able to attend selectively to dimensions specified as relevant to solution, and generated fewer strategies. In addition, the underachieving readers retained disconfirmed hypotheses and rejected confirmed hypotheses more often than normal readers, which suggests that they were also less attentive to feedback. In terms of the present model, then, a deficit in the central processor produced defective functioning in several cognitive subprocesses.

Hartman (1977 and Chapter 4) has provided data that may identify the central (logical) deficit responsible for the depressed performances of underachieving readers. Poor readers in the second and fourth grades showed much less sophisticated classification skills than did normal readers. Their classification skills correlated as highly with reading achievement scores as their reading scores did with each other. Classification skills also predicted the extent to which semantic memory was hierarchically organized (Collins & Quillian, 1972). It is possible, then, that the schemes embodied in the processor, which underlie classification performance and memory organization, also play an important role in the functioning of various attentional processes. Another possibility, of course, is that the logical schemes embodied in the processor affect memory organization directly and attentional processes only indirectly, through memory organization. Unfortunately, neither classification nor memory data were obtained in the present experiment, so these possibilities await direct investigation. Clearly, more precise measures of characteristics of the processor are called for. Only then will it be possible to evaluate the exact role of the processor in organizing and integrating the various cognitive subprocesses. It seems evident, though, that a central-processing deficit of some sort plays an important role in the inferior attentional performance exhibited by underachieving readers (Hagen & Kail, 1975; Hartman, 1977; LaBerge & Samuels, 1974; Shiffrin & Schneider, 1977).

Conclusions

Results of these experiments indicate that task manipulations sometimes radically alter the functioning of various cognitive subprocesses. Because these cognitive subprocesses regulate the flow of information to the processor, the children's problem-solving strategies were also affected by the manipulations. Experiment 5 demonstrated that children who do not normally switch their attention from a disconfirmed stimulus object to one that contains the solution can be taught, through verbal-rule instruction (Beilin, 1976), to voluntarily control this facet of their attention processes. Lower-SES children who were trained using instructional feedback combined with rule provision performed at almost the same level as comparable children who received external attentional guidance in the form of the experimenter pointing to the stimulus that contained the solution on each trial. Middle-SES children showed equivalent performance under the two conditions.

These latter children exhibited strategies in, and solved, about 25% more of their problems than did the lower-SES children given identical training or external attentional guidance. Children of the two SES levels did not differ appreciably on the other dependent measures that were evaluated; although in several cases there were small differences in favor of the middle-SES children. Thus, according to the present conceptualization, the differences in performance resulted from the functioning of the processor. This is qualified, though, because the children's performance was evaluated in two separate experiments and was not compared statistically.

Morello *et al.* (1977) and other (e.g., Gruen, Ottinger, & Zigler, 1970; Odom, 1967; Overton, Wagner, & Dolinsky, 1971) have suggested the cognitive capabilities of lower-SES children lag behind those of middle-SES children during the primary grades due to environmental differences in opportunities to interact with problem-solving tasks. If this is the case, then more precisely designed experiments should reveal the specific deficits.

The normal and underachieving readers of Experiment 8 showed differences which in some respects paralleled those between middle- and lower-SES children. Although statistical comparisons are unwarranted because the data were collected in different schools, under different experimental conditions, and at different times, some of the similarities among the underachieving readers and the lower-SES children were striking, as were the similarities among the normal readers and middle-SES children (Mims & Gholson, 1977; Phillips & Levine, 1975; Expt. 5 of this chapter). The lower SES children of Experiment 5 showed strategies in about 50–56% of their problems, while the poor readers given four-dimensional problems in Experiment 8 did so in 52% of their problems. Middle-SES children have shown strategies in about 65–80% of their four-dimensional problems in various experiments. The normal readers of Experiment 8 exhibited them in about 67%. More precise measures of the logical elements embodied in the processors of children of different SES and reading-achievement levels are clearly indicated.

Experiment 6 was concerned with the distracting effects of material feedback elements. Children who received material–directional feedback attended to, coded, and recoded information at the same high levels as those who received verbal–directional feedback. The material–directional condition, however, did not yield efficient processing. The verbal–directional condition produced significantly more strategies (70 versus 50%) and more solved problems (85 versus 66%). These patterns of performance suggested that the necessity for the child to manipulate tokens during the intertrial interval caused the processor to malfunction. A closer inspection of the data, however, indicated that the differences were probably due to more peripheral attentional processes. The verbal–directional condition produced better performance on the local-consistency measure (88 versus 82%, $p<.10$) along with about 20% more strategies and 20% fewer local-consistency errors in the systems data.

The verbal-only and material-only conditions produced uniformly poor performance (e.g., 13–23% strategies). This indicates that the directional component should be combined with feedback whenever possible when elementary-school children are to be taught conceptual material. Surprisingly, the material-only condition produced better performance than verbal-only on three dependent measures. The differences were not large, but they were significant. This finding was inconsistent with results obtained in closely related research (e.g., Mims & Gholson, 1977; Penney, 1967; Spence, 1970a, 1971; Spence & Dunton, 1967; Spence & Segner, 1967). The discrepancy may have resulted from specific methodological factors inherent in Experiment 6.

Experiment 7 confirmed the effects of task manipulations upon coding, recoding, and attentional processes using a probe procedure in which the stimulus cues were decomposed and the subjects (third graders, sixth graders, college students) were instructed to indicate those that "could still be correct" following feedback on each trial. Interactions of the kind predicted by the model presented in Chapter 3 (cf. Gholson & Beilin, 1979), between age (or cognitive level) and task manipulations, were obtained on three dependent measures and approached significance ($p<.10$) on two others. The hypothesis probe technique that was used permitted an assessment of the subjects' memories for stimulus information and for the hypotheses they exhibited on the previous trial. In general, the children showed almost no memory for stimulus information; they showed some, but not much memory for the hypotheses they exhibited on the preceding trial.

The college students exhibited perfect processing in about 90% of their problems: four hypotheses on the first trial, two on the second, and one hypothesis, the solution, on the third trial. Only two of the children showed this pattern in all of their problems. A few others exhibited the pattern in three or fewer problems. The children showed three different modes of approach to the task:

1. Some exhibited one hypothesis on each trial both before and after solution was attained,
2. Others tended to exhibit three or four hypotheses on each of the first three trials and began narrowing the set only after the trial of last error, if at all,
3. The remaining children mostly exhibited three or four hypotheses on the first trial and began narrowing the set immediately.

The decomposed stimulus array facilitated performance somewhat, relative to earlier research in which blank trials and introtacts were used to monitor hypotheses. Many of the children appeared to approach the decomposed array as a matching-to-sample task in which they were to identify the cues in the correct stimulus object, but the array did serve as a constant reminder as to the possible solutions to the problems (cf. Ingalls & Dickerson, 1969). When hypotheses were selected from the decomposed array in the presence of the stimulus objects the children's coding, recoding, and attention processes were facilitated, but the presence of the stimulus object did not improve memory for stimulus information from the preceding trial or for the hypotheses exhibited on that trial.

III
SUMMARY AND CONCLUSIONS

The model presented in Chapters 3 and 4 (cf. Gholson & Beilin, 1979) guided the research presented in subsequent chapters. The model rests upon three basic assumptions:

1. Prediction hypotheses are consolidated out of more basic components that are acquired independently.

2. A processor, which embodies logical abilities, changes qualitatively with development.

3. The functioning of various cognitive subprocesses changes quantitatively with development.

The purpose of this last section is to evaluate these assumptions in the light of research presented in Chapters 5, 6, and 7, and to provide a more precise restatement of the model. For the most part, the findings were congenial to the model, but some important discrepancies were noted. Consequently, the restatement will require some adjustments relative to the version presented in Chapters 3 and 4.

8
A Developmental Theory of Human Learning

In Chapter 3 an outline of the model was presented (cf. Gholson & Beilin, 1979), and a series of questions were posed concerning the emergence of hypotheses, the role of the processor, and the cognitive subprocesses. Many of these questions were then addressed vis-à-vis the existent literature, and the model was expanded and modified accordingly in Chapter 4. Implications were then explored in research presented in Chapters 5, 6, and 7. It is now time to take stock; that is, qualify and expand the model in the light of subsequent research findings.

The Emergence of Prediction Hypotheses

It was proposed that the acquisition of prediction hypotheses results from a three-tiered process. At the outset of acquisition, the young (preoperational) child's behavior is frequently dominated by response-set hypotheses in which the win and lose components involve the same action (e.g., win–stay object, lose–stay object). These components of response sets must be separated from each other before the acquisition of prediction hypotheses may begin. The individual response components are then acquired independently and at different rates. The results of Experiment 1, in which learning-set procedures were combined with blank-trial probes, provided strong support for these assumptions—except that response sets were not as frequent or dominant as expected. The children showed consistent hypothesis patterns at high levels during all phases of acquisition. At the outset, the preschoolers did sometimes exhibit combinations of components that would yield response-set hypotheses (e.g., win–shift object, lose–shift object). But things were more complicated than expected: They frequently shifted from object to position hypotheses or vice versa, and there was remarkable variability in the strengths of the different components.

The frequencies of object-alternation, position-alternation, and position-preference hypotheses decreased during precriterion sessions, while the frequency of simple object hypotheses increased. The strengths of various win and lose components also changed with practice among the groups of preschoolers who eventually achieved criterion. Win–stay object was very weak at the outset among children who required more than one session to reach criterion. It strengthened from probabilities as low as about .15 in the first session to about .80 or greater in criterion sessions. Lose–shift object was strong from the outset (.61–1.00). Win–stay position was also strong from the outset, but lose–shift position was not strong—not nearly as strong as lose–shift object.

As already indicated, during precriterion sessions the children very frequently shifted from object to position hypotheses and from position to object hypotheses following both wins and losses. As they approached criterion, however, (*a*) the probabilities that they shifted from object to position hypotheses decreased; (*b*) the probabilities that they shifted from position to object hypotheses increased: and (*c*) the overall frequencies of position hypotheses dropped precipitously, from as high as 65% to as low as 7%.

The preschool children who failed to achieve criterion did so for several reasons. First, the strength of the win–stay object component remained weak throughout, never exceeding .30. In addition, they frequently replaced both confirmed and disconfirmed object hypotheses with position hypotheses. After the first day these children exhibited position hypotheses in more than 60% of their probes in each session.

The blank-trial probe data from the two-dimensional problems also revealed that the preschool children's responses were not determined by compound cues (cf. Cole, 1976; House, 1979; T. J. Tighe & L. S. Tighe, 1972; Zeaman & House, 1974). If they had been, the children would have been expected to show response patterns that corresponded to simple object cues at very depressed levels (.50), especially on criterion days. This, of course, was not the case; the children showed simple object hypotheses about 80% of the time on criterion sessions. It is possible that the discrepant findings resulted from differences in the precision of the analyses that are performed. The reversal–extradimensional shift task that has been used previously to study compounding is not fine-grained;

that is, it cannot reveal the specific hypotheses that dictate choice responses and cannot evaluate win and lose components.

Once win–stay object and lose–shift object are consolidated the resulting scheme appears to be durable, because the preschool children showed nearly perfect transfer from the two-dimensional to four-dimensional problems: Only four children required more than one session to achieve criterion.

The findings seem to indicate that left to their own devices, young children do not rigidly exhibit response-set hypotheses. Previous research, in which standard pretraining preceded experimental problems, suggested that either stimulus preference (win–stay object, lose-stay object), position preference (win–stay position, lose–stay position) or position alternation (win–shift position, lose–shift position) response sets would dominate individual children's behavior and would be difficult to extinguish (e.g., Gholson *et al.*, 1972, 1976; Gollin & Saravo, 1970; Rieber, 1969; Schuepfer & Gholson, 1978; Tumblin *et al.*, 1979; Weisz, 1977). This was clearly not the case in the present experiment. The children exhibited considerable flexibility both in their hypotheses and their win and lose components. Rather than bringing performance to asymptotic levels (see Chapters 3 and 4), then, standard pretraining might actually have interfered with young children's functioning; that is, the pretraining itself might have led the children to consolidate components that resulted in response sets. This conclusion is qualified, though, because the children studied in the earlier research were slightly older (kindergarteners). In addition, the preschool children in Experiment 2 exhibited prediction hypotheses most of the time following a modified version of the standard pretraining procedure.

Among the second graders the win–stay object and lose–shift object components were strong from the outset. The children who failed to achieve criterion immediately tested mostly position-alternation and object-alternation hypotheses during early problems. The flexibility with which various combinations of win and lose components were exhibited indicated that most of these children had previously acquired each response component and, consequently, to achieve criterial learning all they were required to do was consolidate the appropriate pair to yield a correct prediction hypothesis.

An important issue that remains to be investigated concerns the relative dominance of position versus object hypotheses during various phases of the acquisition process and the mechanism responsible for the changes that occur (Lane, McDaniel, Bleichfield, & Rabinowitz, 1976; Levine, 1974, 1975; Ryan, 1977). Future research should also consider the acquisition of other learning sets: win–shift object, lose–stay object;

win–stay position, lose–shift position; win–shift position, lose–stay position. This research should provide a description of the acquisition of each component and each consolidation process. It might also be fruitful to study "learning set" that involves combinations of position and object components. One might speculate that because older children and adults test only prediction hypotheses (Gholson *et al.*, 1972; Levine, 1963, 1975; Levinson & Reese, 1967), young children might actually find it easier to consolidate win–shift object with lose–stay position, for example, than would college students or older children. An intriguing issue concerns the relationship between performance during probes as opposed to performance on feedback trials; that is, why did many of the preschool children maintain an hypothesis during a series of blank trials and then replace it on feedback trials regardless of the feedback?

The Processor

This conception involves a processor that operates on information which is processed, transformed, and integrated into ongoing behavior by activated logical schemes, and an organized set of cognitive subprocesses that regulate a continuous flow of information to (and from) the processor. The processor is analogous to an executive system (Klahr & Siegler, 1978; Newell & Simon, 1972) and embodies the logical knowledge available to the individual. It consists of a set of logical operations and a interpreter that determines the sequence in which the logical operations are performed. The processor changes qualitatively with developmental level, but changes in the functioning of the cognitive subprocesses are quantitative.

The processor performs two important functions: (*a*) it integrates the various cognitive subprocesses and, (*b*) depending upon developmental level, permits the individual to construct and execute solution plans of varying sophistication. As a first approximation, gross characteristics of the processor were identified with Piaget's descriptions of the cognitive capabilities of preoperational, concrete operational, and formal operational thought. Implications of Piaget's theory were then considered in relation to the kinds of hypothesis-sampling systems individuals of each cognitive level should be capable of manifesting.

The cognitive capabilities of preoperational children are so impoverished that they should be capable of exhibiting only stereotypes and unsystematic hypothesis sequences. This is because they are capable of only a semilogic that involves one-way dependencies; they assimilate external causes and effects to their own action schemes, show attentional centration, and lack sophisticated classification skills. Research concerned with the behavior of preoperational children that was reviewed in Chapter 4 was generally in line with predictions derived from Piaget's theory (Gholson *et al.*, 1972, 1976; Morello *et al.*, 1977; Rieber, 1969; Weisz, 1977).

The preschool children (experimental group) who were studied in Experiment 2 generated response sequences that corresponded to non-positional stimulus cues in 84% of their blank-trial probes, maintained confirmed hypotheses 80% of the time, and rejected disconfirmed hypotheses 85% of the time. Thus they clearly exhibited prediction hypotheses. These children showed stereotypes in only 11% of their problems, but they showed unsystematic hypothesis sequences in 68%. Even though they were trained with procedures that required them to follow a dimension-checking format, they exhibited hypothesis sequences that corresponded to strategy categories in only 19% of their problems.

Some of our learning-set research that is in progress (Daniel, Schuepfer, & Gholson, 1980) provides an addendum to the data reported in Experiments 1 and 2. Preoperational and concrete operational kindergarten children were brought to criterion in two-dimensional and then four-dimensional learning-set problems of the kind described in Experiment 1. They then received a series of 10 four-dimensional problems in which the feedback-trial sequences involved orthogonal stimuli; that is, the stimulus configurations that were presented on three consecutive feedback trials logically specified a single hypothesis as the solution to the problem. Cognitive level produced no effects upon learning-set performance in either the two- or four-dimensional problems. In the orthogonal problems, however, differences were obtained. The concrete operational children showed strategic behavior in many of their problems; the preoperational children's performance, however, was not strategic and actually deteriorated across problems.

Piagetian stage, then, appears to be a good predictor of performance only when the child is required to process information from trial to trial. When the task demands are simplified and all that is required, for example, is for the child to consolidate win–stay with lose–shift object, no cognitive-level effects are obtained. This conclusion is qualified, of course, in that it would probably be expected to hold only if the children were of roughly the same age range, SES level, level of formal schooling, etc.

In Experiment 3, preoperational kindergarten children who received a visual illustration of the dimension-checking strategy along with verbal-rule instruction exhibited 37% unsystematic sequences and only 15% strategy sequences. The transitional children in this condition, however, showed performance that was *statistically* equivalent to that exhibited by concrete operational children. They showed 34% strategies and only 15% unsystematic sequences. These latter findings, along with those reported by Morello *et al.*, (1977), suggest that the full acquisition of concrete operations, as measured by number and continuous-quantity conservation tasks (Morello *et al*. also used area), may not be necessary for the child to exhibit dimension checking and hypothesis checking in four-dimensional problems. Exactly what logical knowledge transitional children have achieved that preoperational children have not remains to be specified. Fitzgerald's (1977) work suggests that precise measurement of the changing nature of the young child's classification skills might prove fruitful in this regard.

Concrete operational children separate environmental contingencies from their own actions, show logical reversibility, grasp the nature of class-inclusion relations, and decenter. These logical operations imply that the concrete operational child should be capable of exhibiting strategic approaches to problem solving. Cognitive functioning is limited, however, because this child is capable only of a descending mode of classification. This involves a serial ordering and evaluating of the experiential data associated principally with the world of tangible objects. Concrete operational thought can locate the general classes (or dimensions) of the problem materials and formulate a systematic plan to evaluate each. But these children are limited to a mode of processing that brings classes together by a class inclusion that moves from one element (cue, hypothesis, dimension) to the next sequentially. Thus concrete thought is limited to an orderly process of subtracting one single class (hypothesis, dimension) from another, or adding classes to form a single larger class. It follows that concrete operational children should be capable of exhibiting the dimension-checking or hypothesis-checking strategy, but not focusing.

Research investigating the systems exhibited by concrete operational kindergarten children supports the conclusion that concrete operations are *sufficient* to permit the child to exhibit these systems. The children manifested dimension checking and hypothesis checking in 45–75% of their problems (Gholson *et al.*, 1976; Expt. 3, this volume). Attempts to elicit the focusing strategy from second graders by modeling procedures and verbal-rule instruction were singularly unsuccessful (Richman & Gholson, 1978). Not only did they fail to focus, but they actually showed worse performance than controls who received no training. This may have been because they attempted to implement the focusing strategy, but lacked the executive functions necessary to do so. Sixth graders in the same experiment, however, showed about 55% focusing following the training procedures, and their performance was generally comparable to that exhibited by college students (cf. Gholson *et al.*, 1972,

1973; Levine, 1966, 1975). Richman's (see Chapter 4 and Expt. 4) attempts to train focusing in eighth graders and college students who were concrete operational have also proven unsuccessful.

Toward the end of the concrete operational period, however, when children are transitional to formal operations according to Piaget's criteria (they conserve volume, but do not exhibit formal operational performance on tasks designed to assess it), they do manifest focusing at high levels following training in the use of a focusing strategy. This performance is not consistent with Piaget's theory as described in Chapter 4, because formal operations should be *necessary* in order for the individual to exhibit the focusing strategy. Turner (1978; Goodwin & Turner, 1979), however, has determined that only Stage III classification skills (Inhelder & Piaget, 1964) are necessary for focusing in standard four-dimensional problems.

Turner reasoned that once children have fully conceptualized the meanings of "some" and "all" as well as flexibility in "anticipation" and "hindsight," it should be possible for them to exhibit focusing sequences if the task does not require the verification of hypotheses by deduction and implication. Because the stimuli are symmetrical, dichotomous, and available on each trial in conventional hypothesis-testing tasks, the subjects are not required to construct appropriate tests for themselves. Thus focusing sequences may be generated by subjects who simply divide the eight hypotheses into two subclasses: potential solutions and those which are not potential solutions. Because Stage III children have mastered hindsight, anticipation, etc., feedback information may be applied to eliminate more than one hypothesis on a given trial: It is not necessary for the child to construct appropriate tests of each hypothesis (cf. Hook & Cook, 1979; Moshman, 1979), because all stimulus information is present on each trial.

Following this reasoning, Goodwin and Turner (1979) investigated the performance of children (mean CA = 9:8 years) at two levels of concrete operational development: *(a)* those who passed only a differential-criteria sorting task (Inhelder *et al.*, 1974); *(b)* those who also passed the Inhelder *et al.* (1974) class-inclusion quantification task, but failed a combinatorial task (Inhelder & Piaget, 1958) that assessed formal operations. Following the assessment, half the children of each level received explicit training in the use of the focusing strategy. This included visual demonstrations and verbal rule instructions. The children were taught to *name* the four confirmed hypotheses following feedback on the first trial, then the two that remained viable following feedback on the second trial, and the solution following feedback on the third trial. Hypotheses were monitored by this procedure during test problems.

The Level III classifiers exhibited more than 50% focusing following the training. Similar children who did not receive the training showed focusing sequences at about the same level that usually obtains among concrete operational children. The children who passed only the differential-criteria sorting task and received the focusing training showed few focusing sequences—no more than an untrained control group.

These findings, along with the ones obtained among eighth graders (Richman, 1976; Richman *et al*., 1978) and college students (Expt. 4) who were transitional from concrete to formal operations, support Turner's interpretation of the standard hypothesis-testing task vis-à-vis Piaget's theory. This, of course, assumes that transitional performance as assessed by the volume conservation task implies that Level III classification skills have also been achieved. This appears reasonable, but awaits empirical verification.

A serious problem for the model concerns the performance of middle-aged transitional adults and both formal operational and transitional adults who are over 60 years of age (see Expt. 4). These groups exhibited focusing in only 16, 8, and 2% of their problems, respectively. This performance remains a puzzle, but the subjects received no training in the use of any strategy, and thus it remains possible that appropriate training would elicit high frequencies of focusing among all three groups. In the absence of this training research, the puzzle cannot be resolved, but it seems reasonable to suggest (Hornblum & Overton, 1976) that performance factors reflected in the cognitive subprocesses were responsible for the decrements that were obtained among the middle-aged and elderly.

Cognitive Subprocesses

The role of the processor in integrating the various cognitive subprocesses and controlling their functioning remains to be precisely determined. Research reviewed in Chapter 4 indicated that the consolidation of certain logical skills during the concrete operational period has an important bearing on both coding and memory processes. The acquisition of transitive inference skills (Johnson & Scholnick, 1979) and advanced conservation skills (weight and volume) was shown to determine how information is coded into memory. In addition, Hartman (1977) determined that the child's level of classification development determines how semantic memory itself is organized in concrete operational children. Children with advanced classification skills exhibited performance that indicated their memories were hierarchically organized. Those with intermediate classification skills showed some hierarchical organization, but not as much as children with advanced skills. Among the children with low classification skills there was no hint of any hierarchical organization at all in semantic memory.

Hartman also determined that there was a close correlation between level of classification development and reading-achievement level (.61–.72). In Experiment 8 (see Chapter 7) it was shown that underachieving readers exhibit logical deficits that are embodied in their processors. Due to these deficits the children are less able than their normal-achieving peers to selectively attend to relevant stimulus information and disembed it from irrelevant information. The lower-SES children who were studied in Experiment 5 exhibited performance that was similar to the children of comparable age who were underachieving readers in Experiment 8. It was suggested that both groups of children might possess underdeveloped classification skills, and that this defect in their processors was responsible for the relatively poor performance they exhibited. Confirmation of this speculation awaits further research, because classification data were not obtained in either Experiment 5 or 8.

In Experiment 5 it was demonstrated that children who do not voluntarily switch their visual attention from a disconfirmed stimulus object to one that contains the solution under standard conditions may be taught to do so through instructional feedback and rule provision. Following this training, children of both lower and middle SES levels exhibited performances comparable to children for whom feedback included an external attention-directing component throughout: The experimenter said either "correct, the answer is in this picture," or "wrong, the answer is in *this* picture," and pointed to the correct stimulus object for about 4 seconds following the child's response. Under standard conditions, in which subjects are told only "correct" or "wrong" following responses, only college students have shown this kind of voluntary attentional control spontaneously (Gholson *et al.*, 1973; Schonebaum, 1973; Expts. 5 and 6 of this volume).

In Experiment 6 it was shown that even when the attention-directing component is included in the feedback procedure, material feedback impedes the performance of second- and third-grade children. It appeared that the necessity for the children to manipulate the material feedback elements interfered with their attentional processes. These children exhibited fewer strategies and more problems in which they made local-consistency errors than children who received the directional component combined with verbal feedback.

Experiment 7 confirmed the differential effects of task manipulations upon coding, recoding, and attentional processes using a probe procedure in which the stimulus cues were decomposed, and the subjects (third graders, sixth graders, college students) were instructed to indicate those that remained viable following feedback on each trial. Interactions between cognitive level and task manipulations were obtained on three measures of performance and approached significance on two others. The college students showed focusing in about 90% of their problems, but the children rarely exhibited perfect processing. The children exhibited considerable differences in their modes of approach to the set of decomposed cues. Some children selected three or four decomposed cues on every trial before the trial of last error, and then narrowed the set somewhat during the four trials after the last error. Some of these children appeared to approach the task as a matching-to-sample problem. Others exhibited three or four hypotheses on the first trial and began narrowing the set immediately. The final group (20% of the children) exhibited one hypothesis on each trial, both before and after the last error.

Despite the fact that most of the children (80%) showed several hypotheses on at least the first few trials, they did not process them efficiently. This was because the children showed very poor memory for stimulus information from one trial to the next. They did not perform much above chance level on this measure. In addition, the children also had some difficulty in remembering the hypotheses they exhibited from one trial to the next. Whether memory performance can be improved with training remains to be investigated, but the results of attentional training (Expt. 5) were excellent, and hold some promise that the functioning of other cognitive subprocesses may be brought under voluntary control.

In general, then, the model presented in Chapter 3 fared well, but required some adjustments when evaluated in the light of results from a series of experiments specifically designed to investigate some of its previously untested implications. As one might expect, the processes turned out to be more complicated than the earlier version of the model predicted (cf. Gholson & Beilin, 1979). More precise experiments are clearly in order. This research should be designed (*a*) to monitor the time course of all the components out of which various prediction hypotheses are consolidated, (*b*) to elucidate more fully the changing characteristics of the processor within each major stage of development, (*c*) to illuminate the role of the processor in the functioning of each cognitive subprocess and in their integration, and (*d*) to isolate and study each cognitive subprocess and its functioning.

The model appears promising in that it brings together several diverse bodies of research and theory. In addition, it has certain important virtues when compared to current information-processing (e.g., Klahr & Wallace, 1976; Klahr & Siegler, 1978; H. A. Simon, 1972) and neo-Piagetian approaches (Case, 1978; Inhelder *et al.*, 1974; Pascual-Leone, 1970). Information-processing models are clear on the relationship between executive functions and performance, but are vague on the mechanisms that account for developmental change. Neo-Piagetian models provide structural mechanisms that account for development, but are vague on the relationship between structures, operations, and performance. Thus, they are not easily tested. The present model derives operations from structures and specifies the relationship between the (logical) operations embodied in the processor and performance. Thus, it is truly developmental and, at the same time, easily tested.

References

Adams, M. J., & Shepp, B. E. Selective attention and the breadth of learning: A developmental study. *Journal of Experimental Child Psychology,* 1975, *20*, 168–180.

Allport, F. H. *Theories of perception and the concept of structure.* New York: John Wiley & Sons, 1955.

Anderson, R. P., Halcomb, C. G., & Doyle, R. B. The measurement of attentional deficits. *Exceptional Children*, 1973, *39*, 534–539.

Atkinson, R. C., & Shiffrin, R. M. Human memory: A proposed system and its control processes. In K. W. Spence & J. T. Spence (Eds.), *The psychology of learning and motivation*. Vol. 2. New York: Academic Press, 1968.

Baker, R. W., & Madell, T. O. A continued investigation of susceptibility to distraction in academically underachieving and achieving male college students. *Journal of Educational Psychology,* 1965, *56*, 254–258.

Baltes, P. B. Longitudinal and cross-sectional sequences in the study of age and generation effects. *Human Development*, 1968, *11*, 145–171.

Baltes, P. B. (Ed.), *Life-span development and behavior*. Vol. 1. New York: Academic Press, 1978.

Baltes, P. B., & Schaie, K. W. On life-span development research paradigms. In P. B. Baltes & K. W. Schaie (Eds.), *Life-span developmental psychology: Personality and socialization*. New York: Academic Press, 1973.

Bandura, A. *Social learning theory.* New York: General Learning Press, 1971.

Bandura, A., & Harris, M. B. Modification of syntactic style. *Journal of Experimental Child Psychology,* 1966, *4*, 341–352.

Bandura, A., & Walters, R. H. *Social learning and personality development*. New York: Holt, Rinehart, & Winston, 1963.

Barclay, J. R., & Reid, M. Semantic integration in children's recall of discourse. *Developmental Psychology*, 1974, *10*, 277–281.

Barringer, C., & Gholson, B. Effects of type and combination of feedback upon conceptual learning by children: Implications for research concerning academic learning. *Review of Education Research,* 1979, *49,* 459–478.

Battig, W. F. Paired-associate learning under simultaneous repetition and nonrepetition conditions. *Journal of Experimental Psychology*, 1962, *64*, 87–93.

Beilin, H. Learning and operational convergence in logical thought development. *Journal of Experimental Child Psychology*, 1965, *2* 317–339.

Beilin, H. Stimulus and cognitive transformation in conservation. In D. Elkind & J. H. Flavell (Eds.), *Studies in cognitive development: Essays in honor of Jean Piaget*. New York: Oxford University, 1969.

Beilin, H. The training and acquisition of logical operations. In M. F. Rosskopf, L. P. Steffe, & S. Taback (Eds.), *Piagetian cognitive-development research and mathematical education*. Washington, D. C.: National Council of Teachers of Mathematics, 1971.

Beilin, H. *Studies in the cognitive basis of language development.* New York: Academic Press, 1975.

Beilin, H. Constructing cognitive operations linguistically. In H. W. Reese (Ed.), *Advances in child development and behavior*. Vol. 11. New York: Academic Press, 1976.

Berlyne, D. E. *Conflict, arousal and curiosity*. New York: McGraw-Hill, 1960.

Berman, P. W. Stimulus novelty as a variable in children's win-stay, lose-shift discrimination learning set. *Child Development*, 1971, *42*, 1591–1595.

Berman, P. W. Win-stay, lose-shift problem learning by children: Effects of age and experience. *Developmental Psychology*, 1973, *8*, 315.

Berman, P. W., & Meyers, J. Effects of ratio of win-stay to lose-shift problems on children's performance on win-stay problems. *Psychonomic Science*, 1971, *23*, 131–132.

Berman, P. W., Rane, N. G., & Bahow, E. Age changes in children's learning set with win-stay, lose-shift problems. *Developmental Psychology*, 1970, *2*, 233–239.

Bessemer, D. W., & Stollnitz, F. Retention of discriminations and an analysis of learning set. In A. M. Schrier & F. Stollnitz (Eds.), *Behavior of nonhuman primates.* Vol. 4. New York: Academic Press, 1971.

Birren, J. E. *Psychology of aging*. Englewood Cliffs, N. J.: Prentice Hall, 1964.

Botwinick, J. *Cognitive processes in maturity and old age*. New York: Springer, 1967.

Bourne, L. E., & Pendleton, R. B. Concept identification as a function of completeness and probability of information feedback. *Journal of Experimental Psychology*, 1958, *56*, 413–420.

Bourne, L. E., & Restle, F. Mathematical theory of concept identification. *Psychological Review*, 1959, *66*, 278–296.

Bower, G. H. *Properties of the one-element model as applied to paired associate learning*. Technical report No. 31, 1960, Stanford University, Contract NONR 225 (17).

Bower, G. H. Cognitive psychology: An introduction. In W. K. Estes (Ed.), *Handbook of learning and cognitive processes*. Vol. 1. Hillsdale, N. J.: Lawrence Erlbaum Associates, 1975.

Bower, G. H., & Trabasso, T. Reversals prior to solution in concept identification. *Journal of Experimental Psychology*, 1963, *66*, 409–418.

Bower, G. H., & Trabasso, T. Concept identification. In R. C. Atkinson (Ed.), *Studies in mathematical psychology*. Stanford, California: Stanford University Press, 1964.

Bowman, R. E. Discrimination learning-set performance under intermittent and secondary reinforcement. *Journal of Comparative and Physiological Psychology*, 1963, *56*, 429–434.

Brackett, H. R., & Battig, W. F. Methods of pretraining and knowledge of results in paired-associate learning under conditions of repetition and non-repetition. *American Journal of Psychology*, 1963, *76*, 66-73.

Brainerd, C. J. Cognitive development and concept learning: An interpretive review. *Psychological Bulletin*, 1977, *84*, 919-939.

Brainerd, C. J. *Piaget's theory of intelligence*. Engelwood Cliffs, N. J.: Prentice Hall, 1978,

Bransford, J. D., & Franks, J. J. The abstraction of linguistic ideas. *Cognitive Psychology*, 1971, *2*, 331–350.

Brown, A. L. The development of memory: Knowing, knowing about knowing, and knowing how to know. In H. W. Reese (Ed.), *Advances in child development and behavior*. Vol. 10. New York: Academic Press, 1975.

Brown, A. L. Knowing when, where, and how to remember: A problem of metacognition. In R. Glaser (Ed.), *Advances in instructional Psychology*. Vol. 1. Hillsdale, N. J.: Lawrence Erlbaum Associates, 1978.

Brown, A. S. Examination of hypothesis-sampling theory. *Psychological Bulletin*, 1974, *81*, 773–790.

Bruner, J. S., & Goodman, C. C. Value and need as organizing factors in perception. *Journal of Abnormal and Social Psychology*, 1947, *42*, 33–44.

Bruner, J. S., Goodnow, J. J., & Austin, G. A. *A study of thinking*. New York: Wiley, 1956.

Bruner, J. S., Olver, R. R., & Greenfield, P. M. *Studies in cognitive growth*. New York: Wiley, 1966.

Bruner, J. S., & Postman, L. Tension and tension release as organizing factors in perception. *Journal of Personality*, 1947, *15*, 300–308.

Bruner, J. S., & Postman, L. Symbolic value as an organizing factor in perception. *Journal of Social Psychology*, 1948, *27*, 203–208.

Bush, R. R., & Mosteller, F. *Stochastic models for learning*. New York: Wiley, 1955.

Byrd, D. M. *The effects of mnemonic training upon problem-solving strategies as a function of developmental memory level.* Unpublished M. S. Thesis, Memphis State University, 1979.

Cantor, J. H., & Spiker, C. C. Dimensional fixation with introtacts in kindergarten children. *Bulletin of the Psychonomic Society*, 1977, *10*, 169–171.

Cantor, J. H., & Spiker, C. C. The problem-solving strategies of kindergarten and first-grade children during discrimination learning. *Journal of Experimental Child Psychology*, 1978, *26*, 341–358.

Case, R. Structures and strictures: Some functional limitations on the course of cognitive growth. *Cognitive Psychology*, 1974, *6*, 544–573.

Case, R. Intellectual development from birth to adolescence: A neo-Piagetian interpretation. In R. S. Siegler (Ed.), *Children's thinking: What develops?* Hillsdale, N.J.: Lawrence Erlbaum Associates, 1978.

Chumbley, J. Hypothesis memory in concept learning. *Journal of Mathematical Psychology*, 1969, *6*, 528–540.

Cicirelli, V. G. Categorization behavior in aging subjects. *Journal of Gerontology*, 1976, *31*, 676–680.

Clark, L. L., Lansford, T. G., & Dallenbach, K. M. Repetition and associative learning. *American Journal of Psychology*, 1960, *73*, 22–40.

Cohen, R., Weatherford, D. L., Lomenick, T., & Koeller, K. Spatial representation: Role of task demands and familiarity with the environment. *Child Development*, 1979 (in press).

Cole, M. A probe trial procedure for the study of children's discrimination learning and transfer. *Journal of Experimental Child Psychology*, 1976, *22*, 499–510.

Cole, M., Frankel, F., & Sharp, D. Development of free recall learning in children. *Developmental Psychology*, 1971, *4*, 109–123.

Coltheart, V. Memory for stimuli and memory for hypotheses in concept identification. *Journal of Experimental Psychology*, 1971, *89*, 102–108.

Collins, A. M., & Quillian, M. R. How to make a language user. In E. Tulving & W. Donaldson (Eds.), *Organization of memory*. New York: Academic Press, 1972.

Comstock, E. M., & Chumbley, J. I. A model of three-choice discrimination learning under complete and incomplete feedback conditions. *Cognitive Psychology*, 1973, *4*, 117–129.

Cotton, J. W. Mathematical analysis of a multiple-look concept identification model. *British Journal of Mathematical and Statistical Psychology*, 1972, *25*, 257–273.

Covington, M. V., Crutchfield, R. S., & Daves, L. B. *The productive thinking program*. Berkeley, Calif.: Brazelton, 1966.

Cross, H. A., & Vaughter, R. M. The Moss-Harlow effect in preschool children as a function of age. *Journal of Experimental Child Psychology*, 1966, *4*, 280–284.

Dalton, A. J., Rubino, C. A., & Hislop, M. W. Some effects of token rewards on school achievement of children with Down's syndrome. *Journal of Applied Behavior Analysis*, 1973, *6*, 251–259.

Daniel, C., Schuepfer, T., & Gholson, B. *Effects of developmental level and learning-set training upon the strategic behavior of kindergarten children*. Unpublished Manuscript, Memphis State University, 1980.

Day, M. C. Developmental trends in visual scanning. In H. W. Reese (Ed.), *Advances in child development and behavior*. Vol. 10. New York: Academic Press, 1975.

Denney, D. R. Modeling and eliciting effects upon conceptual strategies. *Child Development*, 1972, *43*, 810–823.

Denney, D. R. The effects of exemplary and cognitive models and self-rehearsal on children's interrogative strategies. *Journal of Experimental Child Psychology*, 1975, *19*, 476–488.

Denney, D. R., Denney, N. W., & Ziobrowski, M. J. Alterations in the information-processing strategies of young children following observation of adult models. *Developmental Psychology*, 1973, *8*, 202–208.

Denney, N. W. Classification abilities in the elderly. *Journal of Gerontology*, 1974, *29*, 309–314.

Denney, N. W., & Lennon, M. L. Classification: A comparison of middle and old age. *Developmental Psychology*, 1972, *7*, 210–213.

Denney, N. W., & Wright, J. C. *Cognitive changes during the adult years: Implications for developmental theory and research*. Paper presented at the Meetings of the Society for Research in Child Development, Denver, April, 1975.

Dodd, D. H., & Bourne, L. E. Test of some assumptions of a hypothesis-testing model of concept identification. *Journal of Experimental Psychology*, 1969, *80*, 69–72.

Douglas, V. I. Stop, look and listen: The problem of sustained attention and impulse control in hyperactive and normal children. *Canadian Journal of Behavioral Science*, 1972, *4*, 259–282.

Durost, N. W., Bixler, H. H., Hildreth, G. H., Lund, K. W., & Wrightstone, J. W. *Metropolitan Achievement Tests: Teachers Handbook*. New York: Harcourt, Brace, Jovanovich, 1971.

Dykman, R. A., Ackerman, P. T., Clements, S. D., & Peters, J. E. Specific learning disabilities: An attentional deficit syndrome. In H. R. Myklebust (Ed.), *Progress in learning disabilities*. Vol. 2. New York: Grune & Stratton, 1971.

Dykman, R. A., Walls, R. C. , Suzuki, T., Ackerman, P. T., & Peters, J. E. Children with learning disabilities: Conditioning, differentiation, and the effect of distraction. *American Journal of Orthopsychiatry*, 1970, *40*, 766–781.

Eimas, P. D. A developmental study of hypothesis behavior and focusing. *Journal of Experimental Child Psychology*, 1969, *8*, 160–172.

Eimas, P. D. Effects of memory aids on hypothesis behavior and focusing in young children and adults. *Journal of Experimental Child Psychology*, 1970, *10*, 319–336.

Elkind, D., Larson, M., & Van Doorninck, W. Perceptual decentration learning and performance in slow and average readers. *Journal of Educational Psychology*, 1965, *56*, 50–56.

Erickson, J. R. Hypothesis sampling in concept identification. *Journal of Experimental Psychology*, 1968, *76*, 12–18.

Erickson, J. R., & Zajkowski, M. M. Learning several concept-identification problems concurrently: A test of the sampling-with-replacement assumption, *Journal of Experimental Psychology*, 1967, *74*, 212–218.

Erickson, J. R., Zajkowski, M. M., & Ehmann, E. D. All-or-none assumptions in concept identification: Analysis of latency data. *Journal of Experimental Psychology*, 1966, *72*, 690–697.

Estes, W. K. The statistical approach to learning theory. In S. Koch (Ed.), *Psychology: A study of a science*. Vol. 2. New York: McGraw-Hill, 1959.

Estes, W. K. Learning theory and the new "mental chemistry." *Psychological Review*, 1960, *67*, 207–223.

Estes, W. K. *Learning theory and mental development*. New York: Academic Press, 1970.

Estes, W. K., & Burke, C. J. A theory of stimulus variability in learning. *Psychological Review*, 1953, *60*, 276–286.

Falmagné, R. Construction of a hypothesis model for concept identification. *Journal of Mathematical Psychology*, 1970, 7, 60–96.

Fellows, B. J. *The discrimination process and development*. New York: Pergamon Press, 1968.

Fitzgerald, J. M. Verbalization effects in young children: Classification abilities and the use of verbal labels. *Child Development*, 1977, *48*, 604–611.

Flavell, J. H. *The developmental psychology of Jean Piaget*. New York: Van Nostrand Reinhold, 1963.

Flavell, J. H. Developmental studies of mediated memory. In H. W. Reese & L. P. Lipsitt (Eds.), *Advances in child development and behavior*. Vol. 5. New York: Academic Press, 1970.

Flavell, J. H., & Wohlwill, J. F. Formal and functional aspects of cognitive development. In D. Elkind & J. H. Flavell (Eds.), *Studies in cognitive development: Essays in honor of Jean Piaget*. New York: Oxford University Press, 1969.

Foreit, K. G. Blank trials and hypothesis behavior in young children. *Bulletin of the Psychonomic Society*, 1974, *3*, 1–3.

Gagné, R. M. *The conditions of learning*. (2nd ed.) New York: Holt, 1970.

Gelman, R. Conservation acquisition: A problem of learning to attend to relevant attributes. *Journal of Experimental Child Psychology*, 1969, 7, 167–187.

Geyer, J. J. Comprehensive and partial models related to the reading process. *Reading Research Quarterly*, 1972, 7, 541–587.

Gholson, B., & Beilin, H. A developmental model of human learning. In H. W. Reese & L. P. Lipsitt (Eds.), *Advances in child development and behavior*. Vol. 13. New York: Academic Press, 1979.

Gholson, B., & Danziger, S. Effects of two levels of stimulus complexity upon hypothesis sampling systems among second and sixth grade children. *Journal of Experimental Child Psychology*, 1975, *20*, 105–118.

Gholson, B., Levine, M., & Phillips, S. Hypotheses, strategies, and stereotypes in discrimination learning. *Journal of Experimental Child Psychology*, 1972, *13*, 423–446.

Gholson, B., & McConville, K. Effects of stimulus differentiation training upon hypotheses, strategies, and stereotypes in discrimination learning among kindergarten children. *Journal of Experimental Child Psychology*, 1974, *18*, 81–97.

Gholson, B., & O'Connor, J. Dimensional control of hypothesis sampling during three-choice discrimination learning. *Child Development*, 1975, *46*, 894–903.

Gholson, B., O'Connor, J., & Stern, I. Hypothesis sampling systems among preoperational and concrete operational kindergarten children. *Journal of Experimental Child Psychology*, 1976, *21*, 61–76.

Gholson, B., Phillips, S., & Levine, M. Effects of the temporal relationship of feedback and stimulus information upon discrimination-learning strategies. *Journal of Experimental Child Psychology*, 1973, *15*, 425–441.

Gholson, B., & Schuepfer, T. Commentary on Kendler's paper: An alternative perspective. In H. W. Reese & L. P. Lipsitt (Eds.), *Advances in child development and behavior*. Vol. 13. New York: Academic Press, 1979.

Gibson, E. J. The ontogeny of reading. *American Psychologist*, 1970, *25*, 136–143.

Gibson, J. J., & Gibson, E. J. Perceptual learning: Differentiation or enrichment? *Psychological Review*, 1955, *62*, 32–41.

Glanzer, M., & Clark, W. H. The verbal-loop hypothesis: Conventional figures. *American Journal of Psychology*, 1964, *77*, 621–626.

Glick, J. Cognitive development in cross-cultural perspective. In F. D. Horowitz (Ed.), *Review of child development research*. Vol. 4. Chicago: University of Chicago Press, 1975.

Goldfield, E. *The developmental effects of visual imaging and verbal labeling on the coding of information in problem solving*. Unpublished M.A. Thesis, Hunter College of the City University of New York, 1974.

Gollin, E. S., & Saravo, A. A developmental analysis of learning. In J. Hellmuth (Ed.), *Cognitive studies*. Vol. 1. New York: Bruner/Mazel, 1970.

Goodman, K. S. Reading: A psycholinguistic guessing game. In H. Singer & R. B. Ruddell (Eds.), *Theoretical models and processes of reading*. Newark, Del.: International Reading Association, 1970.

Goodman, K. S. Orthography in a theory of reading instruction. *Elementary English*, 1972, *49*, 1254–1261.

Goodman, K. S. *Theoretically based studies of patterns of miscues in oral reading performance*. Final report. Contract No. OEG-0-9-320375-4269. U.S. Office of Education, 1973.

Goodman, Y. M. Reading diagnosis; qualitative or quantitative? *The Reading Teacher*, 1972, *26*, 32–37.

Goodwin, K. S., & Turner, R. R. *Effects of focusing training on hypothesis testing in concrete operational children*. Unpublished Manuscript, West Virginia University, 1979.

Gottfried, A. E. Effects of instructions and stimulus representation on selective learning in children. *Developmental Psychology*, 1976, *12*, 140–146.

Grassi, J. R. Auditory vigilance performance in brain damaged, behavior disordered, and normal children. *Journal of Learning Disabilities*, 1970, *3*, 302–305.

Gratch, G. Response alternation in children: A developmental study of orientations to uncertainty. *Vita Humana*, 1964, *7*, 49–60.

Gregg, L. W. & Simon, H. A. Process models and stochastic theories of simple concept formation. *Journal of Mathematical Psychology*, 1967, *4*, 246–276.

Gruen, G. E., Ottinger, D., & Zigler, E. Level of aspiration and the probability learning of middle- and lower-class children. *Developmental Psychology*, 1970, *3*, 133–142.

Guilford, J. P. *Psychometric methods*. New York: McGraw-Hill, 1954.

Gumer, E., & Levine, M. The missing dimension in concept learning: Dimensionality or local consistency? *Journal of Experimental Psychology*, 1971, *90*, 39–44.

Guthrie, E. R. *The psychology of learning*. New York: Harper & Row, 1935.

Guthrie, E. R. Conditioning: A theory of learning in terms of stimulus, response and association. In *The psychology of learning*. National Social Studies Education, 41st Yearbook, Part II, 1942.

Guyer, B. L., & Friedman, M. P. Hemispheric processing and cognitive styles in learning-disabled and normal children. *Child Development*, 1975, *46*, 658–688.

Haber, R. N. Effects of coding strategy on perceptual memory. *Journal of Experimental Psychology*, 1964, *68*, 357–362.

Hagen, J. W. The effect of distraction on selective attention. *Child Development,* 1967, *38,* 685–694.

Hagen, J. W. Strategies for remembering. In S. Farnham-Diggory (Ed.), *Information processing in children*. New York: Academic Press, 1972.

Hagen, J. W., & Hale, G. H. The development of attention in children. In A. D. Pick (Ed.), *Minnesota symposia on child psychology*. Vol. 7. Minneapolis: University of Minnesota Press, 1973.

Hagen, J. W., Jongeward, R. H., Jr., & Kail, R. V., Jr. Cognitive perspectives on the development of memory. In H. W. Reese (Ed.), *Advances in child development and behavior*. Vol. 10. New York: Academic Press, 1975.

Hagen, J. W., & Kail, R. V., Jr. The role of attention in perceptual and cognitive development. In W. M. Cruickshank & P. Hallahan (Eds.), *Perceptual and learning disabilities in children*. Vol. 2. Syracuse, N.Y.: Syracuse University Press, 1975.

Hale, G. A., & Green, R. Z. Children's attention to stimulus components with variation in relative salience of components and degree of the stimulus integration. *Journal of Experimental Child Psychology*, 1976, *21*, 446–459.

Hale, G. A., & Morgan, J. S. Developmental trends in children's component selection. *Journal of Experimental Child Psychology*, 1973, *15*, 302–314.

Hale, G. A., & Stevenson, E. E., Jr. The effects of auditory and visual distractors on children's performance in a short-term memory task. *Journal of Experimental Child Psychology*, 1974, *18*, 280–292.

Hallahan, D. P. Distractibility in the learning disabled child. In W. M. Cruickshank & D. P. Hallahan. *Perceptual and learning disabilities in children*. Vol. 2. Syracuse, N.Y.: Syracuse University Press, 1975.

Hallahan, D. P., Kauffman, J. M., & Ball, D. W. Selective attention and cognitive tempo of low achieving and high achieving sixth grade males. *Perceptual and Motor Skills*, 1973, *36*, 579–583.

Harlow, H. F. The formation of learning sets. *Psychological Review*, 1949, *56*, 51–65.

Harlow, H. F. Analysis of discrimination learning by monkeys. *Journal of Experimental Psychology*, 1950, *40*, 26–39.

Harlow, H. F., & Hicks, L. H. Discrimination learning theory: Uniprocess vs. duoprocess. *Psychological Review*, 1957, *64*, 104–109.

Harter, S. Discrimination learning set in children as a function of IQ and MA. *Journal of Experimental Child Psychology*, 1965, *2*, 31–43.

Harter, S. Mental age, IQ, and motivational factors in the discrimination learning set performance of normal and retarded children. *Journal of Experimental Child Psychology*, 1967, *5*, 123–141.

Hartman, T. G. *The relationship among performance on Piagetian classification tasks, retrieval time from semantic memory, and the reading abilities of elementary school children*. Unpublished Doctoral Dissertation, Memphis State University, 1977.

Hayes, K. J., & Pereboom, A. C. Artifacts in criterion-reference learning curves. *Psychological Review*, 1959, *66*, 23–26.

Haynes, C. R., & Kulhavy, R. W. Conservation level and category clustering. *Developmental Psychology*, 1976, *12*, 179–184.

Hill, S. D. Performance of young children on three discrimination-learning tasks. *Child Development*, 1965, *36*, 425–435.

Hilgard, E. R., & Bower, G. H. *Theories of learning.* Third Edition. New York: Appleton-Century-Crofts, 1966.

Hilgard, E. R., & Bower, G. H. *Theories of learning*. Fourth Edition. Englewood Cliffs, N.J.: Prentice-Hall, 1975.

Hohle, R. H. Component process latencies in reaction times of children and adults. In L. P. Lipsitt & C. C. Spiker (Eds.), *Advances in child development and behavior*. Vol. 3. New York: Academic Press, 1967.

Holstein, S. B., & Premack, D. On the different effects of random reinforcement and presolution reversal on human concept identification. *Journal of Experimental Psychology*, 1965, *70*, 335–337.

Hook, J. G., & Cook, T. D. Equity theory and the cognitive ability of children. *Psychological Bulletin*, 1979, *86*, 429–445.

Hooper, F. H., Fitzgerald, J., & Papalia, D. Piagetian theory and the aging process: Extensions and speculations. *Aging and Human Development*, 1971, *2*, 3–20.

Horn, J. L. Human ability systems. In P. B. Baltes (Ed.), *Life-span development and behavior*. Vol. 1. New York: Academic Press, 1978.

Horn, J. L., & Cattell, R. B. Age differences in primary mental ability factors. *Journal of Gerontology*, 1966, *21*, 210–220.

Hornblum, J. N., & Overton, W. F. Area and volume conservation among the elderly: Assessment and training. *Developmental Psychology*, 1976, *12*, 68–74.

House, B. J. Attention to components or compounds as a factor in discrimination transfer performance. *Journal of Experimental Child Psychology,* 1979, *27,* 321–331.

Hoving, K. L., Morin, R. E., & Konick, D. S. Age-related changes in the effectiveness of name and visual codes in recognition memory. *Journal of Experimental Child Psychology*, 1974, *18*, 349–361.

Hull, C. L. *Principles of behavior*. New York: Appleton, 1943.

Ingalls, R. P., & Dickerson, D. J. Development of hypothesis behavior in human concept identification. *Developmental Psychology*, 1969, *1*, 707–716.

Inhelder, B., & Piaget, J. *The growth of logical thinking from childhood to adolescence*. New York: Basic Books, 1958.

Inhelder, B., & Piaget, J. *The early growth of logic in the child*. New York: Norton, 1964.

Inhelder, B., Sinclair, H., & Bovet, M. *Learning and the development of cognition*. Cambridge, Mass.: Harvard University Press, 1974.

Jeffrey, W. E., & Cohen, L. B. Response tendencies of children in a two-choice situation. *Journal of Experimental Child Psychology*, 1965, *2*, 248–254.

Johnson, J. W., & Scholnick, E. K. Does cognitive development predict semantic integration? *Child Development*, 1979, *50*, 73–78.

Kagan, J. Reflection-implusivity and reading ability in primary grade children. *Child Development*, 1965, *36*, 609-628.

Kagan, J., & Kogan, N. Individuality and cognitive performance. In P. H. Mussen (Ed.), *Carmichael's manual of child psychology*. Vol. 1. Third Edition. New York: John Wiley & Sons, 1970.

Kagan, J., Rosman, B. L., Kay, D., Albert, J., & Phillips, W. Information processing in the child: Significance of analytic and reflective attitudes. *Psychological Monographs*, 1964, *78*, (1, Whole No. 578).

Karpf, D., & Levine, M. Blank-trial probes and introtacts in human discrimination learning. *Journal of Experimental Psychology*, 1971, *90*, 51–55.

Kelley, J. E. *Basic psychophysical functions in young children*. Unpublished Doctoral Dissertation, University of Arizona, Tucson, 1974.

Kemler, D. G. *A developmental study of hypothesis-testing in discriminative learning tasks*. Unpublished Doctoral Dissertation, Brown University, 1972.

Kemler, D. G. Patterns of hypothesis testing in children's discriminative learning: A study of the development of problem-solving strategies. *Development Psychology*, 1978, *14*, 653–673.

Kemler, D. G., Shepp, B. E., & Foote, K. E. The sources of developmental differences in children's incidental processing during discrimination trials. *Journal of Experimental Child Psychology*, 1976, *21*, 226–240.

Kendler, H. H., & Kendler, T. S. Vertical and horizontal processes in problem solving. *Psychological Review*, 1962, *69*, 1–16.

Kendler, T. S. An ontogeny of mediational deficiency. *Child Development*, 1972, *43*, 1–17.

Kendler, T. S. Toward a theory of mediational development. In H. W. Reese & L. P. Lipsitt (Eds.), *Advances in child development and behavior*. Vol. 13. New York: Academic Press, 1979.

Kendler, T. S., & Kendler, H. H. An ontogeny of optional shift behavior. *Child development*, 1970, *41*, 1–27.

Kessen, W. "Stage" and "structure" in the study of children. In W. Kessen & C.P. Kuhlman (Eds.), Thought in the young child. *Monographs of the Society for Research in Child Development*, 1962, *28*, (2, Whole No. 83).

Kessen, W., & Kessen, M. L. Behavior of young children in a two-choice guessing problem. *Child Development*, 1961, *32*, 779–788.

Kintsch, W. *Memory and cognition*. New York: John Wiley & Sons, 1977.

Klahr, D., & Siegler, R. S. The representation of children's knowledge. In H. W. Reese & L. P. Lipsitt (Eds.), *Advances in child development and behavior*. Vol. 12. New York: Academic Press, 1978.

Klahr, D., & Wallace, J. G. *Cognitive development: An information-processing view*. Hillsdale, N. J.: Lawrence Erlbaum Associates, 1976.

Koch, M. B., & Meyer, D. R. A relationship of mental age to learning-set formation in the preschool child. *Journal of Comparative and Physiological Psychology*, 1959, *52*, 387–389.

Kofsky, E. A scalogram study of classificatory development. *Child Development*, 1966, *37*, 191–204.

Kornreich, L. B. Strategy selection and information processing in human discrimination learning. *Journal of Educational Psychology*, 1968, *59*, 438–448.

Krechevsky, I. "Hypotheses" in rats. *Psychological Review*, 1932, *39*, 516–532. (a)

Krechevsky, I. "Hypotheses" versus "chance" in the pre-solution period in sensory discrimination learning. *University of California Publications in Psychology*, 1932, *6*, 27–44. (b)

Krechevsky, I. The docile nature of "hypotheses." *Journal of Comparative Psychology*, 1933, *15*, 429–443. (a)

Krechevsky, I. Hereditary nature of "hypotheses." *Journal of Comparative Psychology*, 1933, *16*, 99–116. (b)

Krechevsky, I. A note concerning "the nature of discrimination learning in animals." *Psychological Review*, 1937, *44*, 97–104.

Kuenne, M. R. Experimental investigation of the relation of language to transposition behavior in young children. *Journal of Experimental Psychology*, 1946, *36*, 471–490.

LaBerge, D., & Samuels, S. J. Toward a theory of automatic information processing in reading. *Cognitive Psychology*, 1974, *6*, 293–323.

LaBouvie-Vief, G., Hoyer, W. J., Baltes, M. M., & Baltes, P. B. Operant analyses of intellectual behavior in old age. *Human Development*, 1974, *17*, 259–272.

Lane, D. M., McDaniel, J. R., Bleichfeld, B. E., & Rabinowitz, F. M. Toward the specification of hypothesis domains and einstellung. *Journal of Experimental Psychology: Human Learning and Memory*, 1976, *2*, 489–496.

Langer, J. Werner's theory of development. In P. H. Mussen (Ed.), *Carmichael's manual of child psychology*. Vol. 1. Third Edition. New York: John Wiley & Sons, 1970.

Lashley, K. S. *Brain mechanisms and intelligence.* Chicago: University of Chicago Press, 1929.

Leeming, F. C., Blackwood, H. D., & Robinson, K. D. Instrumental learning in the presence of noncontingent reward. *Journal of Experimental Psychology: Human Learning and Memory*, 1978, *4*, 266–273.

Levine, M. A model of hypothesis behavior in discrimination learning set. *Psychological Review*, 1959, *66*, 353–366.

Levine, M. Mediating processes in humans at the outset of discrimination learning. *Psychological Review*, 1963, *70*, 254–276.

Levine, M. Hypothesis behavior. In A. M. Schrier, H. F. Harlow, & F. Stollnitz (Eds.), *Behavior of nonhuman primates*. Vol. 1. New York: Academic Press, 1965.

Levine, M. Hypothesis behavior by humans during discrimination learning. *Journal of Experimental Psychology*, 1966, *71*, 331–338.

Levine, M. The size of the hypothesis set during discrimination learning. *Psychological Review*, 1967, *74*, 428–430.

Levine, M. Neo-noncontinuity theory. In G. H. Bower & J. T. Spence (Eds.), *The psychology of learning and motivation*. Vol. 3. New York: Academic Press, 1969.

Levine, M. Human discrimination learning: The subset sampling assumption. *Psychological Bulletin*, 1970, *74*, 397–404.

Levine, M. Hypothesis theory and nonlearning despite ideal S–R reinforcement contingencies. *Psychological Review*, 1971, *78*, 130–140.

Levine, M. A transfer hypothesis, whereby learning-to-learn, einstellung, the PREE, reversal-nonreversal shifts, and other curiosities are elucidated. In R. L. Solso (Ed.), *Theories in cognitive psychology: The Loyola symposium*. Potomac, Md: Lawrence Erlbaum Associates, 1974.

Levine, M. *A cognitive theory of learning: Research on hypothesis testing*. Hillsdale, N. J.: Lawrence Erlbaum Associates, 1975.

Levine, M., Leitenberg, H., & Richter, M. The blank trials law: The equivalence of positive reinforcement and nonreinforcement. *Psychological Review*, 1964, *71*, 94–103.

Levine, M., Miller, P., & Steinmeyer, C. H. The none-to-all theorem of human discrimination learning. *Journal of Experimental Psychology*, 1967, *73*, 568–573.

Levine, M., Yoder, R. M., Kleinberg, J., & Rosenberg, J. The presolution paradox in discrimination learning. *Journal of Experimental Psychology*, 1968, *77*, 602–608.

Levinson, B., & Reese, H. W. *Patterns of discrimination learning set in preschool children, fifth-graders, college freshmen, and the aged.* ERIC No. EDOO3032. Bethesda, Md: ERIC Reproduction Service, 1963.

Levinson, B., & Reese, H. W. Patterns of discrimination learning set in preschool children, fifth-graders, college freshmen, and the aged. *Monographs of the Society for Research in Child Development*, 1967, *32*, (7, Whole No. 115).

Liebert, R. M., Odom, R. D., Hill, J. H., & Huff, R. L. Effects of age and rule familiarity on the production of modeled language constructions. *Developmental Psychology*, 1969, *1*, 108–112.

Meichenbaum, D. *Cognition–behavior modification: An integrative approach*. New York: Plenum Press, 1977.

Mercer, C. D., Cullinan, D., Hallahan, D., & LaFleur, N. K. Modeling and attention-retention in learning disabled children. *Journal of Learning Disabilities*, 1975, *8*, 444–450.

Miller, S. A. Nonverbal assessment of Piagetian concepts. *Psychological Bulletin*, 1976, *83*, 405–430.

Mims, R. M., & Gholson, B. Effects of type and amount of feedback upon hypothesis sampling systems among seven- and eight-year-old children. *Journal of Experimental Child Psychology,* 1977, *24,* 358–371.

Mondani, M. S., & Tutko, T. A. Relationship of academic under-achievement to incidental-learning. *Journal of Consulting and Clinical Psychology*, 1969, *33*, 558–560.

Morello, V. J., Turner, R. R., & Reed, N. E. Problem-solving strategies on a partial reinforcement task: Effects of socioeconomic status and cognitive level. *Journal of Experimental Child Psychology*, 1977, *24*, 74–85.

Moshman, D. Development of formal hypothesis-testing ability. *Developmental Psychology*, 1979, *15*, 104–112.

Moss, A. *The developmental effects of irrelevant information on problem solving strategies*. Unpublished Doctoral Dissertation, City University of New York/Graduate School, 1976.

Nahinsky, I. D. A test of axioms of all-or-none concept identification models. *Journal of Verbal Learning and Verbal Behavior*, 1968, *7*, 593–601.

Nahinsky, I. D., & Slaymaker, F. L. Sampling without replacement and information processing following correct responses in concept identification. *Journal of Experimental Psychology*, 1969, *80*, 475–482.

Neimark, E. D. Intellectual development during adolescence. In F. D. Horowitz (Ed.), *Review of child development research*. Vol. 4. Chicago: University of Chicago Press, 1975. (a)

Neimark, E. D. Longitudinal development of formal operations thought. *Genetic Psychology Monographs*, 1975, *91*, 171-225. (b)

Neimark, E. D. The natural history of spontaneous mnemonic activities under conditions of minimal experimental constraint. In A. D. Pick (Ed.), *Minnesota symposia on child development*. Vol. 10. Minneapolis: University of Minnesota Press, 1976.

Neimark, E. D., Slotnick, N. S., & Ulrich, T. Development of memorization strategies. *Developmental Psychology*, 1971, *5*, 427–432.

Neisser, U. *Cognitive psychology*. New York: Appleton-Century-Crofts, 1967.

Nesselroade, J. R., Schaie, K. W., & Baltes, P. B. Ontogenetic and generational components of structural and quantitative changes in adults behavior. *Journal of Gerontology*, 1972, *27*, 222–228.

Newell, A., & Simon, H. A. *Human problem solving*. Englewood Cliffs, N. J.: Prentice-Hall, 1972.

Noland, E. C. & Schuldt, W. J. Sustained attention and reading retardation. *Journal of Experimental Education*, 1971, *40*, 73–76.

Nuessle, W. Reflectivity as an influence on focusing behavior. *Journal of Experimental Child Psychology*, 1972, *14*, 265–276.

Odom, R. D. Problem-solving strategies as a function of age and socioeconomic level. *Child Development*, 1967, *38*, 747–752.

Odom, R. D. Effects of perceptual salience on the recall of relevant and incidental dimensional values: A developmental study. *Journal of Experimental Psychology*, 1972, *92*, 285–291.

Odom, R. D. A perceptual-salience account of décalage relations and developmental change. In L. S. Siegel & C. J. Brainerd (Eds.), *Alternatives to Piaget: Critical essays on the theory*. New York: Academic Press, 1978.

Odom, R. D., Liebert, R. M., & Hill, J. H. The effects of modeling cues, reward, and attentional set on the production of grammatical and ungrammatical syntactic constructions. *Journal of Experimental Child Psychology*, 1968, *6*, 131-140.

Offenbach, S. I. A developmental study of hypothesis testing and cue selection strategies.

Developmental Psychology, 1974, *10*, 484–490.

Offenbach, S. I. *Children's learning as a function of hypothesis set size*. Unpublished Manuscript. Purdue University, 1979.

O'Leary, K. D., & Kent, R. Reversibility: The strength or weakness of behavior modification. In L. A. Hamerlynck, L. C. Handy, & E. J. Mash (Eds.), *Behavioral change: Methodology, concepts, and practice*. Champaign, Ill.: Research Press, 1973.

Overton, W. F. General systems, structure, and development. In K. F. Riegel & G. C. Rosenwald (Eds.), *Structure and transformations: Developmental and historical aspects*. New York: Wiley, 1975.

Overton, W. F., Wagner, J., & Dolinsky, H. Social-class differences and task variables in the development of multiplicative classification. *Child Development*, 1971, *42*, 1951–1958.

Paivio, A. A theoretical analysis of the role of imagery in learning and memory. In P. W. Sheehan (Ed.), *The function and nature of imagery*. New York: Academic Press, 1972.

Papalia, D. E. The status of several conservation abilities across the life-span. *Human Development*, 1972, *15*, 229–243.

Papalia, D. E., & Bielby, D. D. V. Cognitive functioning in middle and old age adults. *Human Development*, 1974, *17*, 424–443.

Paris, S. G., & Landauer, B. K. Constructive aspects of children's comprehension and memory. In R. V. Kail & J. W. Hagen (Eds.), *Perspectives on the development of memory and cognition*. Hillsdale, N. J.: Lawrence Erlbaum Associates, 1977.

Parrill-Burnstein, M. Teaching kindergarten children to solve problems: An information-processing approach. *Child Development*, 1978, *49*, 700–706.

Parrill-Burnstein, M. *Teaching kindergarten children to use complex strategies: An information-processing approach*. Unpublished Manuscript, Emory University, 1979.

Pascual-Leone, J. A mathematical model for the transition rule in Piaget's developmental stages. *Acta Psychologica*, 1970, *32*, 301–345.

Penney, R. K. Effect of reward and punishment on children's orientation and discrimination learning. *Journal of Experimental Psychology*, 1967, *75*, 140–142.

Phillips, S. *Introtacts in children's discrimination learning*. Unpublished Doctoral Dissertation, State University of New York at Stony Brook, 1974.

Phillips, S. Effects of concrete reward/cost contingencies upon discrimination-learning styles of prekindergarten and kindergarten children. *Perceptual and Motor Skills*, 1976, *43*, 273–274.

Phillips, S., & Levine, M. Probing for hypotheses with adults and children: Blank trials and introtacts. *Journal of Experimental Psychology: General*, 1975, *104*, 327–354.

Piaget, J. *The child's conception of number*. London: Routledge and Kegan Paul, 1952.

Piaget, J. *The child's conception of the world*. Paterson, N. J.: Littlefield Adams, 1963.

Piaget, J. *Six psychological studies*. New York: Vintage, 1968.

Piaget, J. Piaget's theory. In P. H. Mussen (Ed.), *Carmichael's manual of child psychology*. Vol. 1. Third Edition. New York: John Wiley & Sons, 1970.

Posner, M. I. Coordination of internal codes. In W. C. Chase (Ed.), *Visual information processing*. New York: Academic Press, 1973.

Postman, L. Repetition and paired-associate learning. *American Journal of Psychology*, 1962, *75*, 372–389.

Postman, L., & Bruner, J. S. Perception under stress. *Psychological Review*, 1948, *55*, 314–323.

Postman, L., & Bruner, J. S. Hypothesis and the principle of closure: The effect of frequency and recency. *Journal of Psychology*, 1952, *33*, 113–125.

Prawat, R. S., & Cancelli, A. Constructive memory in conserving and nonconserving first graders. *Developmental Psychology*, 1976, *12*, 47–50.

Ratliff, R. G., & Root, J. R. Two-choice discrimination learning in children as a joint function of incentive level and punishment. *Journal of Genetic Psychology*, 1974, *124*, 249–257.

Ratliff, R. G., & Tindall, R. C. Interaction of reward, punishment, and sex in a two-choice discrimination task with children. *Developmental Psychology*, 1970, *3*, 150.

Rayner, K., & Kaiser, J. S. Reading mutilated text. *Journal of Educational Psychology*, 1975, *67*, 301–306.

Reese, H. W. Discrimination learning set in Rhesus monkeys. *Psychological Bulletin*, 1964, *61*, 321–340.

Reese, H. W. Imagery and contextual meaning. *Psychological Bulletin*, 1970, *73*, 404–414.

Reese, H. W. The development of memory: Life-span perspectives. In H. W. Reese (Ed.), *Advances in child development and behavior*. Vol. 11. New York: Academic Press, 1976.

Reese, H. W. Discriminative learning and transfer: Dialectical perspectives. In N. Datan & H. W. Reese (Eds.), *Life-span developmental psychology: Dialectical perspectives on experimental research*. New York: Academic Press, 1977.

Reese, H. W., & Lipsitt, L. P. *Experimental child psychology*. New York: Academic Press, 1970.

Restle, F. A theory of discrimination learning. *Psychological Review*, 1955, *62*, 11–19.

Restle, F. Toward a quantitative description of learning set data. *Psychological Review*, 1958, *65*, 77–91.

Restle, F. The selection of strategies in cue learning. *Psychological Review*, 1962, *69*, 329–343.

Restle, F. Significance of all-or-none learning. *Psychological Bulletin*, 1965, *64*, 313–325.

Restle, F., & Emmerich, D. Memory in concept attainment: Effects of giving several problems concurrently. *Journal of Experimental Psychology*, 1966, *71*, 794–799.

Richman, S. *Effects of strategy modeling and age upon information processing among elementary-school children*. Unpublished Doctoral Dissertation, City University of New York/Graduate School, 1975.

Richman, S. *Piagetian stage, strategy modeling, and problem-solving strategies*. Paper presented at American Psychological Association Meetings, Washington, D. C., September, 1976.

Richman, S., & Gholson, B. Strategy modeling, age, and information-processing efficiency. *Journal of Experimental Child Psychology*, 1978, *26*, 58–70.

Richman, S., Shaheen, J., & Montgomery, T. *Strategy modeling and problem solving in concrete to formal operational subjects*. Paper presented at Southeastern Conference on Human Development Meetings, Atlanta, April, 1978.

Rieber, M. Response alternation in children under different schedules of reinforcement. *Psychonomic Science*, 1966, *4*, 149–150.

Rieber, M. Hypothesis testing in children as a function of age. *Developmental Psychology*, 1969, *1*, 389–395.

Riegel, K. F. Dialectic operations: The final period of cognitive development. *Human Development*, 1973, *16*, 346–370.

Robinson, J. A. Category clustering in free recall. *Journal of Psychology*, 1966, *62*, 279–285.

Rock, I. The role of repetition in associative learning. *American Journal of Psychology*, 1957, *70*, 186–193.

Rosenthal, T. L., & Carroll, W. R. Factors in vicarious modification of complex grammatical parameters. *Journal of Educational Psychology*, 1972, *63*, 174–178.

Rosenthal, T. L., Kelley, J. E., & White, G. M. Anchoring and relational judgments by young children and retardates. *Memory and Cognition*, 1974, *2*, 279–282.

Rosenthal, T. L., & Zimmerman, B. J. Modeling by exemplification and instruction in training conservation. *Developmental Psychology*, 1972, *6*, 392–401.

Rosenthal, T. L., & Zimmerman, B. J. Organization, observation, and guided practice in concept attainment and generalization. *Child Development*, 1973, *44*, 606–613.

Rosenthal, T. L. & Zimmerman, B. J. *Social learning and cognition*. New York: Academic Press, 1978.

Rosenthal, T. L., Zimmerman, B. J., & Durning, K. Observationally induced changes in children's interrogative classes. *Journal of Personality and Social Psychology*, 1970, *16*, 681–688.

Ross, A. O. *Psychological aspects of learning disabilities and reading disorders*. New York: McGraw–Hill, 1976.

Rubin, K. H., Attewell, P. W., Tierney, M. C., & Tumolo, P. Development of spatial egocentrism and conservation across the life span. *Developmental Psychology*, 1973, *9*, 432.

Ryan, H. *The effects of stimulus novelty and training on the einstellung phenomenon in sequence learning*. Unpublished M. S. thesis, Memphis State University, 1977.

Saarni, C. I. Piagetian operations and field independence as factors in children's problem-solving performance. *Child Development*, 1973, *44*, 338–345.

Sabatino, D. A., & Ysseldyke, J. E. Effect of extraneous "background" on visual-perceptual performance of readers and non-readers. *Perceptual and Motor Skills*, 1972, *35*, 323–328.

Samuels, S. J., Begy, G., & Chen, C. C. Comparison of word recognition speed and strategies of less skilled and more highly skilled readers. *Reading Research Quarterly*, 1976, *11*, 72–86.

Samuels, S. J., Dahl, P. R., & Archwamety, T. Effect of hypothesis/test training on reading skill. *Journal of Educational Psychology*, 1974, *66*, 835–844.

Savin, H. B., Word frequency effect and errors in the perception of speech. *Journal of the Acoustical Society of America*, 1963, *35*, 200–206.

Schadler, M. Development of relational learning: Effects of instruction and delay of transfer. *Journal of Experimental Child Psychology*, 1973, *16*, 459–471.

Schaie, K. W., LaBouvie, G. V., & Buech, B. U. Generational and cohort-specific differences in adult cognitive functioning: A fourteen-year study of independent samples. *Developmental Psychology*, 1973, *9*, 151–166.

Schlesser, R., Meyers, A. W., & Cohen, R. Generalization of self-instructions: Effects of specific versus meta content, active rehearsal and cognitive level. *Child Development*, in press.

Schneider, W., & Shiffrin, R. M. Controlled and automatic human information processing: I. Detection, search and attention. *Psychological Review*, 1977, *84*, 1–66.

Schonebaum, R. M. A developmental study of differences in initial coding and recoding of hypothesis information. *Journal of Experimental Child Psychology*, 1973, *16*, 413–423.

Schuepfer, T., & Gholson, B. Effects of IQ and mental age on hypothesis testing in normal and retarded children: A methodological analysis. *Developmental Psychology*, 1978, *14*, 423–424.

Schultz, N. R., & Hoyer, W. J. Feedback effects on spatial egocentrism in old age. *Journal of Gerontology*, 1976, *31*, 72–75.

Schusterman, R. J. The use of strategies in the decision behavior of children and chimpanzees. *American Psychologist*, 1961, *16*, 424.

Schusterman, R. J. The use of strategies in two-choice behavior of children and chimpanzees. *Journal of Comparative and Physiological Psychology*, 1963, *56*, 96–100.

Schwartz, S. H. Trial-by-trial analysis or processes in simple and disjunctive concept-attainment tasks. *Journal of Experimental Psychology*, 1966, *72*, 456-465.

Shiffrin, R. M. & Schneider, W. Controlled and automatic human information processing: II. Perceptual learning, automatic attending, and a general theory. *Psychological Review*, 1977, *84*, 127–190.

Siegel, A. W., & White, S. H. The development of spatial representations of large-scale environments. In H. W. Reese (Ed.), *Advances in child development and behavior*. Vol. 10. New York: Academic Press, 1975.

Siegler, R. S., & Liebert, R. M. Effects of presenting relevant rules and complete feedback on the conservation of liquid quantity task. *Developmental Psychology*, 1972, *7*, 133–138.

Silverman, M., Davids, A., & Andrews, J. M. Powers of attention and academic achievement. *Perceptual and Motor Skills*, 1963, *17*, 243–249.

Simon, E. W., & Bohannon, J. N., III. The relationship between conservation of quantity and categorized free-recall in primary-grade children. *Bulletin of the Psychonomic Society*, 1978, *12*, 427–429.

Simon, H. A. On the development of the processor. In S. Farnham-Diggory (Ed.), *Information processing in children*. New York: Academic Press, 1972.

Skinner, B. F. *The behavior of organisms: An experimental analysis*. New York: Appleton, 1938.

Solomon, R. L., & Postman, L. Frequency of usage as a determinant of recognition thresholds for words. *Journal of Experimental Psychology*, 1952, *43*, 195–201.

Spence, J. T. Verbal discrimination performance under different verbal reinforcement combination. *Journal of Experimental Psychology, 1964, 67*, 195–197.

Spence, J. T. Verbal-discrimination performance as a function of instructions and verbal-reinforcement combination in normal and retarded children. *Child Development*, 1966, *37*, 269–281. (a)

Spence, J. T. The effects of verbal reinforcement combination on the performance of a four-alternative discrimination task. *Journal of Verbal Learning and Verbal Behavior*, 1966, *5*, 421–428. (b)

Spence, J. T. The distracting effects of material reinforcers in the discrimination learning of lower- and middle-class children. *Child Development* 1970, *41*, 103–111. (a)

Spence, J. T. Verbal reinforcement combinations and concept-identification learning: The role of nonreinforcement. *Journal of Experimental Psychology*, 1970, *85*, 321–329 (b)

Spence, J. T. Do material rewards enhance the performance of lower-class children? *Child Development*, 1971, *42*, 1461–1470.

Spence, J. T., & Dunton, M. C. The influence of verbal and nonverbal reinforcement combinations in the discrimination learning of middle- and lower-class preschool children. *Child Development*, 1967, *38*, 1177–1186.

Spence, J. T., & Segner, L. L. Verbal versus nonverbal reinforcement combinations in the discrimination learning of middle- and lower-class children. *Child Development*, 1967, *38*, 29–38.

Spence, K. W. The nature of discrimination learning in animals. *Psychological Review*, 1936, *43*, 427–449.

Spence, K. W. The differential response in animals to stimuli varying within a single dimension. *Psychological Review*, 1937, *44*, 430–444.

Spence, K. W. Continuous versus noncontinuous interpretations of discrimination learning. *Psychological Review*, 1940, *47*, 271–288.

Sperling, G. The information available in brief visual presentations. *Psychological Monographs*, 1960, *74*, (11, Whole No. 498).

Spiker, C. C. An extension of Hull-Spence discrimination learning theory. *Psychological*

Review, 1970, *77*, 496–515.

Spiker, C. C., & Cantor, J. H. Introtacts as predictors of discrimination performance in kindergarten children. *Journal of Experimental Child Psychology*, 1977, *23*, 520–538.

Spiker, C. C., & Cantor, J. H. The Kendler levels-of-functioning theory: Comments and an alternative schema. In H. W. Reese & L. P. Lipsitt (Eds.), *Advances in child development and behavior*. Vol. 13. New York: Academic Press, 1979.

Staats, A. W., Minke, K. A., & Butts, P. A token reinforcement remedial reading program administered by black therapy technicians to problem black children. *Behavior Therapy*, 1970, *1*, 331–353.

Stauffer, R. G. Reading as a cognitive function. In H. Singer & R. B. Ruddell (Eds.), *Theoretical models and processes of reading.* Newark, Del.: International Reading Association, 1970.

Stevenson, H. W. Learning in children. In P. H. Mussen (Ed.), *Carmichael's manual of child psychology*. Vol. I. Third Edition. New York: John Wiley & Son, 1970.

Stevenson, H. W., & Swartz, J. D. Learning set in children as a function of intellectual level. *Journal of Comparative and Psychological Psychology*, 1958, *51*, 755–757.

Suchman, R. G., & Trabasso, T. Color and form preference in young children. *Journal of Experimental Child Psychology*, 1966, *3*, 177–187. (a)

Suchman, R. G., & Trabasso, T. Stimulus preference and cue function in young children's concept attainment. *Journal of Experimental Child Psychology*, 1966, *3*, 188–198. (b)

Suppes, P., & Schlag-Rey, M. Observable changes of hypotheses under positive reinforcement. *Science*, 1965, *148*, 661–662.

Tarver, S. G., & Hallahan, D. P. Attention deficits in children with learning disabilities: A review. *Journal of Learning Disabilities*, 1974, *7*, 560–569.

Tarver, S. G., Hallahan, D. P., Cohen, S., & Kauffman, J. The development of visual selective attention and verbal rehearsal in learning disabled boys. *Journal of Learning Disabilities*, 1977, *10*, 491–500.

Tarver, S. G., Hallahan, D. P., Kauffman, J., & Ball, D. W. Verbal rehearsal and selective attention in children with learning disabilities: A developmental lag. *Journal of Experimental Child Psychology*, 1976, *22*, 375–385.

Tighe, L. S., & Tighe, T. J. Discrimination learning: Two views in historical perspective. *Psychological Bulletin*, 1966, *66*, 353–370.

Tighe, T. J., & Tighe, L. S. Stimulus control in children's discrimination learning. In A. D. Pick (Ed.), *Minnesota symposia on child psychology*. Vol. 6. Minneapolis: University of Minnesota Press, 1972.

Tindall, R. C., & Ratliff, R. G. Interaction of reinforcement conditions and developmental level in a two-choice discrimination task with children. *Journal of Experimental Child Psychology*, 1974, *18*, 183–189.

Tolman, E. C. *Purposive behavior in animals and men*. New York: Appleton-Century-Crofts, 1932.

Tolman, E. C. Cognitive maps in rats and men. *Psychological Review*, 1948, *55*, 189–208.

Tomlinson-Keasey, C. Formal operations in females from eleven to fifty-four years of age. *Developmental Psychology*, 1972, *6*, 364.

Tomlinson-Keasey, C., Crawford, D. G., & Miser, A. L. Classification: An organizing operation for memory. *Developmental Psychology*, 1975, *11*, 409–410.

Trabasso, T. Additivity of cues in discrimination learning of letter patterns. *Journal of Experimental Psychology*, 1960, *60*, 83–88.

Trabasso, T. Stimulus emphasis and all-or-none learning of concept identification. *Journal of Experimental Psychology*, 1963, *65*, 395–406.

Trabasso, T., & Bower, G. H. Component learning in the four-category concept problem. *Journal of Mathematical Psychology*, 1964, *1*, 143–169. (a)

Trabasso, T., & Bower, G. H. Presolution reversal and dimensional shifts in concept identification. *Journal of Experimental Psychology*, 1964, *67*, 398–399. (b)

Trabasso, T., & Bower, G. H. Presolution dimensional shifts in concept identification: A test of the sampling with replacement axiom in all-or-none models. *Journal of Mathematical Psychology*, 1966, *3*, 163–173.

Trabasso, T., & Bower, G. H. *Attention in learning: Theory and research*. New York: Wiley, 1968.

Tumblin, A., Gholson, B., Rosenthal, T. L., & Kelley, J. E. The effects of gestural demonstration, verbal narration, and their combination on the acquisition of hypothesis-testing behaviors by first-grade children. *Child Development*, 1979, *50*, 254–256.

Turner, R. R. (Chm), *Symposium: Children's problem solving: Perspectives on a theoretical synthesis*. Presented at the Southeastern Conference on Human Development Meetings, Atlanta, April, 1978.

Watson, J. B. *Behavior. An introduction to comparative psychology*. New York: Holt, Rinehart, & Winston, 1914.

Weir, M. W. Developmental changes in problem-solving strategies. *Psychological Review*, 1964, *71*, 473–490.

Weisz, J. R. A follow-up developmental study of hypothesis behavior among mentally retarded and nonretarded children. *Journal of Experimental Child Psychology*, 1977, *24*, 108–122.

Weisz, J. R., & Achenbach, T. M. Effects of IQ and mental age on hypothesis behavior in normal and retarded children. *Developmental Psychology*, 1975, *11*, 304–310.

White, S. H. Evidence for a hierarchical arrangement of learning processes. In L. P. Lipsitt & C. C. Spiker (Eds.), *Advances in child development and behavior*. Vol. 2. New York: Academic Press, 1965.

White, S. H. The learning theory approach. In P. H. Mussen (Ed.), *Carmichael's manual of child psychology*. Vol. 1. Third Edition. New York: John Wiley & Sons, 1970.

Whitehurst, G. J. Production of novel and grammatical utterances by young children. *Journal of Experimental Child Psychology*, 1972, *13*, 502–515.

Whitehurst, G. J. The development of communication: Changes with age and modeling. *Child Development*, 1976, *47*, 473–482.

Whitehurst, G. J., Ironsmith, M., & Goldfein, M. Selective imitation of the passive construction through modeling. *Journal of Experimental Child Psychology*, 1974, *17*, 288–302.

Wickens, T. D., & Millward, R. B. Attribute elimination strategies for concept identification with practiced subjects. *Journal of Mathematical Psychology*, 1971, *8*, 453-480.

Williams, B. R. Effects of verbal reinforcement combination on children's responses to blank trials. *Journal of Experimental Child Psychology*, 1972, *14*, 30–42.

Williams, B. R. Comment on Levine's blank trial method: A procedure for estimating true hypothesis behavior. *Journal of Experimental Child Psychology*, 1974, *18*, 362–368.

Williams, J. P. Supplementary report: A selection artifact in Rock's study of the role of repetition. *Journal of Experimental Psychology*, 1961, *62*, 627–628.

Winer, B. J. *Statistical principles in experimental design*. Second Edition. New York: McGraw–Hill, 1971.

Witkin, H. A., Dyk, R. B., Fattuson, H. F., Goodenough, D. R., & Karp, S. A. *Psychological differentiation: Studies of development*. New York: Wiley, 1962.

Wright, J. C., & Vlietstra, A. G. The development of selective attention: From perceptual exploration to logical search. In H. W. Reese (Ed.), *Advances in child development and behavior*. Vol. 10. New York: Academic Press, 1975.

Zeaman, D., & House, B. J. An attention theory of retardate discrimination learning. In N. R. Ellis (Ed.), *Handbook of mental deficiency*. New York: McGraw-Hill, 1963.

Zeaman, D., & House, B. J. Interpretations of developmental trends in discriminative transfer effects. In A. D. Pick (Ed.), *Minnesota symposia on child psychology*. Vol. 8. Minneapolis: University of Minnesota Press, 1974.

Zimmerman, B. J., & Rosenthal, T. L. Concept attainment, transfer, and retention through observation and rule-provision. *Journal of Experimental Child Psychology*, 1972, *14*, 139–150.

Zimmerman, B. J., & Rosenthal, T. L. Conceptual generalization and retention by young children: Age, modeling, and feedback effects. *Journal of Genetic Psychology*, 1974, *125*, 233–245. (a)

Zimmerman, B. J., & Rosenthal, T. L. Conserving and retaining equalities and inequalities through observation and correction. *Developmental Psychology*, 1974, *10*, 260–268. (b)

Index